THE BUDDHA
IN YOUR
REARVIEW
MIRROR

Published in 2006 by
Stewart, Tabori & Chang
An imprint of ABRAMS

Library of Congress Cataloging-in-Publication Data

Hochswender, Woody.
  The Buddha in your rearview mirror : a guide to practicing Buddhism in
modern life / by Woody Hochswender.
      p. cm.
  ISBN-13: 978-1-58479-552-0
  ISBN-10: 1-58479-552-2
  1. Religious life—Soka Gakkai. 2. Soka Gakkai—Doctrines. 3.
Nichiren, 1222-1282—Teachings. I. Title.

BQ8420.H63 2007
294.3'444—dc22

2006024823

Editor: Jennifer Eiss
Designer: LeAnna Weller Smith
Production Manager: Anet Sirna-Bruder

The text of this book was composed in Berthold Garamond and Meta

Printed and bound in the
United States of America
10 9 8 7 6 5 4 3 2

ABRAMS
THE ART OF BOOKS SINCE 1949

115 West 18th Street
New York, NY 10011
www.abramsbooks.com

For
Sensei
and
Kate

THE BUDDHA
IN YOUR
REARVIEW
MIRROR

A GUIDE TO PRACTICING BUDDHISM IN MODERN LIFE

WOODY HOCHSWENDER

Stewart, Tabori & Chang
New York

CONTENTS

INTRODUCTION

In the Rearview Mirror

BUDDHISM IS GAINING ON US, WHETHER WE ARE AWARE OF it or not. It is there, in the rearview mirror, following us down the roaring freeway of modern life. Buddhism and its twenty-five-hundred-year-old principles are as ineluctable as technological progress—and destined to become as permanent a part of our lives. Buddhism is everywhere. It is in the Internet café, health-food store, bookstore, and movie theater. It can sometimes be a matter of style—the number of Buddha statues popping up in glossy decorating magazines these days is almost alarming—and often a matter of substance. It infuses popular culture, informs philosophical debate, and is changing the way we think and live.

The twenty-first century will very likely see a flowering of Buddhism. Following a century of military conflicts and great material progress, the stage has been set for a gentle, compassionate philosophy that explains the limits of materialism, without renouncing the yearning of people for comfort and progress. The seed and the flower of this new spiritual awakening will be a powerful and improbable source: science. As more and more people adopt a scientific view of the universe, they move inevitably toward the Buddhist view of life. This happens naturally, almost imperceptibly, without people even knowing it.

In a previous book, *The Buddha in Your Mirror*, cowritten with Greg Martin and Ted Morino, the image of a mirror was utilized as an important symbolic element in ancient and modern Japanese Buddhism. In that earlier work, the mirror was seen as a metaphor for revealing one's true self: the Buddha in your mirror is none other than you. This idea has been stated numerous times throughout the history of Buddhism, and its obverse, the notion that Buddha is someone out there, exterior to oneself, has often been debunked.

"If you see the Buddha in the road, kill him," goes the well-known proverb. It is the sort of cryptic saying with a mental trap-door that has given Buddhism a reputation for being somewhat enigmatic and counterintuitive—and thus alien to the Western mind. The logic behind the proverb seems ironclad. If the goal of Buddhism is to discover the enlightened self within each person, then each person is a Buddha. Therefore anyone looking for (and finding) the Buddha outside his or her self has encountered a mirage of enlightenment that is its own manifest disproof. It's an amusing insight but flawed. For instance, most Buddhist practitioners at one time or another benefit from the wisdom of a mentor, someone who shows them how to practice. Indeed, some kind of mentor is nearly indispensable in the early stages of Buddhist practice. We wouldn't want to run over our teacher, would we? In fact, much progress in Buddhism has to do with our encounters with wise teachers, living and dead. Two of these, Nichiren Daishonin, a thirteenth-century Japanese monk, and Daisaku Ikeda, a contemporary leader of worldwide Buddhism, will be discussed in depth in the course of this book. It is hard to imagine the existence of one of the largest schools of modern-day Buddhism without them.

The "rearview mirror" expresses a very particular view of the spiritual-cultural moment. Buddhism as a notional thing, a respected and venerated philosophy, is out there. But there is a bit of distance between the philosophy and the people, between the actual process of attaining Buddhahood and its cultural emanations. As I write, there is a photograph in my favorite daily tabloid newspaper of the actress Angelina Jolie's back—it has a Buddhist prayer tattooed on it, in Sanskrit, carefully inked in four columns, taking up a good deal of space. When it comes to body ornamentation, Jolie is an equal opportunity consumer—she also has tattoos of a Latin phrase, an Arabic motto ("Strength of Will"), a tiger, and names of past lovers. That is one of the impressive things about it—her eclecticism. Buddhism is frequently an ingredient in the bouillabaisse of American spiritual life, sometimes including yoga, organic foods, social activism, and a deep respect for the preciousness of all life, or pacifism.

In the day's *New York Post*, there is also an advertisement for Charles Schwab, the Wall Street brokerage firm, which says, in reference to the element of risk inherent in stock-market investing, "It would be wonderful to live in Nirvana, but we're not there." This is, roughly, a reference to the Buddhist concept of heaven (or emancipation from the cycle of birth and death). It's wonderful to think of Buddhist philosophy being integrated into the Wall Street ethos. Similarly, there is a headline in *The New York Times* that refers to a Broadway show having entered "financial Nirvana." Elsewhere there is a capsule review of an off-Broadway show entitled *Sidd*, a play about the early life of Siddhartha, the given name of the historical Buddha. In the sports section, an article on a long-suffering baseball franchise refers to its efforts to change its "bad karma." There have been many sports articles in this vein about either the Boston Red Sox or the Chicago White Sox, for obvious reasons. Both teams in recent seasons showed exactly what it means to overcome bad karma—and also how deeply the argot of Buddhism has penetrated our world.

While we're on the subject of karma, there are not one but two contemporary songs of that title by very popular recording artists: "Karma" by Alicia Keyes and "Karma" by the Black Eyed Peas. Buddhism has become pop. The word *karma* has become part of contemporary slang, with various meanings. We roughly translate it as "what goes around, comes around," as in the Black Eyed Peas song. It's a little more than that, but never mind. There is a good reason why the word *karma* keeps popping up in sports pages, financial reporting, and hip-hop lyrics: it accurately describes the complex causality we observe in the real world.

We even name bars and nightclubs in honor of the historical Buddha. In the Meatpacking District of New York, perhaps the most stylish neighborhood in today's Manhattan, cavernous nightclubs like the Buddha Bar and Buddakan entice a chic young crowd. These places appear more concerned about wok-smoked salmon and raspberry vodka than enlightenment, but even Buddhists want to have fun.

While its cultural manifestations can sometimes be overt, Buddhism generally is a quiet, unobtrusive religion. Since the experience is so individual, Buddhism tends to generate few rules, dogmas, commandments, and the like. It is not the stuff of hymnbooks and television sermons. But that is probably all to the good. To a large segment of the American population, schooled in modern science, agnostic on the subject of God, and deeply skeptical of traditional faiths, Buddhism is a kind of default religion. It is a religion, shall we say, for those who have no religion.

Even among the most rigorously nonreligious, the principles of Buddhism seem to come quite naturally. We say, with some seriousness, that we believe in "the oneness of all things," or, in jest, that "in our next life we want to come back as a supermodel." And, of course, we abhor war. These three statements suggest an internalization of three hallmarks of Buddhist philosophy: 1) the essential oneness of man and his environment; 2) the eternity of life, as expressed in the notion of reincarnation; and 3) a resolute opposition to violence.

Everyone wants to feel "one" with the universe or with the rest of mankind. A lot of people try to visualize this ecstatic union or experience it in the great outdoors. The efforts of educated, urban folk to get "this close" to nature can be quite passionate—and at times amusing. In his book *Bobos in Paradise*, about today's "bourgeois bohemians" who seek new modes of moral and spiritual excellence, *New York Times* columnist David Brooks relates this experience:

> I'm sitting on a rock in the Big Blackfoot River in western Montana. The sun is glistening off the water, and the grasses on the banks are ablaze in their fall glory. The air is crisp and silent, and I'm utterly alone but for the hawk gliding by above and the trout lurking in the water below. This is the spot where Norman Maclean set and Robert Redford filmed *A River Runs Through It*, and I'm sitting here waiting for one of those perfect moments when time stops and I feel myself achieving a mystical communion with nature.
>
> But nothing's happening. I've been hanging around this magnificent setting for 30 minutes and I haven't had one moment of elevated consciousness. The ageless rhythms of creation are happening all around me. The crisp air whispers. The branches sway. The ducks wing by silently. . . . "Eventually all things merge into one, and a river runs through it," Maclean writes. When I read that back in my living room a few months ago, it seemed so profound. Now I can't figure out what the hell it means. The only things merging into one are my fingers into a block of frozen flesh.[1]

It's interesting to note that attempts to achieve oneness or communion with nature tend to drive the very feeling away. We often end up feeling as separate and alienated as before. The same could be said of efforts to discover the self through pure introspection: the more one looks, the more the self recedes.

Contemporary books on human development, or self-help books, often use the principles of Buddhism to state their case and inform their methods. Where once such books focused on various forms of psychotherapy—transactional analysis, Gestalt theory, and so on—today they echo the spiritual teachings of the Buddha. You can gather these books up in your arms, take them to a table, and quickly discover within them, applied to the problems of today, the main points of Buddhist philosophy: 1) the oneness of mind and body; 2) the oneness of man and his environment; 3) the need to look inward to discover spiritual truth; 4) the importance of supporting the happiness of others as the gateway to one's own happiness. The best-selling writer Wayne W. Dyer, who appears on the Public Broadcasting Service, regularly invokes the Buddhist view of life. Here he discusses the subject of the oneness of man and his environment:

> The drop of iron that is in your blood today is a part of the total iron supply. Obviously it was someplace else before you were conceived. Fifteen million years ago it might have been part of an iron ore deposit in Afghanistan. Today it is part of the outer energy that is you. And so it is with all particles in the universe.[2]

Dyer calls the innate potential for enlightenment "your sacred self." As he puts it: "When you discover your sacred self, you awaken this dormant inner energy and let it guide your life." This description closely parallels the Buddhist process of awakening one's Buddha nature, or enlightened potential, which exists within everyone. Similarly, a host of psychological approaches now advise us to visualize our happiness or even to "think happy." However, this means nothing in itself. Visualizing yourself as happy is like the early science-fiction fantasies of man flying. Creating absolute happiness through Buddhism is like actually building an airplane as opposed to dreaming about flying. One cannot simply think about happiness and expect to find it. So far, there really is no substitute for actual Buddhist practice itself.

This beautiful philosophy already profoundly influences our culture and touches our lives in ways hard to imagine only a half century ago. A most gentle and tolerant life philosophy, Buddhism has throughout the ages peacefully coexisted with other religions, never conquering a single nation or province through force. But Buddhism is somewhat irresistible, managing to influence other religions even as it does not seek to co-opt them. For in a very broad sense, Buddhism is that part of all religions that highlights the inner truth, which speaks directly to the eternity we sense within. Buddhism, one might even say, is like the core view, the common thread, uniting many of the secular and religious philosophies of our times. It acts as a bridge, not a barrier. Buddhism bridges the gap between believers in the eternity of the human spirit and determined skeptics who think that there is only the phenomenal world as we find it. Buddhism remains the best description of the universe—and the individual human being's place within that universe—that has ever been discovered.

There is no space within a single book to talk about all of Buddhism, its hundreds of schools, its 84,000 *sutras*, or teachings. The subject is vast. Countless books, articles, tapes, lectures, and courses are available today on Buddhism. But it is very difficult at times to get an idea exactly what you are supposed to *do*, right now, to be a Buddhist or, perhaps the ultimate goal, become a Buddha. Some recommend thinking a certain way, but shortly after trying to think that certain way, the disobedient mind wanders right back onto its accustomed path. Life goes on, and nothing really changes. There are some who encourage you to go on retreat, or to rearrange your life in some drastic way, or to give up a lot of what makes you who you are in order to, presumably, be someone better. In Nichiren Buddhism, the Buddhism described in this book, you can become enlightened exactly as you are. Buddhism is also popularly thought to include a series of denials or renunciations: of selfish cravings, negative thoughts, jealousy, and so forth. This view includes a kind of asceticism that may not be easy to accomplish. Practicing austerities, such as eating only certain kinds of foods and meditating for hours a day, seems in this modern age a kind of escapism, since it rules out the possibility of a normal life within society. Getting up and going to work every day is already a modern-day austerity.

Why is the road to enlightenment considered so arduous? Why does it have to take so long? Isn't there an easier way? Well, yes, there is.

NOTES ON INTRODUCTION

[1] David Brooks, *Bobos in Paradise: The New Upper Class and How They Got There* (New York: Simon & Schuster, 2000), 218–19.

[2] Dr. Wayne W. Dyer, *Your Sacred Self* (New York: HarperCollins, 1995), 11.

1

A LIFE PHILOSOPHY

For the Twenty-First Century

A BOOK OPENS LIKE A DOOR, REVEALING A NEW WORLD.
In this one, there are shoes outside the door, lots of shoes. (It is customary before attending a gathering of Buddhists to remove your shoes.) But do come in. In this room, there are cushions on the floor and a bell. The bell sounds and the proceedings begin. In this room you will discover two wonderful things: joy in a bottle and a wish-granting jewel. You will definitely find them—but not yet. First you have to listen to various speeches and presentations. Life is always like that. If you were given the joy and the jewel straight off, instead of having to learn a bit about them first, you would not be able to use them. You wouldn't "get" what they were.

Nevertheless, embedded in these pages are *joy in a bottle* and a *wish-granting jewel*. That means Buddhism contains the secret to discovering the wellspring of happiness as well as the means to tap into it.

Why Buddhism? Buddhism isn't the only way, but it is the way that makes the most sense. The other major religions have had tremendous value as the force behind the great cultures of the world, but as science unravels the mysteries of life, our myths about life are passing into history. In Buddhism there is no creation myth and no Creator. Buddhism is unique among the world religions in that it makes no claim to divine revelation. It is the story and the teaching of a human being who, through his own efforts toward self-perfection, awoke to the truth of life within himself. Some life philosophies seek to change the world by altering man's external environment or by imposing a strict code of behavior, such as moral commandments, dietary habits, dress codes, or social restrictions. These restrictions tend to reinforce the group by separating its members from others. This is the very definition of alienation, "to be separated from others." Buddhism deals with the essence of the problem—man himself.

Buddhism is a life philosophy that explores the phenomenon of the self in an almost scientific way, aiming for individual self-perfection, without reliance on any outside or higher power. That's why Buddhism has been called "the science of life." But Buddhism transcends science, because it actually explains the eternal law that exists in and behind the phenomenal world and the universe. Science is really an introduction to Buddhism.

When we look up at the stars, we are looking back in time. Because the distances of space are vast and the speed of light is finite, the starlight we see was emitted millions or even billions of years before we were born. The twinkle of the stars, while charming, can also be slightly chilling. To contemplate the depths of space and the immensities of time, to think that our precious selves and our most important thoughts and dreams exist for the barest instant in the life span of the universe, can be humbling. We are tiny, transient beings whose hopes and dreams are extremely fleeting in the cosmic scheme of things. This perception or insight was at the heart of the historical Buddha's enlightenment. With his awakened eyes, the Buddha realized that desires and attachments can blind us to the law of life and result in the fiction that one's self is absolute, which leads us to view the world and society egocentrically.

Only a few hundred years ago, our ancestors looked out at this same dazzling vista and were at ease with the thought that they were bound by a finite cubic space, around which the stars revolved. They thought their world was a mere six thousand years old. The human being who contemplates the sky tonight has an entirely different perspective than his or her predecessors, who named the stars for their heroes and appointed gods and goddesses to personify their hopes and dreams. Under the unceasing pressure of facts, human beings have been revising the idea of God as someone "up there." More of us are coming to view God or our spiritual essence as something "in here," closer to the heart than to heaven.

In parallel with modern astronomical discoveries, a new science of the infinitesimal sprang into being. It is now generally accepted that at the subatomic level our material world—the hard surfaces that surround us and form the reality of our everyday lives—is somewhat evanescent. At the particle level, matter both exists and does not exist. Reduced to its submicroscopic fundaments, reality is not really solid but, rather, wavelike or energetic. Quantum physics suggests that the nature of the particles themselves is altered by the method of measurement—a particle one moment, a wave the next, depending on how it is viewed. Matter at its most fundamental level therefore contains an element of uncertainty. Like a chimera, it changes from moment to moment.

Life, too, is a subatomic thing. The heavier elements in the human body—all the ones heavier than iron—are derived from supernovae, giant exploding stars that lit the heavens eons before our own solar system was born. Supernovae, then, are integral to the existence of the human race. They seem so far away, so ancient, yet they are one with us.

You probably have been gradually coming around to this Buddhist view of things for a long time, though you may not know anything about Buddhism. Nearly all educated people now recognize the fundamental oneness of human beings and their environment. Thanks to advances in the life sciences, we now take it for granted that our connection to the fragile ecosystem does not end with our own skin but is part of a complex and subtle interaction. This central tenet of Buddhist philosophy represents a major intellectual departure from the prevailing worldview of only a century ago, when the Western societies, based on monotheistic, anthropomorphic faiths, regarded man as standing at the apex of nature, alone and aloof, frequently at odds with and striving to subdue the natural world around him.

Certainly American writers from Emerson and Thoreau to Melville and Whitman celebrated the miracles of nature and the dynamic harmony of all life, and at times the poets have given voice to the single great unity expounded by Buddhism. But as an underlying view of the world, it is a relatively new insight in the West. We now see, or are beginning to see, the human species as part of the larger pulsing fabric of life, and we realize that our blunt attempts at subduing nature can have terrible, unintended consequences. Many people today feel somehow out of kilter with the environment that surrounds them. We sense that mankind has gone against the rhythm of the natural world. Thoughtful people around the world are gradually coming to the realization that there is a rhythm to the universe, and whether or not our own lives are in harmony with it will determine if we can survive and be happy.

No living organism exists independently of others. This is science. It is also the twenty-five-hundred-year-old Buddhist principle of "dependent origination," articulated by the historical Buddha, Shakyamuni. It means, essentially, that no beings or phenomena exist on their own; everything in the world comes into existence in response to causes and conditions, that is, the law of cause and effect.

Shakyamuni Buddha, who lived in ancient India around the time of Plato and Aristotle, was a man of surpassing wisdom, but he was a man, not a god. That is the first important point in Buddhism. The Buddha may have been a great avatar of wisdom and compassion, but he was, after all, a male mammal. We call him the "historical" Buddha because he was the first documented one, the first to be written about. But other Buddhas preceded him, he said, in time and space. The word *buddha* comes from the Sanskrit for "enlightened one" and predates him. The Buddha, whose given name was Siddhartha and whose family name was Gautama, is known as Shakyamuni, because he was a member of the Shakya clan. Shakyamuni means "sage of the Shakyas." (See Glossary, p. 245, for pronunciations.)

He spoke in stories and parables and tended to use analogy more than theory. To a very large extent, the challenge for modern readers is how to take his philosophy from the realm of ideas and translate it into the realm of everyday life. What was it that the historical Buddha, the Indian prince Siddhartha, realized twenty-five centuries ago at his moment of enlightenment while meditating under the legendary *bodhi* tree? What was this grand epiphany that we are still trying, millennia later, to decipher and share?

It is impossible to know what he knew exactly—or to express it adequately in words—but apparently he reached beyond ordinary consciousness to a place where he perceived himself as one with the life of the universe. It is said that in the early stages of his meditation, he was still riven by the distinction between subject (himself) and object (world). The latter was like a wall surrounding the former. Eventually, he penetrated this illusion, coming to a profound insight regarding the true aspect of reality, which he partly defined as *impermanence*. So what is impermanence? Everything we see, all phenomena, are in a state of flux or constant change. At the subatomic level, this is a fact that modern physicists have explained in exquisite detail. The science of particle physics informs us that at the subatomic level (the subworld of quarks, neutrinos, leptons, positrons, and antipositrons) we cannot speak exclusively of fixed or solid matter but only of ever-shifting waves and energy patterns. The Buddha had an intuitive grasp of this unseen submicroscopic reality, as well as its relationship with the macrocosm and the individual human life. Indeed, the Buddha's depiction of the universe parallels the theory of special relativity by Albert Einstein and the uncertainty principle of Werner Heisenberg. But while Buddhism joins with the physicists in teaching that everything in the universe is in constant flux, it does so with a very different purpose. Instead of attempting a scientific explanation of nature, Buddhism seeks to clarify the human position amid the flux and to discover a point of absolute reliance within the self.

The world and society never cease to change for even a single moment. It looks as if the table at which you sit or the book you are holding in your hands is solidly constructed. But, like Ozymandias' statue, everything will crumble someday. The Buddha explained that suffering emerges in our hearts because we forget or are ignorant of this principle of impermanence and become attached to things. We believe that what we possess, from material comforts to human relationships, will last forever. Of course, they won't; thus we experience the pain of loss. Even the attachment to life itself entails suffering, because someday we must die. Buddhism teaches us to recognize these cycles of impermanence and to have the courage to accept them.

All things fluctuate, rising and falling, living and dying. Amid this perpetual change, you are changing, too. We know from biology that the cells in the human body completely regenerate themselves every seven years or so. Yet, we tend to regard ourselves as fixed entities, immutable, incapable of real change (our spouses and significant others usually feel even more strongly about this than we do!). But the important thing from the perspective of Buddhism is: how are you changing, moment to moment, as you adapt to the ceaseless change around you? In Buddhism, we direct these changes ourselves. In the ceaseless drama between our individual destinies and the outside forces that challenge us, we become the directors. It is as if you have been driving this vehicle, called the self, your whole life, but for the first time you are allowed to place your hands on the controls. We call this process "human revolution," and it is lifelong.

In addition to his realization regarding the iron principle of impermanence, the Buddha, at the moment of his enlightenment, is said to have had a vision of the interrelatedness of all things unfold in his awakened mind. The universe and all things are forever engulfed in change, arising and ceasing, appearing and disappearing, in an unending cycle conditioned by the law of causation (what we would call today the laws of science). All things are subject to the law of cause and effect, and consequently, nothing exists independently of other things.

Nichiren Daishonin, a Japanese monk and founder of a school of Buddhism, wrote seven hundred years ago, "You are the universe and the universe is you." Compare this ancient insight to the late astronomer Carl Sagan's famous statement that we are all made of "star stuff." That is, because the molecules in our bodies are byproducts of dying stars, we are literally "one" with the universe. Unlike most religious philosophies, which teach that ordinary, everyday reality exists on a different plane than the ultimate truth (or God), Buddhism reveals that they are inseparable and one. However, this relationship is beyond our intellectual comprehension, hence it is considered "mystic."

Two but Not Two

There are many, many examples of a concordance between Buddhism and the modern scientific view of nature. For example, advances in medicine and the physiology of the human brain have led to a further important unifying concept: the oneness of body and mind. This dynamic unity is expressed in the Buddhist term *shiki shin funi* (in Japanese, *shiki* means "body," *shin* means "mind," and *funi* means "two but not two"). The validity of this principle has been documented in countless studies that show the interplay between people's psychological state and the health of their bodies. We know now that a person's mental well-being significantly affects his or her corporeal health, especially when it comes to dealing with and recovering from illness.

More important, shiki shin funi explains that happiness is a matter of harmony with the environment in which we live and with ourselves. When your body is in one place and your mind is in another, you can never be truly happy. In a sense, unhappiness is being physically present at one's job each day while thinking of how to find another job—or of vacationing in Maui. A happy person can fit into any situation and create value there. Harmony is being where you want to be and wanting to be where you are. Buddhism aims for the total development of the person, spiritually and physically. Through Buddhist practice, we gain good health and financial fortune as well as a growing awareness of ourselves and a concern for others. These benefits of practice are the spiritual and material proofs of Buddhism's power.

Ultimately, whatever religion you practice and whatever life philosophy you uphold, chances are that it now involves some element of direct seeking into the human heart. The quest or journey of your faith (or even perhaps of your agnosticism) is directed *inward* as a means of seeking truth, rather than *outward* toward some divine figure or symbol. This search for the true or authentic self, amid a world of turbulence and change, has become a characteristic even of traditional faiths.

Mainstream faiths now increasingly tend toward a more inward, direct experience of their god, as in "personal" Christianity and Judaism. Even jihad, the Islamic concept of struggle, is being interpreted by moderate Muslims as an inner struggle with the self in a quest for spiritual transformation, rather than a battle against an exterior enemy. While it would be naïve to suggest that these inklings of Buddhist influence in other religious traditions are completely transformational, the trend is noteworthy. The idea that spirituality exists within the person lies at the heart of Buddhism. We are all Buddhists then, to some degree, simply because we live in this modern age. We are a reflection of our times.

After the Buddha attained his enlightenment in deep meditation under a *pipal* (fig) tree—later called the bodhi tree—he spent the remainder of his life trying to explain it to others and to help them achieve the same state. It was not an easy job. In doing so, he adopted various means of instruction, geared to the knowledge level and experience of his listeners. He spoke in parables and analogies as he tried to lead people away from suffering toward happiness. His earlier teachings contained many precepts or rules. His more mature teachings emphasized compassion and the potential of all people to reach enlightenment in this lifetime. His variable teaching methods are referred to as "expedient means." He taught people according to their level of understanding. Everything in Buddhism, including this book, tends to be organized in this way.

A Buddhism for Our Time

When we talk about Buddhism, we should also talk about *time*. Shakyamuni Buddha had a very sophisticated, almost modern sense of time. He seemed to have had a premonition of modern cosmology.

This he revealed in the "Life Span" chapter of the Lotus Sutra, his greatest teaching. In this luminous work, the Buddha revealed the nature of his own enlightenment and the potential of every human being to achieve this indestructibly happy state. He declared that his own enlightenment had existed, presumably through many reincarnations or rebirths, from the remotest past. He spoke in terms of "major world systems" and *kalpas*. A "world system" would be a group of planets not unlike our own solar system. He postulated the existence of many of them throughout the universe. A "major" world system might pertain to what we call galaxies. A "kalpa" was a Hindu unit of time roughly equivalent to 12 million solar years (other texts say more). He said one would have to take the dust particles from a major world system, each speck, and multiply that times a kalpa to grasp the time span of the universe. Clearly, he meant an unimaginably long time. Yet, in the Lotus Sutra (*sutra* means "teaching"), he was much closer to estimating the life span of the universe than other prophets or holy books that we know. He grasped the grand scale of cosmic time.

In the current model of the origin of the universe, the big bang is thought to have occurred some 15 to 20 billion years ago. However, since the universe has been shown to be an expanding one and could theoretically at some point contract, some cosmologists believe the process is endlessly repeating. This dovetails with the Buddha's realization that all things are in a perpetual state of flux, arising and ceasing in an unending cycle of birth and death conditioned by the laws of causation. The big bang theory, by the way, also conforms to the Buddhist concept of the simultaneous nature of cause and effect (*inga guji* in Japanese), a rather subtle but critical variation on sequential cause and effect as we normally understand it. Buddhism holds that when a cause is made, its effect is already inherent within it. According to the big bang theory, the universe burst forth from an infinitely dense, perhaps even microscopic, cosmic seed, which contained within it all the visible effects of the universe today. Shakyamuni also allowed for the possibility of life on numerous other worlds, and suggested that other Buddhas dwelled in the far reaches of the universe. Buddhism may be said to have no argument with science (or even perhaps with science fiction). The Lotus Sutra, which Shakyamuni termed "most difficult to believe and difficult to understand," is cosmic in scale and rich in human scope.

The Buddha also said that the universe is alive. Even insentient things are capable of enlightenment or Buddhahood. This doesn't jibe with our view of things. How can rocks be enlightened? Upon examination, however, we see that life at the infinitesimal level can sometimes assume a nonliving form. Under certain conditions, for example, some viruses take the form of inert crystals. Under other conditions (higher temperatures, for example), they are able to reproduce and grow as living organisms. So the boundary between living and nonliving, being and nonbeing, can be rather thin, like a very sharp razor. Life, in a sense, is a potential, and sometimes it is in a state of dormancy. This is exactly what the Buddha taught. Someday, centuries (or kalpas) in the future, the iron and the magnesium in that rock may be inside someone's body, enriching cells or coursing through veins. In a sense, then, the life of the universe is coextensive with our lives. This is quite consistent with the Buddhist view that there is a law of life, or *dharma*, that permeates all phenomena, from the outermost reaches of the universe to the tiniest subatomic particles. This same law exists within each and every individual.

In the West, the nonliving world is thought of as two categories, matter and energy—just as we tend to divide the person in two, body and mind. Though matter and energy seem separate, to the Buddha they were really only different aspects of a common essence. Twenty-five centuries later, Albert Einstein had a similar insight, expressed in the mathematical formula energy = mass times the speed of light squared.

The historical Buddha was not particularly interested in science for its own sake. The whole point of his seeking was to relieve the sufferings of human beings. Although he knew that all people were potential Buddhas, he also realized that some effort or exertion on their part was necessary for them to perceive the truth. We may all be capable of enlightenment, but a kind of fundamental darkness pre-

vents us from realizing it. We are animals, after all, instinctive creatures. Our need to survive in a sometimes hostile world induces a
kind of moral tropism that turns us away from others toward our
own selfish desires. Buddhism defines this tendency toward unhappiness in terms of the "three poisons": greed, anger, and foolishness
(stupidity). We revert to them quite naturally in the absence of a correct philosophy and a consistent practice to polish our lives. This
notion has been demonstrated in countless non-Buddhist works of
literature, including William Golding's *Lord of the Flies*, about a
group of English schoolboys' descent into savagery on a desolate
island. Seven hundred years ago, Nichiren Daishonin, who had
plenty of opportunity to experience the dark side of human nature
in feudal Japan, wrote that the human being is a "talented animal."
The noblest qualities of the human being—wisdom, courage, and
compassion—exist innately in each of us, but it sometimes takes
tremendous effort to bring them out. If people want to become more
than talented animals, to be truly human, then they must embrace
a life philosophy powerful enough to give direction to their desires.

Society today is in a situation of runaway desires. We developed
scientific technology to make life more comfortable, but we have lost
the ability to control that technology. The solution, really, is to make
dramatic changes at the most fundamental level, changes to the
human being. Revolutions in politics, economics, and social structures come and go. But nothing ever really changes. The only revolution that matters anymore is human revolution, a core change in
the outlook of individuals. This is what Buddhism aims for and
achieves, person by person, country by country, next year and the
year after, for a thousand years, ten thousand, and so forth. Buddhists
are incredibly patient. Buddhism, as mentioned, is all about time.

Many people are Buddhists without knowing it. They think like
Buddhists in the way they approach the environment, their communities, and the larger world. Plenty more are interested in being
Buddhist but have no clue about how to practice Buddhism. The
important thing is to stop seeing the Buddha, or one's own enlightenment, as tangential to one's life, something to do on weekends or

on retreat—something in the rearview mirror—and to commence the kind of daily practice that will give real meaning to Buddhist knowledge. Studying Buddhism without practicing it is like trying to get rich by counting someone else's money.

A Higher State of Life

Each of us wants to be wiser, more compassionate, and more courageous—to be better than we are. We would like to turn suffering into happiness, affliction to benefit, hardship to ease. We would ideally face both trial and tragedy in ways that could exalt and strengthen us. In every purpose we want and seek these higher tendencies—wisdom, courage, and compassion. These are also the prime qualities of a Buddha.

In *The Wizard of Oz*, one of the most beloved films ever, the Cowardly Lion, the Scarecrow, and the Tin Man embark on a quest to discover three qualities missing from their lives. The Cowardly Lion seeks courage. The Scarecrow wishes to obtain a brain (wisdom). And the Tin Man yearns to have a heart, especially a "kind" one, to feel for others (compassion). In the climactic moment in the film, the all-powerful Oz is revealed to be a kind of bogus guru who nevertheless, in his own folksy way, eventually fulfills their needs. In L. Frank Baum's original novel, the key scene is slightly different, in a way that makes the meaning of the fable even more explicit:

> "I have come for my courage," announced the Lion, entering the room.
> "Very well," answered the little man; "I will get it for you."
> He went to a cupboard and reaching up to a high shelf took down a square green bottle, the contents of which he poured into a gold-green dish, beautifully carved. Placing this before the Cowardly Lion, who sniffed at it as if he did not like it, the Wizard said,
> "Drink."
> "What is it?" asked the Lion.
> "Well," answered Oz, "if it were inside of you, it would be courage. You know, of course, that courage is always inside one; so that this really cannot be courage until you have swallowed it. Therefore I advise you to drink it as soon as possible."

The Lion hesitated no longer, but drank till the dish was empty.

"How do you feel now?" asked Oz.

"Full of courage," replied the Lion, who went joyfully back to his friends to tell them of his good fortune.[1]

The Lion's quest led to that which he already possessed. Likewise, the others receive talismans of what they seek: the Scarecrow gets a bunch of wheat bran inserted under his hat to make a "brand-new brain" (wisdom), and the Tin Man has a silk-and-sawdust heart (compassion) placed inside his metal breast. (In the film, the Tin Man gets a ticking watch and the Scarecrow receives a diploma.) We know from watching them in action that these are qualities they, too, already possess in generous measure. Courage, wisdom, and compassion are not things that exist outside of our lives, nor are they things that need to be acquired.[2] One should add that these three qualities are virtual antidotes to the "three poisons" mentioned above (greed, anger, and foolishness).

It is no coincidence that *The Wizard of Oz* has proved to be one of the most enduring and popular works of art ever produced. It is a perfect Buddhist parable, one Shakyamuni himself could not have improved. As traditional religions decline in persuasive power, modern films have come to express an alternative, secular theology, whether in the form of aliens who descend from the heavens to teach us the healing power of love or human beings in distant galaxies who learn to respect and wield a "force" that permeates both the person and the universe. (See "Top 6 Films with Buddhist Themes," pp. 28–9.)

Oz's creator, Baum, is unlikely to have had a Buddhist message in mind, but however inadvertently, the story identifies three Buddha qualities and also explains the true relationship between their latent aspects and their manifestations. It moves us because it speaks to that part of human nature that we call the "Buddha nature." Buddhism posits the idea of a Buddha nature, or an inherent cause in each individual for attaining Buddhahood, or enlightenment. The history of Buddhism has seen many doctrinal arguments over the Buddha nature, particularly with regard to whether all people possess it or

TOP 6 FILMS WITH BUDDHIST THEMES

Star Wars (series)

The wisdom of the ages seems to pervade The Force, a mystic, unseen power that pulses through the universe. It can be tapped into and harnessed by individuals through assiduous practice and self-discipline. There are two sides to The Force, light and dark, which are wielded by the Jedi and Sith monastic orders. The light side brings out practitioners' courage and compassion for others, while those on the dark side can use it only to benefit the self.

2001: A Space Odyssey

In its final enigmatic sequences, when the actor Keir Dullea, alone in a strange rococo hotel suite on the far side of Jupiter, ages before our eyes and then dies—only to be reborn as a star child—this film provides the most striking visual expression of the idea of reincarnation ever produced. Mysterious "black monoliths," artifacts or religious symbols of an alien civilization that has reached a higher state of being, sketchily resemble the Gohonzon, or object of worship, in Nichiren Buddhism.

The Wizard of Oz

The storyline is practically a parable out of a Buddhist sutra. No wonder audiences for a half century have been touched deeply by this tale. It speaks directly to their Buddha nature, in terms the Buddha himself would approve.

just a (mostly male) elite of monks, scholars, and aristocrats. The Buddhism we are concerned with here holds that all people—men, women, and children—are endowed with the Buddha nature. Everyone has the innate reservoirs of wisdom, courage, and compassion to attain enlightenment.

Where do these qualities come from? Aren't some people born with more brains or courage than others?

Pure intellectual knowledge is no guarantee of wisdom, although many very smart people also turn out to be exceptionally wise (Benjamin Franklin and Abraham Lincoln come to mind). There are numerous counterexamples, people who were brilliant but whose lives were a mess. Brilliant people may even be more

The Buddha in Your Rearview Mirror

Bambi

A moving portrayal of the Great Chain of Being, *Bambi* vividly shows the intricate connections between all living things and the insentient environment that supports them. The scene where raindrops begin falling—plinking in a pond, dappling the leaves, splashing like water bombs on scurrying insects, while the musical score provides a perfectly syncopated accompaniment—captures for a few moments, as no film ever has, the underlying rhythms of life.

Singin' in the Rain

The movie illustrates the key Buddhist principle of *esho funi*, or "oneness of person and environment," in the correct sense that one's environment essentially mirrors one's inner life state—as when Gene Kelly dances undaunted during a rainstorm. Though the outside world may be cloudy or stormy, what matters is how we feel inside. An enlightened person is not swayed by external changes and faces a storm of obstacles with dignity. That is a Buddha.

The Lord of the Rings (trilogy)

These movies portray a panoramic vision of life in which distinctions between living and nonliving are blurred, especially in their portrayal of the Ents, a race of sentient treelike beings. Legolas, the Prince of the Elves, who is very spiritual and takes time to appreciate small things, is a good example of a Buddhist character. Of course, it helps that the character is played by Orlando Bloom, a practicing Buddhist in real life.

prone to psychological instability, a case in point being the physicist in the movie *A Beautiful Mind*. Meanwhile, the "simplest" people, by intellectual standards, often seem to have the most common sense. When it comes to courage, people throughout history have suspected that some were endowed with more *physical* courage than others, and this notion is celebrated in stories, dramas, and films, from *The Iliad* to *Saving Private Ryan*. They are the boys and girls who plunge into the middle of a scrum on a soccer field, feet and elbows flailing, oblivious to harm, or the ones who think nothing of shinnying up a backyard maple so high that their parents beg them to come down. However, the small daily acts of courage that constitute our lives usually are not about physical derring-do. Except for firefighters and police, few are called on to perform physical acts of bravery as part of everyday life. That does not mean we never have to act resolutely, to show real guts. It might require considerable courage, for example, to tell someone you care about that he or she has a drinking or substance-abuse problem. It sometimes takes guts to tell someone in your office, "I'm not going to do it that way, because it's unethical." It might even take a certain amount of courage just to tell a child, "No." Most of all, it takes a good deal of fortitude to refuse to go along with the group when you know that something is wrong—that is, to stand up for justice when you know it will make you unpopular. That can be a truly courageous thing.

Genuine grown-up courage involves making difficult decisions. Nevertheless, in our culture the concept of courage is typically conflated with the idea of physical courage. Our ideas of compassion are similarly deluded. Compassion for others can become like a fetish, especially for the rich and famous. One can appear altruistic and still have a "sensitivity chip missing." In Buddhism, the dignity of human life is most precious. Each person has inestimable value. As one comes to value one's own life in this way, one's lesser, egotistic self recedes and the lives of other people become precious, too. This greater self is better equipped to work for the happiness of all.

That courage, wisdom, and compassion tend to be buried or hidden from view most of the time is not surprising. Ancient Buddhist teachings and parables refer to this very fact. In the story of "The Jewel and the Robe," as told by the Buddha himself, the quality of Buddhahood or enlightenment is likened to a precious jewel that has been sewn into the robe of a traveler while he is sleeping. He journeys long and far, begging for food and shelter, never realizing he possesses an incredible treasure sewn into the very garment he has been wearing. Our own reservoirs of wisdom, courage, and compassion are no different. They are "the treasure too close to see." By sincerely practicing Buddhism, according to the teachings of Nichiren Daishonin described in this book, all people can discover and display a magnificent quiet courage, genuine compassion, and real wisdom as they face and overcome the obstacles in their lives. Buddhism is a life philosophy that systematically enables anyone, regardless of circumstances, to manifest these three universal qualities at will. It presupposes that a "higher tendency" exists in everyone and is ever present. The trouble is it remains dormant, like the bulb of a flower, waiting for the right conditions to nurture it. How does Buddhism bring it forth? The answer is a long-form subject–the mystery of enlightenment–and the subject of this book.

Buddhism 3.0

When the historical Buddha, Shakyamuni, was in the advanced stages of practice, he embarked on a program of self-mortification and renunciation. He did yoga and practiced all kinds of austerities, including prolonged fasting. According to legend, at one point he touched his belly and could feel his spinal column, and, reaching around to his back, he could touch his belly.[3] Villagers who saw him said his skin turned black. He was starving. At one point, he began to recall his boyhood days in the gardens of his father's palace, sitting under an apple tree–and happiness welled up inside him. He thought: Could this feeling of happiness, which arose from neither greed nor desire, be evil? What was the point of suffering so extremely in order to conquer suffering? He began to think–surely it is by happiness that one achieves happiness!

In many religious traditions people are taught that desires are the cause of unhappiness, that they are in fact sinful and destructive. Many of us learn from childhood to deny our desires or to ignore them. But whenever we try to deny our desires, we just seem to think about them even more. Nichiren Daishonin, a profound Buddhist thinker who wished to reform and elevate religious life in medieval Japan, realized that the attempt to extinguish all desire was a kind of living death and that it excluded the vast majority of human beings from Buddhism. Even the yearning to achieve enlightenment is a desire. Nichiren (pronounced KNEE-chee-ren;

see Glossary, p. 245) revered Shakyamuni Buddha and based his philosophy on a close reading of his teachings, particularly the Lotus Sutra. However, he recognized the astonishing variety of the historical Buddha's methods and the "tactfulness" of the various sutras, with respect to the level of learning of the audience. The Buddha's sermons had been geared to the ability of his listeners. After studying the various teachings of the many schools of Buddhism that existed in Japan during his time, Nichiren came upon what he called "the direct path" to enlightenment. He discovered this "secret," as he termed it, hidden in the depths of the Lotus Sutra, which was the second to last teaching of the historical Buddha's life. (The last was called the Nirvana Sutra.) Here is what he wrote about this tantalizing secret:

> The benefit of all the other sutras is uncertain, because they teach that one must first make good causes and only then can one become a Buddha at some later time. With regard to the Lotus Sutra, when one's hand takes it up, that hand immediately attains Buddhahood, and when one's mouth chants it, that mouth is itself a Buddha, as, for example, the moon is reflected in the water the moment it appears from behind the eastern mountains, or as a sound and its echo arise simultaneously.[4]

There will be much more about chanting later, but for now it should be added that this *gosho,* or letter, was written to a woman, a lay nun named Ueno. The inclusion of women in the ranks of enlightenment was a shocking idea in Japan at the time.

Even more revolutionary was Nichiren's method. He formulated a relatively simple practice for each person—the same exact practice for everyone—to realize that enlightened aspect, to polish it and make it shine brightly for everyone to see, in this lifetime, now, just as we are. This involves chanting and venerating the *daimoku,* or title, of the Lotus Sutra, and reciting portions of its key chapters. This practice can be performed easily and consistently, morning and evening, in the privacy of one's home or in other people's homes, without altering one's lifestyle one iota. It involves no self-mortification or complex meditations. This is Buddhism for the layman and lay-woman.

It built very carefully on Buddhist tradition, especially the sutras. It also benefited from the deep wisdom and theoretical refinements of the Chinese scholars who transmitted Buddhism. In a sense, Nichiren's approach is like Buddhism 3.0, just as Windows and Macintosh have updated refinements of their original breakthrough computer programs. The underlying operating system is the same, but more sophisticated software is used to access it. Nichiren's Buddhism is like a tremendous advance in the "software" of Buddhist practice. For our own time period, Daisaku Ikeda, the president of the lay organization of Nichiren believers around the world, has emerged as the foremost interpreter of Nichiren Buddhism. (His books, lectures, and guidance might be compared to a version 4.0, except that today's practice adheres quite strictly to Nichiren's original vision.) This particular school of Buddhism is practiced by millions of people worldwide and in more than 190 nations and territories. Does that mean that the reader should expect a singular, proprietary version of enlightenment—the sort of presumptive I-know-best view? Not exactly.

For starters, we may want to revise our understanding of the term *enlightened*. Perhaps it is not something that you reach, like the top of the Empire State Building, and only by taking the stairs (Buddhism usually is portrayed as a long, hard climb). Nor is it some sort of giant epiphany, like a bolt of lightning or a bang on the head from your master. Enlightenment may just be an incremental thing, with certain instant results and deeper long-term benefits. You may not have to be a saint to achieve it.

Of all the pop Western views of enlightenment or *satori* or whatever you call the ultimate aim of Buddhist practice, the ones that seem the most persistent involve what could be called "fool on the hill" moments, from the Beatles song of the same name written by Paul McCartney. "The Fool on the Hill" is about someone who favors isolation from society, preferring to commune with nature, no matter what people may think about him. Other people get on with their lives, but he prefers to watch the sun go down and see "the world spinning round." This corresponds to the widespread view of enlightenment as some kind of brilliant sunset or dawn, the whole universe spread out before us, our minds embracing everything all at once. Of course, actual first-person descriptions from famous gurus and saints typically have that cosmic, all-embracing sound. Here is one from the classic (and quite marvelous) book, *Autobiography of a Yogi* by Paramahansa Yogananda, who is describing an encounter with his *guruji*, or master:

> We looked into each other's eyes, where tears were shining. A blissful wave engulfed me. I was conscious that the Lord, in the form of my guru, was expanding the limited ardors of my heart to vast reaches of cosmic love. . . . All objects within my panoramic gaze trembled and vibrated like quick motion pictures. My body, my Master's, the pillared courtyard, the furniture and the floor, the trees and sunshine, occasionally became violently agitated, until all melted into a luminescent sea; even as sugar crystals, thrown into a glass of water, dissolve after being shaken. The unifying light alternated with materializations of form, the metamorphoses revealing the law of cause and effect in creation. An oceanic joy broke upon the calm endless shores of my soul. The Spirit of God, I realized, is exhaustless Bliss; His body is countless tissues of light. A swelling glory within me began to envelop towns, continents, the earth, solar and stellar systems, tenuous nebulae, and floating universes. The entire cosmos, gently luminous, like a city seen afar at night, glimmered within the infinitude of my being.[5]

Enlightenment in Yogananda's view was like an ecstatic vision. We should not derogate or make light of direct religious experience, and Yogananda's book is quite a beautiful journey, but this is not really what Nichiren Buddhists are after. Enlightenment in Nichiren Buddhism is more like a day-by-day process of elevating one's consciousness and life condition. This is not to say that your results will seem any less real or even spectacular. There just are not that many fool-on-the-hill moments in real life. The view of enlightenment as some sort of ecstatic, all-at-once, blissful realization tends to confuse and intimidate regular, workaday people from exploring Buddhism.

The Buddha in Your Rearview Mirror

It seems so exotic. Only a true iconoclast could achieve it. You would have to become an entirely different person to get to that state. And then, who would you be?

Many of us know people who have adopted esoteric practices and religions and then maintained a kind of self-satisfied air about them. The symptoms are somewhat common. Such people are remarkably gentle, even excessively so. They speak softly and wouldn't harm a flea. They wear flowing, diaphanous clothing. There is about them a kind of hauteur, a spiritual grandeur, an aura of rectitude. You feel you can't eat a candy bar or drink a beer in their presence.

In Nichiren Buddhism, you can become enlightened exactly as you are. Buddhism is not about sitting in the corner of a room and feeling superior. It is something you can actually *use* in your life to improve your life, without turning yourself into some kind of smiling, unrecognizable automaton. Each person's path toward enlightenment is unique. Some people who practice this Buddhism become calmer and more serene. Some become more highly strung, ambitious, and full of energy. This Buddhism is propulsive. It moves and inspires people into action—at their jobs, within their families, and in their communities. It is also highly individual. What you get from it ultimately depends on you.

The idea that enlightenment or Buddhahood is not a destination, pursued year after year, lifetime after lifetime, but an immanent quality, present in every person, ready to be awakened at any moment, is a bracing one. Suppose you could turn it on, like a light. If this were so, wouldn't you want to know where the switch was, how to flick it on?

Buddhism in America

It has been said that there are three kinds of Buddhists in America: baggage Buddhists, nightstand Buddhists, and practicing Buddhists.

Baggage Buddhist is a term applied to immigrants who bring their traditional life philosophy with them when they resettle in this country. Buddhists from Japan, Korea, Sri Lanka, Thailand, Myanmar, Vietnam, and other Asian nations bring with them the rich traditions of their homelands. The Buddhism they practice can be any one of the many schools that have flourished over the centuries. Of the approximately 372 million Buddhists in the world, about three million reside in North America.[6]

The Buddhist schools fall into two main streams: Theravada and Mahayana. Followers of Theravada, also called Hinayana Buddhism, tend to come from south Asian nations, where the earlier teachings of the Buddha spread. Since *Hinayana* means "lesser vehicle" and *Mahayana* means "greater vehicle"—in the sense of a vehicle to transport one to enlightenment—one can sense immediately that invidious comparisons exist between these two major streams. So we will use the more neutral term, *Theravada*. For an objective capsule description of the two main streams of Buddhism, there is this from Joseph Campbell's classic book *The Hero With a Thousand Faces*:

> Hinayana Buddhism (the Buddhism surviving in Ceylon, Burma, and Siam) reveres the Buddha as a human hero, a supreme saint and sage. Mahayana Buddhism, on the other hand (the Buddhism of the north) regards the Enlightened One as a world savior, an incarnation of the universal principle of enlightenment.[7]

Note the difference in emphasis: in Theravada, there is strong personal identification with the historical Buddha as the source of wisdom, while in Mahayana there is the centrality of salvation and the Buddha as representative of a *principle* of enlightenment, which is universal. Theravada Buddhism bases its practice on the Pali Canon, the teachings of the Buddha that were orally transmitted centuries after his death. They believe this represents the purest, most original form of Buddhism, since it is based on the Buddha's words. Their practice includes ethical behavior, meditation, and insight. Some branches of Theravada can be characterized by strict adherence to precepts or rules, and it also sometimes involves worship of images of the historical Buddha (hence the ubiquitous "fat" statues). Theravadans sometimes revere Shakyamuni Buddha so deeply that they give up the idea of becoming Buddhas themselves (at least in this life). Another key feature of Theravada Buddhism is the goal of diminishing and eventually extinguishing the fires of human desire through practice. About 38 percent of Buddhists living in North America define themselves as Theravadan, and 56 percent as Mahayanan.

While Theravada Buddhism migrated to the south of India, especially to Southeast Asia, the Mahayana stream flowed along trade routes from northern India into Nepal and Tibet, thence to China, where it came under the influence of Confucianism. It later spread to the Korean peninsula and Japan, where it coexisted with the native Shintoism. The Mahayana philosophy emphasizes the sutras from the later period of the Buddha's life. In Mahayana Buddhism, compassion is more important than adherence to any set of codes or moral laws. Saving others often is viewed as more important than one's own enlightenment. Zen Buddhism, Tibetan Buddhism (or Vajrayana), and the Nichiren school can all be characterized as forms of Mahayana Buddhism.

All these points are necessarily quite broad and general. There can be considerable overlap between the two main Buddhist traditions. Both Theravadans and Mahayanans will surely find something to disagree with here, and that is because there is quite a bit of diversity within the two main streams—and even within the various schools. "Baggage" Buddhists come from either of the two broad streams. They represent a small but influential minority of Buddhists in America. For example, without the pioneering Nichiren baggage Buddhists, there would be no Nichiren Buddhism in America.

Nightstand Buddhists refers primarily to Americans raised in other traditions. They may have encountered the explanatory books of Alan Watts, a best-selling writer on Buddhist subjects in the sixties and seventies, or others. It would not be presumptuous to say that this paperbound philosophy is often linked with various forms of lifestyle experimentation. Beginning in the late 1950s, the tenets of Zen Buddhism in particular, popularized by Watts and writers like D. T. Suzuki, influenced a generation of Americans whose bohemian critique of mainstream values and religions bloomed in the hippie movement. It was not long before armies of long-haired, blue-jean-clad young people were proclaiming their pacificism, their disdain for material things, and their respect for the environment, while clutching well-thumbed copies of Buddhist texts as their ultimate spiritual references. In many cases, though, the Buddhist element in their lives was more of an intellectual orientation than a rigorously practiced faith. They accepted the tenets as wise and logical and per-haps superior to the religious teachings they had been brought up with, but in their day-to-day experience there was nothing specifically Buddhist—aside from a loose vegetarianism and occasional medita-tion sessions—about their lives.

In recent years, the Dalai Lama, the spiritual leader of Tibetan Buddhism, has made many appearances in this country. He is revered as a teacher, respected for his gentle wisdom, and supported in his quest for justice for his countrymen. Like Zen Buddhism, the Tibetan school entails a thoroughly demanding discipline of strict meditation, study, and ascetic practices. Tibetan Buddhists use a variety of methods including hand gestures (*mudras*), mystic dia-grams (*mandalas*), and various invocations (*mantras*) to point fol-lowers to enlightenment. Tibetans also practice a form of tantric meditation known as "deity yoga" to assist practitioners in over-coming their lesser selves.

Zen Buddhists practice *zazen* (sitting meditation) as a method of reaching enlightenment, and followers often attend retreats fea-turing many periods of meditation per day. Enlightenment in Zen can be achieved in an instant, known as *satori*, when you suddenly "get it." Both Zen and Tibetan schools are heavily influenced by their monastic traditions. Leaving your regular daily life to go on retreat can be an important part of practice. Renunciation of desire is a feature of both schools.

In the realm of *Practicing Buddhists*, an important distinction should be made between *daily* practice and the sporadic retreat. Since the traditional Western faiths, Christianity and Judaism, involve pri-marily a Sabbath practice, with perhaps some brief daily devotions, most Americans are fully involved in their religion only once a week. Buddhism, on the other hand, in whatever form it appears, typically entails a strong daily discipline. In the Nichiren school of Buddhism, this is called *gongyo,* which in Japanese means "assiduous practice." Followers of Nichiren perform gongyo twice a day, seven days a week, 365 days a year. This is integral to the practice and is performed in the exact same manner around the world.

So which kind of Buddhist are you, baggage, nightstand, or practicing? If you were born in this country, you are probably not in the first category. If you are reading this book, you certainly are a bit of the second. Perhaps by the end of this book, you will have joined the ranks of the third.

It is perhaps not so easy to settle down and practice in a particular way. The Buddha is said to have left 84,000 sutras. Since he wrote nothing down himself—the written word was considered untrustworthy twenty-five hundred years ago—his legacy has been subject to various interpretations. His teachings were first passed down orally. Then as many as 400 years later they were written down by monks and scholars. As his teachings spread north and south in the centuries after his death, they came under the influence of many different translators, who, in turn, were creatures of the cultures into which they were born.

Consequently, the Buddhist tradition is extremely varied and the sects or schools based on his philosophy are numerous. So what, then, is the essence of Buddhism? To get an idea of the dilemma, consider the Parable of the Elephant, which is widely repeated in Buddhist scriptures. At a time when wandering monks living near the Buddha began to be convinced of the rightness of their views, the Buddha gathered them together and told them the following story. In former times a raja sent for all the blind men in his kingdom and placed an elephant in their midst. One man felt the head of the elephant, another an ear, another a tusk, another the tuft of its tail. Asked to describe the elephant, one said that an elephant was a large pot, others that it was a big fan, or a ploughshare, or a branch. Thus each depicted the creature as the part that he first touched. The raja was highly amused.

To the Buddha, the wandering monks, sure of their beliefs, were like the blind men, unseeing and unaware of the whole truth.

The state of Buddhahood is the life condition one reaches through the practice of Buddhism. But such a state is difficult to explain in concrete terms since our inner lives can be experienced only subjectively. It is thus problematic for one who has not yet practiced Buddhism to comprehend the state of Buddhahood. The door to understanding is through faith. That may seem contradictory with regard to a life philosophy with no God or metaphysical being to speak of and thus no apparent need for faith. But faith in Buddhism is more like the process we call "suspension of disbelief," which describes what we do every time we go to the movies or watch television. We suspend disbelief for a time in order to enjoy, say, a suspense thriller or a horror movie. In Buddhism, we suspend our disbelief in order to gain great benefit and insight. Since the role of Buddhist faith is so important, we need to examine it in the context of other versions of faith.

A Crisis of Faith

In the West, faith has traditionally meant belief in something higher than oneself. It has often been defined in terms of a belief in a "higher power." This supreme being is typically the source of wisdom, truth, forgiveness, and, ultimately, eternal salvation. In addition, faith has been closely linked to revelation or divine inspiration, and sometimes is said not to exist at all without it. Most faith depends for its strength and conviction on understanding or internalization of certain precepts and a carefully delineated transcendental history—the Bible, for instance, or the Koran.

In Buddhism, faith means something quite different. It can sometimes seem like a subtle difference, but it is crucial to understanding the importance of Buddhism at this time in history. Buddhism is filling a vacuum in the world of faith, a terrible void caused by a succession of shocks, both scientific and historical. By tracing a thumbnail history of faith, particularly the decline of traditional faith, we can perhaps begin to see how the Buddhist redefinition of faith precisely suits the moment.

Without a doubt, there has been a tremendous erosion of faith in modern intellectual life. While it has its roots in nineteenth-century philosophy, beginning with Friedrich Nietzsche, who famously proclaimed that "God is dead," this loss of faith accelerated in the wake of two world wars, the Holocaust, and other bloody tragedies of the twentieth century. Faith in man, particularly in international institutions, was shattered in the trenches of World War I. Faith in God, in both his benevolence and his compassion, was seared in the ashes of Hiroshima, Nagasaki, and Dresden, and amid the inhuman horrors of Dachau, Belsen, and Buchenwald. If God was not dead, it seemed he was not paying attention anymore.

Nietzsche himself never intended to declare God literally dead, which, if one accepted God as eternal and all-powerful to begin with, would be an absurdity. What Nietzsche really meant was that our *belief* in God was dead. That is a very different thing. Even in his time, the concept of God had been battered for decades by the rise of empiricism, the great waves of science and reason that had altered our view of the world. Without faith in a just God, Nietzsche suggested, there was no longer any framework for morality. What Nietzsche proposed was that human beings had now to find the will within themselves to become gods in their own right—"supermen," he called them, who would be strong, courageous, joyful, and free of their childlike dependency on God. To Buddhists, this sounds an awful lot like the idea of Buddhahood, and Nietzsche himself wrote glowingly about Buddhism.

While Nietzsche's emphasis on the individual and his call for an inner transformation share some ground with Buddhism, the overall thrust of his philosophy was quite gloomy and not especially life-affirming. As is well known, the Nazis in Germany twisted Nietzsche's ideas to justify their concept of a super race. More important, sincere and thoughtful intellectuals around the world took up his theme of a godless world, devoid of moral meaning, and saw in it a kind of cold nothingness. Nietzsche was a forerunner of existentialism and the dispiriting gloom that has suffused much of modern philosophy, drama, fiction, and poetry.

A thread of loneliness and alienation runs from Fyodor Dostoyevsky to Albert Camus to Jean-Paul Sartre, from Sylvia Plath to Allen Ginsberg, whose epic poem "Howl," a cry of despair, really, with its awful foreboding of "the crack of doom on the hydrogen jukebox," seemed to epitomize the beat generation's fearful response to modern existence. (Later in life, Ginsberg was devoted to first Zen and then Tibetan Buddhism.)

Then there was Einstein. To say that space and time were relative concepts, indeed, that our most dearly held conceptions about the universe were wrong, was one thing. Throughout history, the implications of science—first heliocentric astronomy, then Darwinian evolution, and finally the general theory of relativity—have all dealt serious blows to faith. But the final blow was the realization of the terrible energy dwelling within the atom, bringing along with it the prospect of mutual assured destruction, the end of all civilization's dreams and hopes in a terrible mushroom cloud—it was almost too much to contemplate. As a result, modern thinking tends to be skeptical, cynical, and even nihilistic. There is very little that we will accept these days "on faith." We have little faith in churches, government, corporations, or even our neighbors, whom we often don't even know.

Einstein himself was not necessarily without faith. Indeed, Einstein sought to establish a cosmology that was both empirically true and expressive of ultimate spiritual truth. Einstein did not deny God. He merely said that God was not some sort of grand puppeteer, continually involved in and manipulating his creation. In an enlightening book, *God in the Equation: How Einstein Transformed Religion*, Corey S. Powell suggests that to Einstein, the laws of physics and God were one and the same. In Einstein's view, Powell writes, "God embodies cosmic law."[8] In other words, the spiritual content of the universe was actually contained within itself, not standing apart from physical reality and the laws that described it. It *was* the laws, and to discover the nature of reality, the underlying spirit of the universe, was therefore a matter for scientific inquiry. Einstein, according to Powell, believed the path to God lay in understanding the way the universe works today:

In creating his radical cosmology, Einstein stitched together a rational mysticism, drawing on—but distinct from—the views that came before. Galileo had tried to define a line of demarcation between science and religion by insisting that the Bible tells how to go to heaven, not how the heavens go. Einstein endlessly violated that boundary by redefining God both as an ally and an end in his search for scientific truth. "God does not play dice with the universe," and "the Lord God is subtle, but malicious he is not" are just the most famous of Einstein's sci/religious declarations. His deity was not the interventionist God of Abraham and Isaac, but something more complex and abstract—not so much the Creator of the universe as the embodiment of a beautiful and economical set of physical laws.[9]

Similarly, Buddhism asks us to worship not a person but a law (dharma), a great single law that pervades the universe, which somehow compresses the truth of the human heart and the music of the spheres into one all-embracing principle.

In his book on Einstein, Powell offers many views that closely parallel the Buddhist position. Powell even advances the notion of a new science-based religion, which he calls "sci/religion," based on a universe governed by empirically knowable laws. In the twenty-first century, we need a religion that answers Einstein's call for a "rational mysticism," a life philosophy that reconciles ancient belief with the modern hunger for scientific certainty.

Initially the upheavals created by the discoveries of twentieth-century physical science led to a kind of intellectual despair. While existentialism became the dominant view among the intellectual elites in Europe, it also had a significant influence in the United States. There are many examples in our literature of this peculiarly modern sensibility. A typical example is from the novel *The Floating Opera* by John Barth, whose hero's plight can be summarized in a single despairing passage:

It seemed to me that all my life I'd been deciding that specific things had no intrinsic value—that things like money, honesty,

> strength, love, information, wisdom, even life, are not valuable in
> themselves, but only in reference to certain ends . . . *nothin*g is
> intrinsically valuable; the value of everything is attributed to it,
> assigned to it from outside the thing itself, by people.[10]

This idea that the objective world, the world outside of us, "the thing itself," is essentially blank, without meaning, can be somewhat depressing. Yet it seems a hallmark of modern philosophy and a continuing pose or attitude among Western young people. This feeling of otherness, or alienation, is more than a dominant theme in the arts and literature. It is the natural reaction of the thinking mind. When we look at the outside world, in all its vivid concreteness, it seems different in kind from our ever-shifting mind. A perceptual gulf exists between our consciousness and the physical world. Without some extraordinary means to bridge this divide, a sense of existential dread or anxiety shadows our otherwise modern, comfortable lives. We suffer from an apprehension of the meaninglessness, the nothingness of existence. We live, we love, we accumulate, we die, and the rest, as Hamlet says, is silence.

In response to this awesome feeling of emptiness, traditional monotheistic religions seem relatively powerless. Our faith in them has been shaken. As the philosopher Sam Harris argues forcefully in his book *The End of Faith*, our God-centered creeds do not always stand up to the discoveries of science and scrutiny of logic. If the traditional Western God, a personified man, were benevolent and all-powerful, how could he stand by while a child was born deformed or a short, talentless Austrian tried to rule the world? The problem of vindicating an omnipotent God in the face of evil, known as the problem of theodicy, is a formidable one. To Harris, it is insurmountable:

> The anthropocentrism that is intrinsic to every faith cannot help
> appearing impossibly quaint—and therefore impossible—given what
> we now know about the natural world. Biological truths are simply
> not commensurate with a designer God, or even a good one. The

perverse wonder of evolution is this: the very mechanisms that create the incredible beauty and diversity of the living world guarantee monstrosity and death. The child born without limbs, the sightless fly, the vanished species—these are nothing less than Mother Nature caught in the act of throwing her clay. No perfect God could maintain such incongruities. It is worth remembering that if God created the world and all things in it, he created smallpox, plague, and filariasis. Any person who intentionally loosed such horrors upon the earth would be ground to dust for his crimes.[11]

✳

Under this analysis, faith becomes worse than a simple delusion—it is socially and politically dangerous, even despicable. Theology, says Harris, "is ignorance with wings." Examining such disparate theological phenomena as the Inquisition, witch trials, slavery, vivisection, the terror attacks of Sept. 11, 2001, and the Islamic practice of "honor killings," Harris concludes that religious ideology is so retrograde, it threatens the continued existence of civilization. "We have been slow to recognize," he writes, "the degree to which religious faith perpetuates man's inhumanity to man."[12] Certainty about the next life, he writes, seems to be incompatible with tolerance in this one.

Faith-based religion, according to this view, is obsolete. Yet we all need to believe in something, don't we? In 2004, a *Time* magazine cover story reported on the discovery of a "God gene" in human beings, a genetic predisposition to believe or want to believe in the eternal.[13] In other words, the article suggested, a spiritual essence or religious nature might be hard-wired into our bodies. The article further supposed that this religious gene, as a byproduct of natural selection, must somehow serve an evolutionary purpose, whether it be binding people together in spiritual communities or making them better able to face the demands of survival. Unfortunately, it posited, some may have an overactive genetic makeup for religious faith, resulting in extremes of faith and radical fundamentalism.

Buddhism solves this problem—the terrible choice between believing in the stark nothingness of existence and overblown faith in the supernatural—but only by stepping outside the formal categories of Western thought. This requires a bit of explanation. It is often said that the difference between Asian religions and Western faiths can be reduced to profound differences in language, in the way our language systems identify objects. In the West, for example, we have the word *fist*, which we all know as a clenched hand. However, when a hand positioned in this way is suddenly uncurled, it is no longer a fist. The described object disappears, yet it remains essentially the same. We have English words to describe this change in a linear way (from *fist* to *open hand*). But many Chinese and Japanese words function as both nouns and verbs. This elasticity in language permits great subtleties in thought not easily grasped by the Western mind.

We say nowadays that the person and the environment are one. Yet that tree over there is clearly beyond the boundary of your body, and should you get in your car and drive away, the tree bears no visible connection to you. You are literally separate from it. However, you are still breathing the oxygen the tree's leaves produce from photosynthesis. In Japanese, this relationship is defined as *eshofuni*: in basic terms, oneness of person and the environment. *Esho* is actually a contraction of two words: *eho,* meaning "man," and *shoho*, meaning "environment." *Funi* means "two but not two." The true relationship between man and his environment is *two but not two*. The separation is an illusion created by language to define certain temporary conditions or situations. This more subtle, accurate description of the relationship of person to outside environment is embedded, so to speak, in language.

In the same way, faith in Buddhism, while it refers to the idea of belief, also implies action. It is like the word *karma*, which in Sanskrit literally means "action," but also means the *effects* of all the actions or causes you have made in your life. In Buddhist faith, the idea and the action are quite inseparable. Faith in Buddhism is both belief and action. If you think about it, this is purely logical. We are most faithful when we are performing our acts of faith. Therefore, we say that faith is performing the daily ritual of Buddhist practice, notwithstanding your state of mind or the current strength of your belief. It is enough that you practice. Thus *faith equals practice* becomes the first and foremost definition of faith in Buddhism.

FAITH = PRACTICE

Of course, it helps to have some conviction, a semblance of belief, behind the practice. This will bring a better result. When you get results (we call them "benefits"), they in turn reinforce your practice and increase your underlying faith. This is a second important definition of faith in Buddhism:

FAITH = EXPECTATION OF BENEFIT

To the Western mind, there may seem something almost mechanistic about this definition. Like Pavlov's dog, we respond to the good things that happen—like pulling a lever and getting a food pellet. But that is all right. We are human beings, after all. Faith and hope are eminently matters of rational expectation. Do you have some hope or expectation that your practice will bring improvements to your career, health, or relationships? Then keep on practicing. That is faith. But this is far different from the doctrinally driven faith of most world religions.

Nichiren constantly emphasized the importance of faith. It might seem curious in the Buddhist context. Isn't Buddhism the religion Westerners turn to when they have lost faith? With its focus on the individual and its insistence on an enlightened potential within the ordinary human being, doesn't Buddhism have a special appeal to the agnostic or even the atheist, one who does not believe in the existence of God? Why would Nichiren return over and over again to the concept of faith?

Nichiren was sharply critical of Buddhist temples that emphasized a paradise beyond this world, specifically the Pure Land School of Buddhism that was sweeping Japan in his day. In Nichiren Buddhism, faith is not a respite from struggle but an immersion in it. Faith is action. In Buddhism, tangible benefits are not something to be awaited after death. They are for now, in this life. In terms of enlightenment, Nichiren wrote that one can "gain entrance through faith alone." Does this mean that one cannot become a Buddha unless one believes wholeheartedly in Buddhism? Well, yes and no. It may not be necessary at the outset to believe in all the principles of Buddhism. Indeed, a healthy skepticism combined with a seeking spirit is usually considered a correct attitude for the beginner. For example, very few Buddhists I know make explicit their belief in reincarnation. While Hollywood stars seem to love to talk about reincarnation, among hard-core Buddhists it is just not discussed much, except jokingly. One does not necessarily have to *believe* in reincarnation to be a very sincere practicing Buddhist. In fact, I don't myself. I'm more or less agnostic on the subject. I'll find out when the time comes (preferably later rather than sooner).

In this Buddhism, faith is a prerequisite for enlightenment, but it is natural to have doubts. In fact, at crucial moments doubts can fuel one's practice. The line between faith and nonfaith can be infinitesimal. It is like a razor's edge, to borrow the image from the Somerset Maugham novel about a Westerner who travels to the East in search of ultimate truth. In other words, we are always living on a kind of razor's edge, suspended between doubt and belief. The cup is half full, the cup is half empty. It is the condition of the modern human being.

Unlike fundamentalist faith, which can be a kind of unquestioning fervor where even a spark of doubt must be extinguished, Buddhist faith always involves a degree of skepticism and a willingness to experiment. We call this "seeking spirit." In Nichiren Buddhism, there are said to be two kinds of faith: faith like fire and faith like flowing water. One who has faith like fire can start out practicing head-first, with no doubts, burning to see and learn everything. But such a person frequently burns out quickly and becomes disenchanted when confronted with obstacles, bumps on the road of life or practice. In Buddhist practice, faith is essential, but ideally it will be steady and continuous, like flowing water.

The Value-Creating Society

We have said that the roots of modern despair and loss of faith, as expressed in the existentialist's creed, stemmed from both history and science. But let us rewind a little bit in order to compare the different way Buddhism approaches the phenomenal world.

The underlying philosophy that led most specifically to existentialism was known as phenomenology, a school of thought developed before World War I in German universities. Its principal exponents were Edmund Husserl and Martin Heidegger (Husserl's student), and both were studied deeply by the Nobel Prize winner Jean-Paul Sartre, whose magnum opus carried the somewhat dismal title *Being and Nothingness*.

Phenomenology had to do with the study of the structures of experience in the world in which we live—a world, its proponents insisted, devoid of moral, spiritual, and human purpose. Perhaps the apotheosis of this view was contained not in a philosophical treatise but in Sartre's controversial novel *Nausea* (1938), whose protagonist, Antoine Roquentin, has a most peculiar, obsessive relationship with the objective world. Simply put, the world of objective reality makes him sick. The objects he sees—stones, chestnut trees, the litter-strewn gutters of city streets—overwhelm him with their, well, *objecthood*, and he is filled with meaningless, anarchic visions. Objects, in and of themselves, he decides, have no value. Life itself, then, has no intrinsic value. Nothing—not love, not music, not laughter, not hope—can rescue him from his predicament. He is an emblem, if an extreme one, of the modern alienated sensibility.

If all there is to life are atoms—or even smaller, subatomic things— and their various interactions, all whizzing and vibrating to an unfathomable tune, what then is life in the end? Perhaps Sartre was right.

Now let us turn to another view of the value of things, that of a Japanese educator named Tsunesaburo Makiguchi, a follower of John Dewey who set out to reform the educational system in early twentieth-century Japan. Makiguchi was also a devoted follower of Nichiren Buddhism and wanted to apply its ideas to the Japanese educational system, which he thought was rigid, formalistic, and insensitive to the learning needs of the individual child. Until the 1930s the followers of Nichiren were known as the Hokkeko. They were a relatively small group of lay believers, led by the priesthood of the Fuji School (Nichiren Shoshu). In 1930, Makiguchi founded an organization which became known as the Soka Gakkai. The words in Japanese mean "value-creating society." It was an absolute tenet of Makiguchi's faith that human beings, in the face of the forces of modernity, had a choice: either succumb to the impersonal demands of society or try to create the most value in every single moment of life. The objective world may be morally neutral and meaningless in its own right, but the important thing was for each person to bestow value on the world—to create value throughout each moment of existence. This outlook was firmly grounded in the Buddhism he practiced.

Both Makiguchi and Josei Toda, his disciple, were imprisoned during World War II for daring to stand up against Japanese militarism. They resisted all pressure from the Japanese government to accept the state Shinto religion, which was used to unify the public in support of the war. Makiguchi died in prison. Toda emerged to reestablish Nichiren Buddhism throughout Japan. In turn, his disciple Daisaku Ikeda helped bring the teachings of Nichiren Buddhism, through his various lectures and books, to the rest of the world, making the value-creating society an international phenomenon. Today, more than ten million Japanese practice Nichiren's philosophy, and the lay organization of this Buddhism, Soka Gakkai International, has chapters in more than 190 nations and territories around the world.

The life philosophy of this Buddhism is derived from the same phenomenological approach as the dreary existentialism already mentioned, but with astonishingly different conclusions. How can this be? We have said that Nichiren took Shakyamuni Buddha's core teaching, the Lotus Sutra, and reinterpreted it for modern times, or what in Buddhism is known as the "Latter Day of the Law." But that is a bit of a simplification. Actually, the Buddhist canon, including the Lotus Sutra, had migrated along trade routes north from India, into Nepal and Tibet, and from there to China, where it was translated and retranslated and merged somewhat with the ideas of Confucianism. But among all the Chinese Buddhist scholars, one named T'ien-t'ai (also known as Chih-i) was perhaps the most accomplished. Interestingly, T'ien-t'ai was a proponent of the Chinese school of phenomenology. But unlike the modern German and French varieties, this ancient Chinese phenomenology sought to classify all the various structures (experiences) that a human being could have of the phenomenal world–to actually list them as an inventory or catalogue of psychological moments. This resulted in quite a vast system, what T'ien-t'ai eventually termed "three thousand realms in a single moment of life," or, to use the Japanese term, *ichinen sanzen.* It was a detailed portrait of the ebb and flow of consciousness, the stream of thought and emotion that constitutes our being. Everything the human being can think, feel, or express was seen as a potential in each moment of life. According to this view, all universal phenomena are contained in a single life moment, in the depths of our lives, and each single life moment vibrates with all the phenomena of the universe. It expresses the totality of human life resonating in harmony with the universe.

As an aspiring monk, Nichiren was a follower of the Tendai School (the name given to the teachings of T'ien-t'ai) in Japan, and eventually adapted its ideas to his own brand of Buddhism. But this phenomenological system was not limited to the gloomy side of human existence. The three thousand realms included anger, animality, hopelessness, and the hell of despair. But included, too, were the realms of learning, realization, compassion, and, above all, Buddhahood. The human personality, according to the phenomenology of the Chinese, was more like a kaleidoscope than a fixed thing. This view, clearly, more accurately renders the way most of us experience the world. (A more detailed exposition of this principle appears in Chapter 3.)

Shakyamuni Buddha himself was deeply aware of the formlessness and conditioned nature of thought and consciousness. As a result of his meditations, he viewed individual consciousness in terms of a continual process or unfolding, rather than as a fixed self with its own essential nature. This is exactly how it seems to us. One's response to the information of the senses, to the outside objective world, is constantly shifting and changing–calm one moment, a bit bored the next, suddenly sad or angry (perhaps after a disturbing phone call), then excited and stimulated (losing yourself in work), and finally, exalted and happy (drinks with a friend). What realm you are in depends somewhat on the situation itself and also on you and what causes you have made during your life (upbringing, experiences, education, etc.). In other words, how you react—what realm you are plunged into—depends on your karma, defined as the net total of all your words, thoughts, and deeds. This is another way of saying who you are and how you experience life depends on all the things you have done (causes) and the resulting impact on you (effects)—sort of a printout of all your acts and influences—and how these interact with your environment. For each individual on the planet, such a printout would challenge a supercomputer. The amount of data would be staggering. But, on reflection, isn't this depiction of the reality of life much more sophisticated than the French and German phenomenological view? It is certainly denser and more complex. Nichiren Buddhism is based on two powerful streams of thought: value creation in modern Japan and phenomenology in ancient China. While it runs almost precisely parallel to the currents in Western philosophy—the existential gloom and rigorous phenomenology described above—it also represents a virtual antithesis of those intellectual movements.

Buddhism looks at a world that has been stripped of its meaning and says "create value." Buddhism sees the depths of despair and suffering, and encourages us to tap into our Buddha nature, a realm of life that is always there, waiting to be discovered. An expansion of this inner realm encourages empathy for others, strengthens the desire to contribute to society, and brings the light of wisdom from within the depths of one's life.

Kooks with Nukes

Unfortunately, in a world where simple, old-fashioned faith is diminishing or lapsing, the most fervent believers, to use Yeats' phrase, are full of passionate intensity. To the degree that traditional faiths lose ground, there seems to be a concomitant rise in fundamentalism. It is as if the death of mainstream faith has led to a rise in fringe ultrafaith.

Isn't there a third way, a path between the extremes of no faith/no religion and blind faith/superstition—between atheism and fundamentalism? Buddhism clearly offers a Middle Way or path between these two extremes. Buddhism never asks you to abandon your reason. Buddhism *is* reason. It requires a different kind of faith, a faith based on one's individual experiments in consciousness, and the various "proofs" derived from those transactions. It is the closest thing to a science of life that we are going to get.

Contemporary critics like Sam Harris can be harsh and logically ruthless in their views on traditional faith, particularly what he calls "idolatrous faith," like that of Muslim terrorists and Christian ideologues. But Harris leaves the door open to mystical experiences based on investigating the nature of consciousness directly, in other words, techniques for transcending the self and experiencing the oneness of human beings and their environment. Mysticism, he writes, is a rational enterprise, but religion is not:

> For millennia, contemplatives have known that ordinary people can divest themselves of the feeling that they call "I" and thereby relinquish the sense that they are separate from the universe. This phenomenon, which has been reported by practitioners in many spiritual traditions, is supported by a wealth of evidence—neuroscientific, philosophical, and introspective. Such experiences are "spiritual" or "mystical," for want of better words, in that they are relatively rare (unnecessarily so), significant (in that they uncover genuine facts about the world), and personally transformative.[14]

For such a rational mysticism to be compatible with a healthy, scientific skepticism, Harris contends, it must contain explicit instructions, with no more ambiguity or artifice than we might find in a manual for operating a lawn mower.

The Buddhism of Nichiren Daishonin, which abandons the esoteric practices and austerities of older forms of Buddhism in favor of a simple daily practice that anyone can do, seems to meet this standard. There are no priests or religious authorities in Nichiren's

Buddhism to interpret or place sacred truth beyond the reach of ordinary people—or to insert themselves as intermediaries. Such authoritarianism has no place in Nichiren Buddhism. It is entirely up to the individual. As each individual practices Buddhism, which is a kind of paradigm of the ultimate truth, the knowledge and experiences acquired lead toward greater explanatory and predictive power, just as the history of paradigms in science tends toward a convergence with the true nature of the phenomenal world. Melvin E. Klegerman, a biochemist and practicing Nichiren Buddhist, puts it this way: "The concept of religion as universal paradigm means that each person becomes a scientist experimenting with his or her own life, over which he or she has total control. Practice of such a religion would link a positive inner human reformation with the healing and flourishing of the environment."[15]

This is the opposite of basing one's existence on untestable hypotheses about what happens after death or what an unseen deity says about your neighbor's faith. In an age of fanaticism and portable weapons of mass destruction, we can no longer give credence or make concessions to any faith sanctified by something other than evidence. Buddhism offers the great hope of transforming the world because it gently erodes people's egotism and fanaticism. Buddhism can coexist with almost any creed, mildly asserting its own subtle hegemony through strength of logic and proof of practice. Best of all, Buddhism never asks or requires you to behave in a certain way. That is, it is almost entirely devoid of moral rules. It is simply a philosophy created by human beings for the benefit of other human beings.

Buddhism doesn't ask you to believe in God. It teaches you how to believe in yourself.

What Only a Buddha Can Know

To understand Buddhism, one first has to practice it. Practice precedes understanding. In a world in which many of us want to know exactly what we are getting into before we get into it, this concept may seem unsatisfying. We want to be utterly convinced of the correctness and truth of something before we will become involved with it. Unfortunately, the scope of Buddhism is so vast that our minds are not really capable of fully understanding it through initial study. This is not some novel or argumentative notion developed here to enshroud the subject in fog. Listen to the golden words of the Buddha himself in the Lotus Sutra, speaking to Shariputra, his disciple considered foremost in learning:

> Shariputra, to sum it up: the Buddha has fully realized the Law that is limitless, boundless, never attained before. But stop, Shariputra, I will say no more. Why? Because what the Buddha has achieved is the rarest and most difficult to understand Law. The true entity of all phenomena can only be understood and shared between Buddhas.

These words are recited daily (in translation) by millions of Nichiren Buddhists around the world. By "the true entity of all phenomena," the Buddha meant a complete understanding of reality or the ultimate truth. He asserted that this ultimate understanding "can only be understood and shared between Buddhas." It does present a paradox. If you must first be a Buddha before you can comprehend Buddhahood, then the process of enlightenment seems circular. Yet this is the Buddha himself telling us how it is, so we must ponder his words deeply.

Upon reflection, it really is not that puzzling. Consider other areas of human inquiry, for example, astrophysics. An astronomer cannot really explain the latest developments in the field to a neophyte without first referencing many fundamental laws of science, previous research papers, highly technical data, and so forth. He or she assumes a certain level of knowledge in the listener and adjusts the level of sophistication of the explanation accordingly. To really grasp, say, a presentation at an astronomy conference, one would have to be familiar with complex mathematical equations that go way beyond the typical high school trigonometry class. In fact, to really understand, one might have to be led through the intricate measurements and data, photon by photon, red shift by red shift, produced by incredibly sophisticated telescopes. Similarly, to grasp Buddhist principles fully, one ideally should be conducting one's own "experiments," which are like experiments in individual consciousness, during one's daily

Buddhist practice. This opens the door to additional understanding through study. In that sense, the knowledge exchanged among various practitioners can be compared to that "shared between Buddhas."

If Buddhism really does represent the "ultimate truth" of the universe most accurately, what kind of truth would it be if you could simply read about it and quickly absorb it from articles and books? It would be just intellectual knowledge. The world is filled with intellectual knowledge, some of it useful, some not. So, at the outset, let us be clear about the limits of this book, or any book, when it comes to explaining Buddhist philosophy. It can never provide a full explanation in the absence of a daily practice. As the founder of this Buddhism, the prophet and reformer Nichiren Daishonin, wrote more than seven hundred years ago: "Exert yourselves in the two ways of practice and study. Without practice and study there can be no Buddhism." Study is intertwined with practice. One thing Buddhists continually study, not surprisingly, is the life of Nichiren himself, which is the subject of the next chapter. One might reasonably ask, if Shakyamuni Buddha of ancient India was the originator of Buddhism, why should we be interested in this fellow Nichiren? To use an analogy, Benjamin Franklin is known in this country as the father of electricity, which he harnessed by flying a kite with a metal key attached to the string during a lightning storm. Yet his discovery meant very little to the daily lives of the majority of Americans. It was not fully actualized in practice, so to speak, until a century later when Thomas Edison invented the lightbulb. In the same way, Nichiren used the Buddha's essential insights to come up with a dynamic method for attaining enlightenment, making it accessible to the common person.

Although Nichiren lived and died more than seven centuries ago, at a time when Europe was in the midst of the Dark Ages and Japan itself was dominated by a distinctly martial form of feudalism, contemporary readers typically find it remarkable how modern and relevant his insights are for today. What can be especially interesting, from today's perspective, are the strong human bonds formed between this pacifist monk and the stalwart samurai who became both his protector and his disciple.

[1] L. Frank Baum, *The Wizard of Oz* (Chicago, IL: Reilly & Lee, 1956), 187.

[2] "Courage," *Seikyo Times* (December 1990), 45.

[3] Betty Kelen, *Gautama Buddha: In Life and Legend* (New York: Avon, 1967), 66-7.

[4] The Gosho Translation Committee, *The Writings of Nichiren Daishonin* (Tokyo: Soka Gakkai International, 1999), 1099.

[5] Paramhansa Yogananda, *Autobiography of a Yogi* (Los Angeles: Self-Realization Fellowship, 1972), 165-7.

[6] *The World Almanac 2005* (New York: World Almanac Books, 2005), 734.

[7] Joseph Campbell, *The Hero With a Thousand Faces* (New Jersey: Princeton University Press, 1949), 150.

[8] Corey S. Powell, *God in the Equation: How Einstein Transformed Religion* (New York: Norton, 2005), 172.

[9] Ibid., 15.

[10] John Barth, *The Floating Opera* (New York: Avon, 1956), 238.

[11] Sam Harris, *The End of Faith: Religion, Terror, and the Future of Reason* (New York: Norton, 2005), 172.

[12] Ibid., 15.

[13] Jeffrey Kruger, "The God Gene," *Time* (Oct. 25, 2004), 62-72.

[14] Harris, *The End of Faith*, 40.

[15] Melvin E. Klegerman, "Science and Buddhism," *Living Buddhism*, Vol. I, no. 3 (March 1997), 18.

2

THE SAGE & THE SAMURAI

Mentor and Disciple

THE HISTORY OF NICHIREN BUDDHISM CONTAINS PROFOUND lessons for modern times. It is the story of a man of humble origin who persevered against enormous odds, defying tyranny and intolerance, to battle for the truth and the people. Amazingly, relatively few in the West have ever heard of Nichiren or studied his teachings. Fewer still, even among Buddhists, know much about his loyal follower, the samurai Shijo Kingo.

Nichiren Daishonin was born on February 22, 1222, to a fisherman's family in Awa province on the coast of Japan, perhaps fifty miles as the crow flies from present-day Tokyo. As he wrote later, he was the "son of a *chandala* family," *chandala* being the lowest group in the Indian class system. He was given the childhood name of Zennichi-maro. After his enlightenment, he changed his name to Nichiren, or Sun Lotus. (*Daishonin* means "great sage.") Little is known about his early days. Tidal waves have washed away the section of seashore where his father's house once stood. Only the blue waters and salt air of his childhood remain. The inspiration of nature and the simple virtues of seaside folk stayed with him all his life. In later years, after his retirement to the mountains, when a follower sent him an offering of seaweed, he wept in memory of his youth.

Nichiren lived in a time of great turmoil, known as the Kamakura period. The site of the new military government, Kamakura, located near what would be Yokohama today, was fewer than a hundred miles from his home, but a world away in intrigue and sophistication. Throughout Japan feudal lords vied for power, and hereditary shoguns ruled with an iron fist. Periodic earthquakes wreaked cataclysmic damage on rickety wooden villages and provincial cities; famines decimated the population; and threats of foreign invasion, particularly from the Mongols of Kublai Khan, were constant.

The new farmer-warrior class, or *samurai*, practiced a rigorous ancient code of honor called *bushido*, but they were subject to the whims and ambitions of their lords. Buddhism, introduced to Japan some six centuries earlier, had become the religion of state, but the clerics and the people were deeply divided over what form the correct practice of Buddhism should take. The various schools of Mahayana Buddhism practiced then, which had come by way of China and Korea, were concerned with abstruse theological doctrines and characterized by rigorous monastic discipline. Buddhism therefore was a religion for the courtly class. There was not much that the common, mostly unlettered people could understand. While it inspired beautiful artworks and astonishing architecture during this period, Buddhism in Japan was ruled by rigid formality and divided by clashing sects.

At the age of twelve, Nichiren left home to join a monastery at the nearby Seichoji Temple. He was ordained a monk at fifteen. Filled with questions, he determined early on to solve the fundamental problem of life and death. Later he would write:

> Ever since my childhood, I, Nichiren, have studied Buddhism with one thought in mind. Life as a human is pathetically fleeting. A man exhales his last breath with no hope to draw in another. Not even dew borne by the wind suffices to describe this transience. No one, wise or foolish, young or old, can escape death. My sole wish has therefore been to solve this eternal mystery. All else has been secondary.[1]

Studying the various schools of Buddhism that dominated the spiritual life of Japan at the time, Nichiren came to the conclusion that the core of the Buddha's enlightenment was contained in the Lotus Sutra (or The Lotus of the Perfect Truth, *Saddharma-pundarika* in Sanskrit), one of the last and most revered teachings of the Buddha's life. He thought that the truths contained there were eternal, but that the method for revealing them should be a simple one, available to all, without regard to differences in wisdom and virtue. Nichiren thus began the historic process of returning Buddhism to its origins.

In his biography *Nichiren: The Buddhist Prophet*, Masaharu Anesaki, a professor of religion at Harvard University, described the Lotus Sutra, which held an honored position in most schools of Buddhism, in this way:

> The whole composition is a symphony in which the chief motive is the identifying of Buddha and Dharma [Law], but the melodies, the instruments, the movements, and even the keynotes vary from part to part; and naturally, the inspirations imparted by the book varied from time to time, in accordance with the temperaments, the needs and aims, of different ages and persons.[2]

In April of 1253, at the age of thirty-one, after studying for a period at the large Buddhist monastery at Mount Hiei, Nichiren returned to his old monastery near home. He visited his parents, and they became his first converts. His old master, Dozenbo, and his fellow monks welcomed him, but they regarded him as nothing more than a promising young man who had seen the world. Remaining silent about what he had learned, Nichiren retired to a forest near the monastery. Everyone thought he was occupied with the typical methods of self-purification and meditation that Buddhist monks practiced. But Nichiren was engaged in something altogether different, an original idea of his own. He spent seven days in prayer and seclusion, before launching his plan. One night he climbed a hill that commanded an unobstructed view of the Pacific Ocean. As dawn broke, he began to invoke or chant the title, or *daimoku*, of the Lotus Sutra, with the rising sun as his witness.[3] At noon on the same day, April 28, 1253, Nichiren proclaimed the primacy of the Lotus of the Wonderful Law at an assembly of his fellow monks and denounced the prevailing forms of Buddhism. When the local magistrate got word of his remarks, he and a group of hostile monks set out to arrest the young apostate. Nichiren, with the aid of sympathetic priests, was able to escape along a hidden forest trail.

He remained determined to spread his teachings, convinced that they were the only way to save Japan from disaster. For this he was ostracized by his peers, subjected to persecution, and twice exiled by the government authorities. He eventually settled in Kamakura, where he attracted a band of loyal followers and continued to engage in vigorous debates with established religious figures. When a politically connected priest named Ryokan was asked by the government to pray for rain, Nichiren issued a challenge to him: he offered to become Ryokan's disciple if his prayers succeeded and rain fell. If none did, Ryokan was to become his follower. No rain fell. Instead, Kamakura was struck by a fierce windstorm. Ryokan began to plot against him. In the fall of 1271, under pressure from the authorities, Nichiren was taken to a desolate beach called Tatsunokuchi, or "Dragon's Mouth," a place used for the execution of criminals. Preparations for a beheading were made. Nichiren calmly requested a message first be sent to his most loyal disciple, the samurai Shijo Kingo, who, accompanied by his brothers, came rushing to his side. It is said that Kingo, in his haste, ran out of his house barefoot to be by his master's side. He found Nichiren calmly arrayed on a straw mat, exposing his neck. Just as the executioner's blade was about to fall, the sky was filled with light. As Nichiren later wrote:

> A brilliant orb as bright as the moon burst forth . . . shooting across the sky from southeast to northwest. It was shortly before dawn and still too dark to see anyone's face, but the radiant object clearly illuminated everyone like bright moonlight. The executioner fell on his face, his eyes blinded. The soldiers were terrified and panic-stricken.[4]

Whether it was a comet or a meteor is not precisely known (though astronomers and scholars have spent considerable effort researching possible celestial phenomena on that particular day), but the execu-

PLACES RELATED TO NICHIREN DAISHONIN

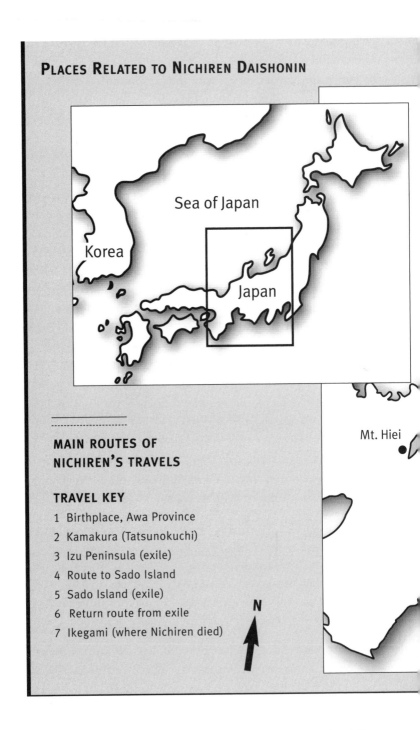

Sea of Japan

Korea

Japan

Mt. Hiei

MAIN ROUTES OF NICHIREN'S TRAVELS

TRAVEL KEY

1 Birthplace, Awa Province

2 Kamakura (Tatsunokuchi)

3 Izu Peninsula (exile)

4 Route to Sado Island

5 Sado Island (exile)

6 Return route from exile

7 Ikegami (where Nichiren died)

N

The Buddha in Your Rearview Mirror

Sado Island

⑤

④

⑥

Minobu

▲
Mt. Fuji

③
Ito

⑦

②

①

Kominato
(Komatsubara)

tion became impossible. His persecutors fled in terror, and Nichiren was instead sent into exile.

His relationship with Shijo Kingo continued to flourish, as expressed in numerous heartfelt letters. These letters, or *gosho*, as they are known (*go* is an honorary prefix, and *sho* means "writings"), form an impressive body of literature on the theory and practice of Buddhism in feudal Japan. Some of these are major treatises, while others are simple notes of encouragement to lay followers. Thirty-seven were addressed to Shijo Kingo.

All the important world religions have their sacred scriptures. Judaism and Christianity have the Old and New Testaments, Islam has the Koran, and Hinduism has its Vedic songs. Buddhism has many sutras, or teachings, that contain the original wisdom of Shakyamuni Buddha of northern India. The scriptures of Buddhism mainly consist of translations of the Buddha's words and sermons compiled some time after his death (the Buddha himself left nothing in his own hand). Because of the varying quality of the translations, from Sanskrit to Chinese to Japanese, as well as the sometimes contradictory messages they contain, the sutras have given rise to many interpretations regarding their meaning and hierarchy of importance and, therefore, to the many schools of Buddhism.

But the scriptures of Nichiren's Buddhism are somewhat unusual in the annals of religion. First, the founder wrote them himself, in his own words. Second, while some have been lost, a great many are extant. Of the 476 documents collected in the Japanese canon known as the *Gosho Zenshu* (*The Complete Works of Nichiren Daishonin*), 176 exist in Nichiren's own handwriting. Many others have been preserved in old manuscripts made by his disciples.

Finally, Nichiren's writings are distinguished by their incisive analysis of the Buddhist sutras themselves. Building on the works of the Chinese master T'ien-t'ai (538–597), he makes persuasive arguments, based on references within the actual sutras, concerning which ones are most important and which are to be regarded as "provisional," or products of the Buddha's early teaching methods. While Shakyamuni Buddha's own self-perfection and enlightenment were explicit throughout many sutras, how he achieved this marvelous state—a kind of unshakable happiness, free from the transient satisfactions and disappointments of everyday life—was not always clear. The road or path came without detailed directions. When it comes to being a Buddha, the important question for modern readers has always been: sounds great, how do we get there? Relying on the superb sutra translations of Kumarajiva, a fifth-century scholar from central Asia, Nichiren decided that the way to enlightenment was implicit, or as he put it, "hidden in the depths," of the Lotus Sutra. Broad hints are contained in the document itself. At various times in the Lotus Sutra, the Buddha tells his listeners to disregard his previous writings in favor of the overriding truth he was revealing for the first time.

Nichiren was both a master calligrapher and a brilliant narrative stylist. Since the picture-like forms of Chinese ideographs—the scholarly language of Japan in his time—are imbued with rich interpretive content, his writings are said to provide an especially vivid portrait of his own ideas and sentiments.[5] These writings are still widely studied today by millions of Nichiren followers, and they open a window onto the social and spiritual landscape of his age.

Imagine what it was like to live and seek enlightenment in feudal Japan. What were the special conditions and settings that inspired Nichiren to promulgate a virtual revolution in Buddhist thought? The hereditary aristocracy ruled the land with the aid of mercenary armies. Beginning with the arrival of Sino-Buddhism in the sixth century, Buddhist doctrines had swept the highest circles of the ruling class and the scholarly elite, but these groups were riven by uncertainty regarding the teachings. The sutras were profound, but what did they actually *mean*? The great Chinese masters, seeking to clarify things, had systematized the historical Buddha's insights, but these theoretical advances were not easily accessible to the common person. High on the list of these insights were those of nonsubstantiality, temporary existence, and the Middle Way. These were later codified by the Chinese scholar T'ien-t'ai as the "three truths":

1. THE TRUTH OF NONSUBSTANTIALITY means that all phenomena are essentially nonsubstantial—that is, at the deepest level reality isn't really rock solid or even "matter." As mentioned, this has been confirmed or at least seconded by particle physics.

2. THE TRUTH OF TEMPORARY EXISTENCE refers to the idea that although things are nonsubstantial, they do exist temporarily. But even so, they are in constant flux. (The chair that you sit upon or the glasses that rest on your nose seem solid enough, but they, too, are changing and will eventually turn to dust.)

3. THE TRUTH OF THE MIDDLE WAY consists in regarding the first two propositions as true, that reality is both nonsubstantial and temporary—yet it is in essence neither. In other words, the true nature of things cannot be defined as either existence or nonexistence.

It was enough to make your head hurt. One can readily see why Nichiren sought to simplify the often obscure intellectual framework of Buddhism and make it understandable to all.

Meanwhile, unsure or unaware of the historical Buddha's actual message, the Japanese monasteries vied with each other for influence. By the ninth century, divergent schools of Buddhism centered at these monasteries had firmly aligned themselves with various ruling clans. Intersect rivalry was bloody and common. Some monasteries began supporting what amounted to small standing armies, fighting men who would defend the temples from assaults by rival temple militias. Most of these militants were not monks or priests, but fighting men sworn to protect their order. However, there was some blurring of roles, as in the case of the legendary Musashibô Benki, a giant warrior monk, or *sôhei*, who fought in the service of the Minamoto clan. Many samurai were renowned as men of letters and the arts, skilled with both the brush and the sword. As the monasteries grew in wealth and power, so did the ranks of the sôhei. The Tendai Temple on Mount Hiei maintained a force of several thousand of these men, also called *yamabushi*, or mountain warriors.[6]

It was therefore incredibly risky for Shijo Kingo to remain loyal to Nichiren, himself a former student at the Tendai temple on Mount Hiei, just as it was perilous for Nichiren to assert and reveal his own vision of the truth. In 1264, on a visit to his home village, Nichiren and some followers were attacked by the local steward and a band of soldiers at a place called Komatsubara. Two of his followers were killed. Nichiren received a sword cut to the forehead and suffered a broken wrist. It was a narrow, hairbreadth escape. But he continued to remonstrate with the government and religious leaders about what he considered their reliance on incorrect teachings and false doctrines. Everything we know today about Nichiren and his followers compels us to appreciate the extreme courage and compassion that underlay their quest to reform Buddhism. If we were to encounter Nichiren and his samurai follower in the pine forests of ancient Japan, what would we see?

Nichiren, who had been educated at the leading monasteries of Kyoto, Nara, Kamakura, and Mount Hiei, was a monk. So he would be tonsured, his skull shaven except perhaps for a topknot of dark hair. He would be wearing belted robes, the traditional dress of a Buddhist monk. Since he was out of favor with the court aristocracy, his robes would be made of a simple gray fabric. On his travels he might have worn a straw umbrella hat. By modern standards, he might be considered somewhat short in stature. A famous line from one of his writings states that the world of enlightenment exists nowhere but "within this 5-foot body," which suggests that Nichiren and his countrymen, in addition to being shorter in general than Westerners, came from an epoch when human beings were physically smaller than they are today. However, in his biographical study, Professor Anesaki at one point calls Nichiren a "huge monk," without specifying whether he was referring to height or weight. So while we do not know his actual dimensions, we can imagine that Nichiren was an imposing figure.

Shijo Kingo, his loyal follower, might be clad in samurai armor, which was much lighter and more flexible than the heavy, clanking protective garb worn by the knights in our own Middle Ages. There would be individual strips of iron, fitted loosely over the body, and held together by colored thongs. Depending on the situation, he would probably wear a *horo*, a sort of billowing cape, and his *kabuto*, or helmet. Shijo, of course, would be armed. Typically, the samurai carried two lethal swords, made of curved steel, and a bow and arrow. The long sword, suspended cutting-edge down, was known as a *tachi*. The short sword, *wakizashi,* was worn in the belt. The samurai was so fond of his swords, he gave them pet names. He would be able to use his bow and arrows either from the ground or while riding on horseback.

Born in 1231, Shijo Kingo was, like his father before him, a samurai in the service of Lord Ema Mitsutoki, who belonged to the ruling Hojo clan. Shijo was an honorable fellow and loyal to a fault. He strictly adhered to the bushido, or Way of the Warrior, a code of honor analogous to the chivalry of medieval knights. Bushido emphasized virtuous behavior, a sense of martial duty, and, above all, devotion to one's lord. His was a life of roughness, discipline, and action, amid constant danger and death. In addition to being a warrior, Shijo Kingo was a skilled physician and a family man widely respected in his community. He was a man who liked his sake and enjoyed the company of his fellows.

Many samurai practiced Zen Buddhism, introduced in Japan during this period by the priest Eisai (1141–1215). Its austere practice and relative simplicity appealed to both the samurai and their feudal lords. Zen practitioners aimed to become enlightened just as the Buddha had, spending hours meditating in the lotus position. Dispensing with the sometimes difficult concepts found in the Buddhist sutras, as well as shunning the elaborate idol worship and ceremonies of other schools, Zen promised its adherents enlightenment based purely on their mental discipline and meditation practice. To the provincial soldier, this approach had great appeal. Samurai often retired into the priesthood after their warrior days were over.

Shijo Kingo, for reasons unknown to historians, was not an acolyte of Zen, nor was he a follower of the Nembutsu school of Buddhism, another sect popular among the warrior class. Nembutsu believers followed the teachings of the priest Honen (1133–1212) and worshipped a mythic figure from the sutras named Amida Buddha, who promised rebirth in a pure land (hence the name Pure Land School). Instead, Shijo seems to have encountered Nichiren, probably in Kamakura, and was converted to Nichiren's philosophy at the age of twenty-five.

The Opening of the Eyes

After his near-execution on the beach at Tatsunokuchi, Nichiren was exiled by the authorities to the island of Sado, in the Sea of Japan. Although it is a summertime resort area today, Sado Island then was a desolate, forbidding place. The northwestern coastal regions of Honshu, the main Japanese island, experience heavy winter snows fed by frigid winds that sweep down from Siberia and pick up moisture over the Sea of Japan. The chief heating device in the Japanese hinterland was a charcoal brazier or *hibachi*. In some farmhouses there was a sunken heating pit, or *kotatsu*, to keep one's limbs warm. In Nichiren's hut, there was neither. Snowflakes drifted down through holes in the roof. There was no chinking between the wall boards. Nichiren and his companion, a devoted priest named Nikko, huddled in animal skins and capes of straw to keep warm. Their hut was set beside a graveyard, filled with the corpses of criminals. Of those who had been exiled to Sado, few returned alive.

Yet somehow Nichiren managed to survive and write some of his most influential treatises and goshos. He was sustained by the offerings of his followers, who sent him strings of coins and horse-loads of rice, salt, fruit, sake, and, most precious of all, paper. In a letter to Shijo Kingo known as "The Hero of the World," he writes: "Buddhism concerns itself with victory or defeat, while secular authority is based on the principle of reward and punishment. For this reason, a Buddha is looked up to as the Hero of the World."[7] Nichiren believed that Buddhism should not be an abstract thing but a method for transforming the individual from within, a way to make one a better person. Proof of a philosophy's validity, he thought, would be demonstrated in the visible victories achieved in life—this life, not some dreamy future existence as postulated by other sects. As Professor Anesaki puts it, "the characteristic feature in Nichiren's ideas is that he never was content to talk of abstract truth, but always applied the truth taught to actual life."[8] To this day, Nichiren Buddhism emphasizes winning and losing, not right and wrong. It is a practical life philosophy, not a moralistic one. In any event, Nichiren on Sado was determined to win, to survive.

Nichiren not only survived, he began to write concise expositions of his doctrines and to examine critically the virtues of other religious and ethical systems. After a few months on Sado, he wrote a gosho to Shijo called "The Heritage of the Ultimate Law of Life" in which he made clear his own enlightenment. But he did not ask his followers to worship him. Instead, he stressed the importance of worshiping the law of the universe, which existed in each individual. He explained that all his followers, many of them humble people like himself, contained the potential for Buddhahood. He declared that Shakyamuni's enlightenment and "we ordinary human beings are in no way different or separate from each other." This was a revolutionary view at the time.

He firmly believed that in matters of ultimate truth—especially the eternal truth discovered by the Buddha—the people of Japan were looking at things through squinted eyes. When people see with squinted eyes, though not totally blind, they hold distorted views. He began to expound a Buddhism that involved, above all, a new way of seeing life clearly. Several months later, he finished composing one of his major works, more than 40,000 words in two volumes, entitled "The Opening of the Eyes." It was addressed to Shijo Kingo and sent from Sado Island by messenger.

One can only imagine the anticipation and excitement surrounding the arrival of such a long work after its transport across the Sea of Japan in a leaky boat and then many miles over mountains, through forests and fields. The manuscript would have arrived at Shijo's door, a tight bundle of scrolls wrapped in oil cloth or hidden in a length of hollow bamboo, sealed with tallow and string.[9] Shijo and his wife would wait until after dark before smoothing the stiffened scrolls, using stones to weigh down the corners. Then they would light their lamp and begin to peruse the elegant calligraphy. It had been written on their own paper! (One of the things Shijo had always remembered to send to his mentor on Sado was paper—paper was essential to Nichiren's mission.) Later, they would share the contents with Nichiren's followers in the Kamakura area.

In "The Opening of the Eyes" Nichiren reveals, among many things, his own identity as the Buddha of the Latter Day of the Law.

THE PERIODS OF BUDDHIST HISTORY

AREA	STAGE OF PRACTICE	DATE	SIGNIFICANT EVENTS	AGE
INDIA	Hinayana Buddhism	949 BC	Death of Shakyamuni Buddha	SHOHO
	Provisional Mahayana Buddhism	274–232 BC	Reign of King Ashoka in India (Buddhism becomes state religion)	
CHINA	Translation of the Sutras	4–7 BC	Birth of Christ	ZOHO
		27 BC–284 AD	Roman Empire	
		538 AD	Birth of Chinese master T'ien-t'ai	
		552	Buddhism reaches Japan	
	Building of Temples	767	Birth of Dengyo in Japan	
		794–1185	Heian Period (3 centuries of peace)	
JAPAN	Decline of Shakyamuni's Buddhism	1095–mid-1400s	Christian Crusades	MAPPO
		1222	Birth of Nichiren Daishonin	
		1279	Establishment of Great Gohonzon	
	Rise of Nichiren Buddhism	1517	Martin Luther's Reform Posted	
		1930	Soka Gakkai Founded in Japan	

The phases of Buddhist history, from the death of Shakyamuni Buddha to the rise of modern-day Nichiren Buddhism, are divided into three periods: Shoho, Zoho, and Mappo (our current age, characterized by religious confusion and strife).

The "latter day" refers to the age that began two thousand years after Shakyamuni's death, when Buddhism had lost its power and influence. In this view, the Buddha's death is given as 949 B.C. (other scholars put it nearly five hundred years later). The unfolding future of Buddhism, as predicted by Shakyamuni himself, is then divided into three periods: 1) *Shoho*, or the Former Day, the first thousand years after his death, when Buddhism would have the maximum power to benefit its believers, based on their proximity to the founder, the currency of his doctrines, and the consequent strong faith of the followers; 2) *Zoho*, or the Middle Day of Law, the second thousand years, during which others, including T'ien-t'ai in China, taught "transient" or theoretical interpretations of the Lotus Sutra. During this period Buddhism gradually lost its power among the people, remaining primarily in the form of sutras, statues, and temples; and 3) *Mappo*, or the Latter Day of the Law, the age of strife and conflict in which Nichiren lived, when Buddhism had lost its power and heretical versions were rampant. Only sixty years before Nichiren was born, the last remnants of Buddhism had been extinguished in India by the Islamic invasion. But according to the historical Buddha's predictions, another Buddha would appear in this age to effect a restoration of its true principles. A new Buddhism of Mappo was born in Japan just as the old Buddhism of India was eclipsed. (By the way, this age of Mappo continues in our own times. We live in the Latter Day of the Law. See chart, p. 71.)

In the "Opening of the Eyes" gosho, Nichiren said of Shakyamuni's sutras: "Each word, each phrase he spoke is true; not a sentence, not a verse is false." He asserted this despite the evident doctrinal contradictions between earlier and later sutras expounded by Shakyamuni and the fact that many Japanese practitioners of the period had stopped reading and valuing the sutras altogether. Followers of the Nembutsu School, as mentioned, invoked the name of Amida Buddha, who promised peace and joy upon death and rebirth in the Western Paradise, or Pure Land. Some Nembutsu followers even committed suicide so as to reach the Pure Land sooner. They ignored Shakyamuni's sutras, except the ones that mentioned Amida. Speaking of the multiplicity of the Buddha's 84,000 teachings or sutras, Nichiren went on:

> The World-Honored One of Great Enlightenment [Shakyamuni] designated a specific period of the preceding forty years and more,

and defined the sutras preached during that period, numerous as the sands of the Ganges, as the sutras in which he had "not yet revealed the truth." He designated the Lotus Sutra preached during the eight years [near the end of his life] as the sutra in which he "now must reveal the truth."[10]

In other words, the teachings previous to the Lotus Sutra were to be considered provisional. Shakyamuni had used the word itself in the text of the Lotus Sutra. "Honestly discard provisional teachings," he said. When Shakyamuni began to preach his law, he realized early on that the people of India were already steeped in religion, Brahmanism or Hinduism, and it would take certain "expedient means" (the title of a chapter in the Lotus Sutra) to break their ties with erroneous beliefs. In the early, elementary forms of his Buddhism, Shakyamuni handed down numerous commandments and a strict practice of austerity for his disciples to follow. Women had an astounding 500 commandments to obey; men got off easy with 250. This is not particularly surprising. In ancient times, social organization was minimal. The difference between the barbarian and the civilized human being was somewhat slim and usually marked by adherence to formal codes. Religious laws often tended to be the law of the land as well. Such commandments or precepts were like a dam restraining the flood of human passions. It was natural for religions to be built around a set of rules, and it was natural for the Buddha to prepare his followers for wisdom through a rigorous code. As Pankaj Mishra writes in *An End to Suffering*, his illuminating biography of Shakyamuni Buddha:

> Self-discipline was the way to realizing the essential moral nature of man. At Sarnath, the Buddha spoke of the stages by which gold was refined: how coarse dust and sand, gravel, and grit had to be removed before the gold dust could be placed in a crucible and melted, and its impurities strained off. The way to higher consciousness required this gradual purging of impure deed, work, and thought, through gross impurities to coarser ones, until the time when the dross disappeared and there remained only the pure state of awareness.[11]

As Mishra points out, the Buddha's early followers were required, upon ordination, to cut off their hair and beards, wear yellow robes that covered one shoulder (the left), and maintain lives of chastity and poverty. "They could not possess anything more than three robes, a begging bowl, a razor, needle, belt, water strainer, and medicine," Mishra writes. They also had to walk "with measured steps" and could eat only what they had been given as alms.

In the later period of Shakyamuni's life, known as the Hodo period, many of his followers assumed they had attained the summit of knowledge based on what the Buddha had so far revealed. Shakyamuni scolded his disciples for being complacent and conceited, refuted his earlier sutras, and began preaching what has become known as Mahayana Buddhism. In the last eight years of his life, he thus discarded the teachings of the previous forty years and revealed the true substance of his philosophy. Unfortunately, the Lotus Sutra was so cosmic and revolutionary that few of his contemporaries were able to comprehend it. They were still beseeching the Buddha on his deathbed to explain the nature of the true way.

Nichiren suffered no such doubts or confusion. He knew that the purpose of the Buddha's advent and the role of Buddhism in the world were to relieve the sufferings of the people. In "The Opening of the Eyes," he clarified the correct relationship between the historical Buddha, Shakyamuni, and Buddhist practice: everything Shakyamuni said was true, he was the basis for Buddhism, and his own words indicated the Lotus Sutra to be the lodestar of his enlightenment. Of his own interpretation of the importance of the sutra's title and practice, Nichiren wrote:

> Though the teaching that I am now propagating seems limited, it is extremely profound. That is because is goes deeper than the teaching expounded by T'ien-t'ai . . . and others. It is the three important matters in the "Life Span" chapter of the essential teaching [Lotus Sutra]. Practicing only the seven characters of Nam-myoho-renge-kyo seems limited, but since they are the master of all Buddhas of the three existences, the teacher of all the bodhisattvas in all ten directions, and the guide that enables all living beings to attain the Buddha way, it is profound.[12]

Nichiren issued no commandments, other than to admonish people to abandon mistaken views and to devote themselves to the truth contained within the Lotus Sutra, particularly its title, *Myoho-renge-kyo*, or "Lotus of the Wonderful Law." He realized that if the people were to behave as Buddhas, a peaceful society would follow naturally. In the modern age, more and more people view religious commandments as fraught with relative judgments, frequently illogical, and generally unnecessary. Laws born from the wisdom of experience, the common law, are the basis of modern jurisprudence. In civilized contemporary society, a sense of right and wrong is almost intuitive. To Nichiren, people didn't need more rules in order to make sound judgments. Wisdom—practical knowledge—was what was most needed.

Nichiren also was wary of the purely contemplative methods that characterized much of the Buddhism of his era. To reach spiritual contentment, the meditator must get away from the confusion of the world and find solitude. That may have been easy in ancient India, but it was not in Nichiren's turbulent time—and it is not now. When a person is involved in meditation, seeking the self through a self-conscious process of introspection, a curious phenomenon results. Rather than emerging clearly, the more the self is pursued, the more it seems to recede. This is similar to looking into an ordinary mirror. When you look in the mirror persistently or for an extended period of time, instead of revealing something truly significant about yourself, your face instead becomes, strangely, less recognizable than before. It begins to seem like someone else, not you. Like Narcissus, who fell into the waters of his own reflection, the self in contemplation seeks clarity but encounters confusion. Nichiren realized that the commandments of the Hinayana teachings in their time had been necessary to hold society together and that the meditation techniques of the Mahayana were useful in uplifting people from the sordid conditions of their world. But he knew them to be expedient means compared to the ultimate humanistic philosophy of the Lotus Sutra, which intended all mankind to realize the condition of absolute freedom that was Buddhahood.

After his near-execution, Nichiren began to view himself in a new light. The stark confrontation with death caused him to refocus and deepen his philosophy. This is not unheard of in the history of great ideas. When the Russian writer Fyodor Dostoyevsky incurred the displeasure of the Tsarist regime, he was put before a firing squad and blindfolded, only to be spared at the last possible moment. Thereafter, his works took on extraordinary depths. These include the short fictional piece *Notes from the Underground*, widely considered a precursor of modern Existentialism. In it he deals with the central issue of the limits of self-knowledge in a way familiar to Buddhist epistemology. Here is his obsessively introspective narrator, trying to get a grip on reality by observing the workings of his own mind:

> How am I to set my mind at rest? Where are the primary causes on which I am to build? Where are my foundations? Where am I to get them from? I exercise myself in reflection, and consequently with me every primary cause at once draws after itself another still more primary, and so on to infinity. That is just the essence of every sort of consciousness and reflection.[13]

Nichiren responded to his own crisis with clarity and conviction. He remained utterly convinced that the Buddha nature was present in every human being, but most of all, he recognized and accepted his own unique mission as the votary, or contemporary representative, of the Lotus Sutra. Since he alone had recognized the sutra's full implications, that Buddhahood was open to all, it was up to him to lead the people from suffering based on its teachings. He had an unshakable belief that Buddhahood was *there*, undiscovered, within the body of every human being. Awakening to this belief was the essence of faith. The more certain you were of Buddhahood's existence as an enlightened potential—the more faith you had in it—the more likely it was that you would be able to access it. Believing it was there was like the doorway to finding it. This was implicit in the title "The Opening of the Eyes." When one awakens, the eyes open. To his disciple, Shijo, who perhaps had come to wonder about Nichiren's teachings in light of the difficult life his master was leading, he wrote:

> Although I and my disciples may encounter various difficulties, if we do not harbor doubts in our hearts, we will as a matter of course attain Buddhahood. Do not have doubts simply because heaven does not lend you protection. Do not be discouraged because you do not enjoy an easy and secure existence in this life. . . . Shakyamuni Buddha, the lord of teachings, was cursed by all the followers of non-Buddhist teachings and labeled as a man of great evil. . . . To be praised by fools–that is the greatest shame.[14]

In the same letter, he tells Shijo, "I, Nichiren, am sovereign, teacher, and father and mother to all the people of Japan." The benevolent functions of parent, teacher, and sovereign are known as the "three virtues" all Buddhas are said to possess. In other words, he had discarded his transient self and realized fully his Buddhahood, which was closely tied to his mission to dispel the illusions of the religious and political establishment of Japan. In Buddhism, this moment is known as *hosshaku kempon*, meaning that a Buddha reveals his true identity (*kempon*), and sheds his expedient one (*hosshaku*). This principle also applies to Shakyamuni Buddha. In the sixteenth chapter of the Lotus Sutra, Shakyamuni revealed that he had already attained Buddhahood in the unimaginably distant past, countless eons before his well-known realization beneath the bodhi tree.

This realization can be compared to that moment in which Buddhist practitioners realize that their egoistic self–the self which they regarded as absolute, as No. 1–is not their true self. Their true self is the Buddha nature. You may be a person called Tom, who wants to be a vice president of your firm before you are forty, and who would like to have a five-bedroom house instead of a three-bedroom, and who would like his daughter to attend Vassar, but your eternal, changeless self, your Buddha self, transcends these matters and is beyond Tom. Tom is a social construct. Buddhahood is the eternal reality that underlies Tom's temporary existence. It is this greater self that aspires to enlightenment and works for the happiness of all.

Despite the terrible hardships he was undergoing on Sado, in "The Opening of the Eyes" Nichiren wrote, with fingers numbed by the cold, that he was "the happiest man in all Japan." True happiness, in other words, can be found right where you are, in the here and now, not in some distant place or future time. As mentioned, many Japanese had thought that the Buddha dwelled apart from mankind in some remote and special realm, or "Buddha land." Nichiren insisted that enlightenment could be manifested by the ordinary person living in less than ideal circumstances. Indeed, the challenge for people was to achieve enlightenment, not on some mountaintop retreat, but right here, doing what they do, right where they are.

Happiness, the Goal Other Buddhisms Forgot

During Nichiren's exile on Sado Island, Shijo Kingo made several journeys to visit his master. The trip from Kamakura to the northwest coast would have been arduous, taking several days. The risk was heightened by the fact that Nichiren was a political prisoner, a persona non grata with the regime. Shijo could be attacked anywhere along the way. The roads were plagued by bandits, not to mention members of opposing sects and their armed agents. To all appearances, however, the highway would be quiet and pastoral. A general visual idea of the tranquil countryside along these roads can be gathered from the picturesque landscape prints of the nineteenth-century artist Hiroshige (1797–1858). His scenic guidebooks were filled with woodblock prints of the feudal highways, the peasants and traveling merchants, pilgrims and itinerant priests, guardhouses and roadside shrines. Shijo would have passed field after field sown with rice. There would have been few animals. Cattle were used to haul carts or plow fields, but rarely for food (it was, after all, a Buddhist country now, and the people adhered to traditional Indian precepts about eating meat). The road would stretch long and hard, lined with giant pines.

On these visits and in his letters, Shijo no doubt confided in Nichiren about certain troubles he was experiencing with respect to his samurai colleagues and their feudal overseer, Lord Ema. Doubtless, too, he did not want to trouble the monk with such worldly matters, but it appeared that Lord Ema was considering seizing Shijo's land and transferring him to another, less favorable estate. The situation was urgent and seemingly insoluble.

Nichiren was more than willing to bring the full measure of his wisdom to bear on such issues. Indeed, he considered it absolutely imperative that Buddhism be relevant to the lives and everyday problems of people. The fact that Buddhism had become distant from such everyday matters was precisely what bothered him most. In his gosho "The Hero of the World," a reply to a letter from Shijo, Nichiren revealed his suspicion that Shijo's fellow samurai were conspiring against him and were determined to do him in. He advised Shijo to be careful, to bide his time, but most of all to exercise self-control:

> No matter how furiously a fire may rage, it burns out after a while. On the other hand, water may appear to move slowly, but its flow does not easily vanish. Since you are hot-tempered and behave like a blazing fire, you will certainly be deceived by others. If your lord coaxes you with soft words, I am sure you will be won over, just as fire is extinguished by water. Untempered iron quickly melts in a blazing fire, like ice put in hot water. But a sword, even when exposed to a great fire, withstands the heat for a while, because it has been well forged. In admonishing you in this way, I am trying to forge your faith. Buddhism is reason. Reason will win over your lord.[15]

Buddhism, from Nichiren's point of view, was eminently reasonable. *Buddhism is reason.* He had rejected the occult and mystical practices that were common among other Buddhist sects during his day. He was determined that Shijo show actual proof of the efficacy of Buddhist practice in his own daily life. It was crucial that Shijo demonstrate an upsurge in wisdom, courage, and compassion—three key properties of the Buddha—to prove that Nichiren's methods worked.

After one of Shijo's visits, Nichiren conveyed some of his deepest insights and a concept revolutionary in Buddhism in another letter entitled "Earthly Desires Are Enlightenment." Traditionally, Buddhist monks had preached the necessity of extinguishing one's desires as a step on the road to enlightenment. The Buddha himself had stated that the source of suffering was selfish craving. This was emphasized particularly in the Hinayana teachings. Nichiren's Buddhism for the first time in history elaborated on the true nature of life and desire. Rather than merely suppressing desire or dismissing it as evil or unclean, Nichiren Buddhism harnesses desire for constructive purposes. This is because desire is part of life, and to deny it is to stop living. Desires in themselves are not evil. We would never enjoy food if we were not hungry. The desire for shelter led to architecture. There would be very little literature or art without love. Even the desire for enlightenment is a kind of desire.

We have said that many religions build a dam of rules and commandments to hold the raging waters of people's emotions and desires in check. This is true of the Judeo-Christian and Islamic faiths. It was also quite true of intermediary forms of Buddhism, which emphasized meditation to clear the mind of impure thoughts and various ascetic practices and precepts to cleanse a person of human cravings, presumably freeing the person to concentrate on higher things.

Mahayana Buddhists took a different view of desire than Hinayanans, who thought extinguishing desire was a prerequisite for enlightenment. Some Mahayanans viewed earthly desire and enlightenment as inseparable, since both were manifestations of the same underlying reality of life. While a dam controls the wild power of water, the calm lake thus formed is static. It produces little value. To utilize the force and power of water, controlled outlets are made in a dam and the rushing water can be used to mill grain, to drive saws, and, in modern times, to generate electricity or hydroelectric power. In terms of unlocking human potential, Nichiren saw that "earthly desires" could be channeled or used as a driving force toward enlightenment.

The great Chinese philosopher T'ien-t'ai had compared earthly desires to the persimmon fruit. The persimmon is bitter to the taste, but its sweetness can be drawn out by soaking it in a lime solution and leaving it in the sun. There are not two persimmons, one bitter and one sweet; there is only one. T'ien-t'ai compared desire to the bitter persimmon, enlightenment to the sweet persimmon, and the method of bringing out the sweetness to Buddhist practice.[16] In other words, by practicing Buddhism we can *transform* our desires in the direction of the life-enhancing values of wisdom, courage, and compassion. As Daisaku Ikeda has written:

> The innate function of desire within our individual lives can be thought of as neutral; it has the potential either to harm or to benefit human existence. Rather than suppress our desires, the real question is how to control and direct them so that they enhance human virtues. This is where Buddhism comes in. According to Buddhist teachings, once we activate the supreme state of Buddhahood inherent in each of us, the workings of our desires are redirected toward furthering our individual growth and enlightenment. If, by contrast, we give our desires free rein without first orienting them in a higher state of life, they will only operate destructively, bringing us anguish and perhaps even threatening our continued existence.[17]

Exactly how to accomplish this channeling of desire in a positive direction will be the subject of our discussion of the Ten Worlds in the next chapter ("How to Practice"). In the meantime, the significant point is that Nichiren understood that desire, when properly channeled, can fuel spiritual development.

Nichiren wrote all sorts of messages to Shijo Kingo and his other followers, including simple notes of encouragement and expressions of compassion and condolence. In 1271, Nichiren wrote to Shijo and his wife, Nichigen-nyo, to reassure them at the time of the birth of their first child, Tsukimaro. Later, when their second child, Kyo'o, became ill, Nichiren wrote memorable words of guidance and inspiration. In this letter, he referred to a scroll he had sent, which he called the Gohonzon (or "object of fundamental respect"), that he had inscribed for the infant's protection. It was a beautifully lettered mandala, or devotional symbol, on which he had depicted the title of the Lotus Sutra and various Buddhas and bodhisattvas, representing the gist of enlightenment. This scroll was a forerunner of the modern Gohonzon that appears in millions of practitioners' homes.

(For a detailed description of the Gohonzon, see Chapter IV.) While most of the letters are filled with warm personal encouragement, there are also many examples of Nichiren's strict view of matters of faith and realistic assessments of worldly situations. For a great philosopher, he was also a remarkably practical man.

In 1274, two momentous events caused Shijo Kingo's faith in his master's words to burn brightly. Nichiren was pardoned by the government in Kamakura and allowed to return from Sado Island. At the same time, the Mongols threatened an invasion of Japan, just as Nichiren had predicted years earlier. Heartened by his master's return and the confirmation of his wisdom, Shijo tried to persuade Lord Ema, his superior, of the greatness of Nichiren's Buddhism. Ema, however, was a lay priest of the Nembutsu School and unlikely to be awakened easily. The repercussions were immediate and difficult, leaving Shijo at odds with both his lord and his fellow samurai. Shijo's predicament was addressed in one of the most famous of all the letters written by Nichiren, known as "The Eight Winds" gosho. The concept of "eight worldly winds" that buffet us during our lives is traditional in Buddhist scriptures, including *The Treatise on the Stage of Buddhahood Sutra*. But in Nichiren's gentle words to his samurai follower, it has a special modern resonance.

The Eight Winds

In the letter, Nichiren advised Shijo Kingo on how to conduct himself during the crisis caused by his feudal master, Lord Ema, who had decided to transfer Shijo to another, less favorable estate in a distant province. Land meant everything in feudal Japanese society, and Shijo was crushed at this setback to his fortunes and respect. Nichiren surmised that Shijo's rivals had spoken ill of him to his lord, specifically slandering the loyal samurai's strong faith in Nichiren's form of Buddhism. On the most fundamental level, he advised Shijo to discover the true nature of the situation. "You must beware and act cautiously," he wrote.

More surprising, Nichiren strictly counseled Shijo to bury his resentment toward his lord, and, instead, acknowledge the debt of gratitude he owed him for not seizing his estate earlier. "Even if he never shows you the slightest further consideration, you should not hold a grudge against your lord." In other words, be steadfast and appreciative, not hotheaded. He knew Shijo to be a man with a strong temper. In a famous passage, cherished by Nichiren Buddhists everywhere, he wrote:

> A truly wise man will not be carried away by any of the eight winds: prosperity, decline, disgrace, honor, praise, censure, suffering, and pleasure. He is neither elated by prosperity nor grieved by decline. The [forces of the universe] will surely protect one who does not bend before the eight winds. But if you nurse an unreasonable grudge against your lord, they will not protect you, not for all your prayers.[18]

These words can be read over and over again. In them Nichiren defined a vital quality of the enlightened person, or Buddha: one who is unswayed by the winds of fortune. We all know people who react to a setback or crisis with panic or emotionalism, compounding the problem. We may also know someone who is unfazed by disaster, who responds with equanimity to urgent problems and sets about calmly to solve them. Ernest Hemingway called this quality "grace under pressure" and used it to describe matadors, fishermen, hunters, soldiers, and the like who performed with great skill under trying conditions. But one does not have to work in a macho profession in order to manifest such grace; it is equally desirable in the classroom, a bank, an insurance office, or a suburban home. It requires wisdom and courage to act with equanimity and restraint.

To take a prime example from history, in his Pulitzer Prize–winning book, *1776*, the historian David McCullough notes that in the darkest days of the American Revolution, George Washington hid the grim truth of his ragtag army's predicament from even his most trusted generals and adjutants, because he did not want to discourage them. One might say that Washington merely suppressed his own despair. But based on his convincing displays of confidence–his proud bearing astride his horse among his bedraggled troops, offering words

"THE EIGHT WINDS" GOSHO

I had been anxious about you because I had not heard from you in so long. I was overjoyed to receive your messenger, who arrived with your various offerings. I am going to bestow the Gohonzon on you for your protection.

About the problem of your transfer to another estate: I have studied your lord's letter to you and your letter to me, and compared them. I anticipated this problem even before your letter arrived. Since your lord regards this as a matter of the utmost importance, I surmise that other retainers have spoken ill of you to him, saying: "He shows a lack of respect for you in his unwillingness to move to a new estate. There are many selfish people, but he is more selfish than most. We would advise you to show him no kindness for the time being." You must beware and act cautiously.

As vassals, you, your parents, and your close relatives are deeply indebted to your lord. Moreover, he showed you great clemency by taking no action against your clan when I incurred the wrath of the government and the entire nation hated me. Many of my disciples had their land seized by the government and were then disowned or driven from their lords' estates. Even if he never shows you the slightest further consideration, you should not hold a grudge against your lord. It

of hope and encouragement—it is probably more accurate to say that he refused to *succumb* to the anguish that seemed to accompany the reality of their situation. After his troops won an important early victory by ejecting the British from Boston, Washington was quickly hailed as a national hero. But he did not take this adulation to heart either. "Just as he had shown no signs of despair when prospects looked bleak," McCullough writes, "he now showed no elation in what he wrote or in his outward manner."[19] He was neither carried away by decline nor elated by honor. So much of the story of *1776* revolves around Washington's ability to be unswayed by the "eight winds" and the salutary effect this had on the nation that followed him into being.

Let us take a closer look at the "eight winds." There are four positive winds: prosperity, honor, praise, and pleasure; and four negative ones: decline, disgrace, censure, and suffering. It's hard to think of anything wrong with the positive winds, since they are the marks of success in life. Why should we not be swayed by them?

is too much to expect another favor from him, just because you are reluctant to move to a new estate.

A truly wise man will not be carried away by any of the eight winds: prosperity, decline, disgrace, honor, praise, censure, suffering, and pleasure. He is neither elated by prosperity nor grieved by decline. The [forces of the universe] will surely protect one who does not bend before the eight winds. But if you nurse an unreasonable grudge against your lord, they will not protect you, not for all your prayers.

When one goes to court, one may win one's case, but then again one may lose, when satisfaction could have been obtained outside of court....As for your own problem, I advise you not to go to court. Neither harbor a grudge against your lord, nor leave his service. Stay in Kamakura. Go to attend on your lord less frequently than before; wait upon him only from time to time. Then you can expect that your wish will be fulfilled. Never conduct yourself in a shameful manner. Be unmoved by greed, by the desire for fame, or by anger.

—WRITTEN BY NICHIREN IN 1277

However, if they become objects of devotion, in and of themselves—that is, if we begin to revere wealth, success, and praise—then they will become obstacles to the development of wisdom, courage, and compassion. If they stand in the way of our progress toward enlightenment, then they become negative forces in our lives. People are often sidetracked by their attachment to prosperity, honor, praise, and pleasure. This is not to say that genuine accomplishment and good fortune are to be avoided. Success (prosperity) and fame (honor, praise) are not in themselves problematic. Just by observing the sad personal histories of lottery jackpot winners and young Hollywood stars, we can see how these things can be traps. When someone who has achieved a sudden success begins to stay up to all hours in nightclubs, trailed invariably by a hard-drinking posse, it is no big leap to the notion that success can be a snare on the road to spiritual progress. Indeed, people who are truly infatuated with their own success are often prone to treat subordinates rudely and to ignore the sufferings of those closest to them. This is something we can read about every day.

Turning to the negative side, decline, disgrace, censure, and suffering are not things any of us want to experience. But to some extent, all are inevitable sometimes. Too great an aversion to these sufferings, again, would be an obstacle to one's enlightenment. We all must suffer sometime. It is part of life. Nichiren wrote this to Shijo in another context: "Suffer what there is to suffer. Enjoy what there is to enjoy." (And, he added, in a memorable line, "When you drink sake, stay at home with your wife.") Life entails a certain amount of suffering. This notion is fundamental to Buddhism. A Buddha is someone who can accept misfortune and move on.

Understanding philosophical concepts is admirable, but Buddhism would not be what it is if it did not address the problems of life with logic and common sense. This emerges from Nichiren's counsel concerning Shijo's growing estrangement from his lord. Within the context of the feudal society of the time, the samurai was utterly dependent on his lord. The feudal vassal was a combination governor, military leader, landlord, and boss. Because Shijo had protected Nichiren Daishonin, considered a heretical priest in high Kamakura circles, and had visited him during his exile on Sado Island, he was naturally regarded with suspicion by his fellow samurai and his lord. It soon became clear that Lord Ema was going to take away Shijo's fief and transfer him to the less desirable lands in the faraway province of Echigo. Nichiren's advice in this situation was both logical and counterintuitive. Do not complain. Instead, show appreciation.

How many of us at one time or another have felt resentment toward our boss? At such times, isn't it natural to suppose that our coworkers and erstwhile friends are secretly plotting against us? Is not the bitterness we manifest in these situations the beginning of an almost irrevocable downward slide? The important thing, according to Nichiren, is not to rage against some imagined unfairness but to carefully discern the reality of the situation, to bring your own subjective wisdom to bear against the objective circumstances you face. In any case, Nichiren went on to advise Shijo to maintain a confident state of mind, neither hating nor kowtowing to his lord, and to be prudent until the situation turned in his favor.

In contemporary America, when one encounters even minor difficulties on the job, it has become almost a reflex action to complain about the boss or to rage against the "system." You can complain to your fellow workers, who often nod their heads in disgusted agreement, or you can complain more publicly or legally (consider the vast number of employment lawsuits). This culture of complaint has become a feature of our business world. Many movies, books, and magazine stories detail the evils of the modern boss (and other figures of authority), with the plotline carefully crafted so that the boss is humiliated and the hero eventually triumphs. But is this how things turn out in real life? By contrast, even within the ancient context, Nichiren depicted a realistic view of the issues of duty, loyalty, and authority.

Nichiren counseled Shijo to be unswayed by his lord's threats, and, for the time being, to keep a very low profile. Importantly, he shifted the responsibility from Lord Ema back to Shijo Kingo himself. In other words, in whatever situation you find yourself, ultimately it is up to you to change it for the better. It is not easy to change another person. In Buddhism, everything starts from the standpoint of you—what you can do to change. In addition, Nichiren cautioned Shijo against consorting with his enemies or venturing out alone. In a modern context, such advice would be comparable to saying one should stop engaging in either gossip or confrontations with one's coworkers, who clearly, in this situation, are not on one's side.

Nichiren also cautions Shijo against suing. There were lawsuits in medieval Japan, and Nichiren gives a detailed and enlightened argument against needless litigation. Nichiren instead counsels Shijo to rely solely on the wisdom gained through faith to negotiate the complex minefield of human relations. If one looks at contemporary society, with its mania for litigation, it is fairly easy to see how a lack of wisdom and dialogue has resulted in a breakdown in human relations. This is clearly a major worldwide problem.

Of course, Nichiren Daishonin's Buddhism is not really about office politics or litigation. It is about the realities of life. In this and subsequent letters, Nichiren gradually brought his disciple to a new level of wisdom that enabled him to overcome his problems with his lord. In one, he counseled Shijo, "you must not heedlessly go out drinking at night with your associates or others at places beside your own home." He tells him that if his lord should summon him during the daytime, he should respond "with all haste." However, if Lord Ema were to summon him at night, "then plead some sudden illness for the first three times he calls you." If his lord were to persist, Nichiren advised, then Shijo should have his own men standing guard at the crossroads before he set out. At one point, in 1276, Nichiren advised Shijo to continue to act in a circumspect manner regarding his lord, but also encouraged him to write to Lord Ema, informing him that he would not abandon his estate for another year's time, because to do so would leave Ema unprotected in case of foreign invasion. He instructed him to say, "At this moment I am resolved to sacrifice my life for my lord if anything grave happens," but also to remind Lord Ema that if a sudden crisis should occur, the proposed new estate in Echigo was too far away for Shijo to be of any service.

Finally, in October 1278, Nichiren was overjoyed to receive word from Shijo that not only had Lord Ema decided to allow him to keep his lands, he had also granted Shijo three new fiefs, greatly expanding his original estate. This improvement was to some extent the direct result of Shijo acting in his capacity as physician to cure Lord Ema of a serious illness. But Nichiren certainly viewed it in terms of Shijo's steadfastness and faith in adhering to a course of appreciation and service, rather than one of contention and complaint. Considering the previous threats to transfer him and the ongoing hostility of his fellow samurai, the outcome had been astonishing. Nichiren wrote:

> So your lord has granted you new fiefs! I cannot think it to be true; it is so marvelous that I wonder if it is a dream. I hardly know what to say in reply. . . . No more gratifying thing has ever happened to any member of your lord's clan, whether priest or layman. When I say this, it may seem as if it is a desire of the present existence,

but for ordinary people, that too is only natural, and moreover, a way exists to become a Buddha without eradicating desires.[20]

Eventually, after his various published treatises and public remonstrations against the Kamakura government failed to bring about the religious reforms he desired, Nichiren retired to a mountain cabin on Mount Minobu, to the northwest of Mount Fuji, where he devoted the remainder of his life to writing and teaching. He continued to correspond with and offer encouragement to Shijo. In 1278, after Nichiren fell ill, probably from a form of dysentery, Shijo sent him medicines and his master recovered. Nichiren continued to express concerns for the samurai's safety, advising him not to forget the danger, and when he traveled not to "begrudge the cost of a good horse" to carry him easily in his armor and to "bring along your best men to defend you against surprise attack." He then turned to matters of faith and determination, recounting the story of General Stone Tiger:

> The mighty warrior General Li Kuang, whose mother had been devoured by a tiger, shot an arrow at the stone he believed was the tiger. The arrow penetrated the stone all the way up to its feathers. But once he realized it was only a stone, he was unable to pierce it again. Later he came to be known as General Stone Tiger. This story applies to you. Though enemies lurk in wait for you, your resolute faith in the Lotus Sutra has forestalled great dangers before they could begin. Realizing this, you must strengthen your faith more than ever.[21]

As archaic and mysterious as it seems, this letter contained a very vivid description of a unique dimension of the concept of faith in Nichiren Buddhism. The tremendous *intention* of General Stone Tiger to shoot an arrow through a tiger, the tiger he fervently believed had killed his mother, enabled him to accomplish an impossible feat. So, too, many of our dreams seem distant and unrealizable. But through tremendous efforts in practice, Buddhism is about making the impossible possible in our lives. In his final known letter to Shijo Kingo, Nichiren wrote that the samurai had surely attained enlightenment, based on his sincere practice and his service to his master.

Nevertheless, Nichiren's last words to him were: "You should exert yourself all the more."

In his sixty-first year, in failing health, Nichiren set off on a journey from Mount Minobu to the hot springs at Hitachi. Too ill to continue, he stopped at the home of another follower, Ikegami Munenaka, in what today would be part of metropolitan Tokyo. On October 13, 1282, surrounded by his followers solemnly chanting *Nam-myoho-renge-kyo*, he died peacefully. Shijo Kingo continued to prosper and flourish in the service of his lord and remained faithful to Nichiren Daishonin's Buddhism. He followed it to the end of his life, at age sixty-nine in 1300.

Mentor and Disciple

The mystic bond between Nichiren Daishonin and Shijo Kingo is a storied one in the literature of Nichiren Buddhism. Nichiren wrote many other important letters and treatises—more than a thousand pages of them—to other significant followers. The roster of their names may not trip lightly off the Western tongue, but they are legendary to longtime practitioners: the Ikegami brothers, the lay nun Ueno, Nanjo Tokimitsu, Toki Jonin, and many more. But the correspondence with Shijo Kingo was the largest, and it epitomizes a concept integral to Buddhism: that of mentor and disciple.

Nichiren taught that a common mortal, without eradicating his desires and changing his identity, could attain Buddhahood right here in this world. When Shijo found himself in a desperate situation, Nichiren encouraged him with a steady stream of letters, conveying both patient guidance and his own determination in faith. If a religion is true, Nichiren thought, then it must be able to help people resolve their troubles and find joy in life. That is why he stressed actual proof of practice. In the final analysis, whether or not we can confirm the validity of a life philosophy depends on the qualities we are able to manifest in daily life and society. Life is the stage on which one's Buddha nature is tested. As Nichiren wrote to Shijo, "The real meaning of Shakyamuni Buddha's appearance in this world lay in his behavior as a human being."[22] (See "The Three Kinds of

"THE THREE KINDS OF TREASURE"

It is rare to be born a human being. The number of those endowed with human life is as small as the amount of earth one can place on a fingernail. Life as a human being is hard to sustain—as hard as it is for the dew to remain on the grass. But it is better to live a single day with honor than to live one hundred and twenty and die in disgrace. Live so that all the people of Kamakura will say in your praise that [Shijo] is diligent in the service of his lord, in the service of Buddhism, and in his concern for other people. More valuable than the treasures of the storehouse are the treasures of the body, and the treasures of the heart are the most valuable of all. From the time you read this letter on, strive to accumulate treasures of the heart!

The heart of the Buddha's lifetime teaching is the Lotus Sutra, and the heart of the practice of the Lotus Sutra is expanded in the Fukyo ["Bodhisattva Never Disparaging"] chapter. The real meaning of Shakyamuni Buddha's appearance in this world lay in his behavior as a human being. How profound! The wise may be called human, but the thoughtless are no more than animals.

—NICHIREN, SEPTEMBER 11, 1277

Treasure," above.) Shijo eventually recovered his estate, receiving lands three times larger than his original holdings, and came to be highly regarded as a samurai by the people of Kamakura. His courageous spirit and moving story still shine brightly today.

More important than the material benefits he reaped, however, were the spiritual rewards of his practice. Amid the gale of criticism and intrigue that he faced, it would have been convenient for him to cease his practice of Nichiren Buddhism. In fact, it would have been eminently logical. As we have mentioned, in shogunate Japan, it was a life-or-death situation for him. In a later gosho, Nichiren wrote to Shijo, "To accept is easy; to continue is difficult. But Buddhahood lies in continuing faith." Somehow Shijo remained steadfast, becoming a pillar among Nichiren's lay followers. This, in turn, was tremendously encouraging to Nichiren himself. In his lonely quest to bring a more humanistic version of Buddhism to medieval Japan, he not only needed the precious food and paper that

Shijo provided; he was also nourished by the fruits of Shijo's practice. Their development was mutually reinforcing. One might say that Shijo's courageous efforts fueled Nichiren's deepest insights. Through the master-disciple bond, Nichiren was called upon to manifest wisdom and compassion, and Shijo responded with courage. They each called forth the other's Buddha nature. Who can really say to what extent Nichiren's profound wisdom and compassion grew out of his genuine concern for Shijo? This is the ineffable nature of the master-disciple relationship.

Modern readers may find the words *master* and *disciple* anomalous or even anachronistic in today's society, where we highly value our privacy and independence of spirit. Nowadays this bond is more generally expressed as "mentor and disciple." In our own times, Daisaku Ikeda, the president emeritus of the Soka Gakkai International, the lay organization of Nichiren Buddhism worldwide, is regarded as the mentor and spiritual leader of millions of Buddhists around the world. He is a prolific author and speaker, as well as a peripatetic advocate for the advancement of world peace through dialogue. That is why, in addition to the insights of his words, he is quoted repeatedly in this book. That is the larger or public sense of the historic bond of mentor and disciple in today's world. On the more individual level, it is simply the relationship between you and the person who tells you about the practice or teaches you how to practice. You may have several different mentors along the way.

One cannot practice Buddhism in complete isolation. Since Buddhism makes no distinction between the individual human being and the environment in which that person lives, our happiness is linked to the happiness of others. In a sense, Nichiren Buddhism is an immersion in, not a retreat from, this world. It is essential that we practice for the sake of others as well as ourselves.

Notes on Chapter 2

[1] "The Life of Nichiren Daishonin," *Seikyo Times* (February 1978), 26.

[2] Masaharu Anesaki, *Nichiren, the Buddhist Prophet* (Cambridge, MA: Harvard University Press, 1916), 18.

[3] Ibid., 34.

[4] *The Writings of Nichiren Daishonin*, 767.

[5] Anesaki, *Nichiren, the Buddhist Prophet*, vi.

[6] Anthony J. Brandt, *The Samurai* (Osprey, 1989), 8.

[7] *The Writings of Nichiren Daishonin*, 835.

[8] Anesaki, *Nichiren, the Buddhist Prophet*, 83.

[9] Faye Hovey, "No Distance Can Separate Two Hearts," *Living Buddhism*, Vol. I, no. 11 (November 1997), 30.

[10] *The Writings of Nichiren Daishonin*, 223.

[11] Pankaj Mishra, *An End to Suffering: The Buddha in the World* (New York: Picador, 2004), 209.

[12] Ibid., 317.

[13] Fyodor Dostoyevsky, *Notes from the Underground*, trans. Constance Garnett (Mineola, NY: Dover, 1992), 12.

[14] *The Writings of Nichiren Daishonin*, 283, 287.

[15] Ibid., 839.

[16] Daisaku Ikeda, *Unlocking the Mysteries of Birth & Death* (Santa Monica, CA: Middleway Press, 2003), 8.

[17] Ibid., 181–2.

[18] *The Writings of Nichiren Daishonin*, 794.

[19] David McCullough, *1776* (New York: Simon & Schuster, 2005), 107.

[20] *The Writings of Nichiren Daishonin*, 945.

[21] Ibid., 953.

[22] Ibid., 852.

3

HOW TO PRACTICE

Making Waves

SILVER WILL EVENTUALLY TARNISH IF NOT POLISHED. In the same sense, Buddhists continually strive to polish and uncover the gleam of enlightenment from within. These strenuous efforts to buff and polish one's character are repeated twice daily.

Nichiren Daishonin declared that "the voice does the Buddha's work." The primary practice of Nichiren Buddhism involves chanting the *daimoku* (or "title") of the Lotus Sutra—*Nam-myoho-renge-kyo*—the opening words of the Buddha's highest teaching. We also recite portions of two chapters from the Lotus Sutra—the "Expedient Means" and the "Life Span" chapters[1]—morning and evening. This is the prime point of one's individual practice. Unlike silent meditation, chanting is extremely concrete. You know you are doing it. When you chant each morning your voice resounds throughout the universe. It heralds daybreak for your own life.

I am going to ask you to try it before I explain it.

Find a quiet place. Seat yourself in a comfortable way: in a straight-back chair, on a pillow on the floor, or on the edge of your bed. Be sure to maintain an erect posture. Your attitude initially, no matter how deep your skepticism, should be one of respect—not necessarily devotional respect, more like Aretha Franklin–type respect. If you wish, place your palms together, fingertips touching, with your hands at the center of the chest, as in traditional prayer. Now recite the words *Nam ... myoho ... renge ... kyo ...* slowly at first, then as you gain confidence, more rapidly. The chant should be rhythmical. You will find that the words shape themselves into a rhythmic pattern without much conscious effort on your part. No particular emphasis should be placed on any of the words. It should sound like a rich, pulsing single tone, not a singsong. This is the rhythm of the universe, more a wave than a melody.

When you chant and recite the sutra, it is like a symphony in which you fuse the microcosm of your own body with the song of the macrocosm, the universe. The mystic law is both within you and without you (to paraphrase the Beatles). When you chant, you harmonize your little private world with the larger world outside.

Note that the second word, *myoho*, would normally have three syllables (me-oh-ho), but you must compress it into two, crushing the *myo* into a single syllable. Do the same for the last word, *kyo*; make it one syllable. This is not hard to do. In fact, it comes naturally. *Renge* takes the standard two beats. When you've got it going well, there will be six beats, just like musical beats, per line. If it helps, write the phrase down and read it while you repeat. Some people prefer to read it vertically. You may copy it off this page and place it somewhere so you can read it while you chant.

Nam

Myoho

Renge

Kyo

Now it is important at this very early stage to realize that the majority of the world's practitioners have a tool for visualizing and focusing their attention on these words. It is a beautiful scroll with

Nam-myoho-renge-kyo written boldly down the middle (in Chinese characters). It is called the Gohonzon, based on the scrolls Nichiren personally inscribed to his followers, like Shijo Kingo and his wife, seven centuries ago. The scroll (or mandala) is more than a simple representation of the chant (or mantra); it actually describes the state of enlightenment itself. By merging or fusing your life with it, you bring forth your own enlightened nature. It is therefore desirable eventually to have a Gohonzon of your own (for more on the Gohonzon and how to get one, see Chapter IV). It makes everything, including life in general, a lot easier. Meanwhile, you can chant and receive benefit, with or without the scroll.

Do not chant so loudly that you disturb your neighbors, freak out your roommates, or convince your spouse, in case any further evidence were necessary, that you have gone completely mad. Chanting a Chinese translation of Sanskirt words (with Japanese pronunciation) may sound strange to some Westerners. Chant with consideration. Yet it is quite important to chant with some conviction, with a strong, sonorous voice. It needn't be loud and the tone should be steady. You can be soft and strong at the same time. Remember, we are summoning the Buddhahood that lies within. Chanting Nam-myoho-renge-kyo is the cause that brings your highest potential forward. I don't know you, but it could be that your highest potential is buried under many layers of causes, or karma, which have accumulated like a crust, obscuring the potential that you possess. Therefore, the summons to your Buddha nature should be put forth with vigor.

This simple chant is the "primary practice" that Nichiren taught more than seven hundred years ago and is daily performed by millions of people around the globe. As Daisaku Ikeda succinctly points out, "This phrase incorporates the two essential aspects of Buddhism: the truth itself and the practice to develop the wisdom to realize that truth."[2] The "secondary practice," which is chanting two portions of the Lotus Sutra in conjunction with Nam-myoho-renge-kyo, takes less than five minutes, morning and evening. When you chant Nam-myoho-renge-kyo, then recite the sutra, the two practices together are called *gongyo* (meaning "assiduous practice"). Gongyo will be explained in more detail later. For now, it should be quite clear that the primary practice is easy enough for anyone to do. I've been doing it for more than thirty years.

The relationship between the primary practice and the secondary practice is frequently compared to wine and the bottle that holds it. Nam-myoho-renge-kyo is like the wine, reciting the sutra is like the bottle. This is what was meant at the outset by "joy in a bottle." As Nichiren put it, "Nam-myoho-renge-kyo is the greatest of all joys." This means that chanting itself is a deeply satisfying, joyful activity, and also that you can chant to achieve joy in all life's other activities.

Immediately, you will want to know, what do the words *mean*? That is only natural. It is an expression of seeking spirit, and anyone who has come this far obviously has a full measure of that. In our monthly Buddhist discussion meetings, we typically begin with an explanation of the basics, including Nam-myoho-renge-kyo and the Gohonzon, for the benefit of new people (and others who just forgot). First it must be said that it is not necessary to understand the words in order to gain benefit from chanting them. This sounds like a riddle, but it is not. A baby gains nourishment from breast milk and, later, regular milk, without any knowledge whatsoever of the vitamins, minerals, and protein contained in the milk. Likewise, you will gain nourishment from chanting Nam-myoho-renge-kyo whether or not you know what the words mean.

This process can be compared to driving a car. You may drive a car and enjoy its convenience in getting from place to place without really knowing very much about how it works. You put the key in the ignition, and it goes. Certainly a basic knowledge of the engine can be helpful in getting maximum performance from your car. Knowing when to have the oil changed or when to rotate the tires can be helpful. But one can easily think of hypothetical circumstances where there is a huge difference between a good driver and an expert mechanic. The excellent mechanic, for all his intimate knowledge of piston rings and valve timing, may have piled up dozens of speeding tickets and become a menace on the highway. Let us further stipulate, for the sake of argument, that the mechanic likes to drink. The good driver, on the other hand, though ignorant of the workings of the internal combustion engine, may understand just enough to maintain and operate a car safely.

This example closely parallels the words spoken by the Buddha himself in the opening section of the "Expedient Means" chapter of the Lotus Sutra, which Nichiren Buddhists recite daily. In that section, Shakyamuni Buddha addresses his disciple Shariputra, who is considered foremost in knowledge. Shariputra's knowledge, however, was considered a hindrance to his gaining enlightenment, not an advantage. Those who have reached a relatively sophisticated stage of knowledge about life and the universe, known in Buddhism as people of the "two vehicles" (Learning and Realization), are often prone to arrogance about what they know. Think of important scholars, researchers, and intellectuals in our own time. They may have a tendency to be totally absorbed in their work, their point of view, and their importance, to the exclusion of other people. In Shakyamuni's time such people were thought to be capable of only partial enlightenment.

Therefore people with vast amounts of knowledge about Buddhism are not necessarily more enlightened than you are. Knowledge alone is much less important than a willingness to experiment. Eventually you will gain detailed knowledge of how this practice works. This comes through study, a vital component in Buddhist practice, and from practicing with others, with whom you can exchange views. But since the ultimate truth and validity of Nam-myoho-renge-kyo is beyond intellect, theoretical explanations can never really suffice. Buddhism can only be completely understood through chanting Nam-myoho-renge-kyo. You have to take the car on the road.

In any case, assuming you've already put in a few minutes of vigorous daimoku—remember, "practice precedes understanding"—let's proceed with the definitions.

The Rhythm of the Universe

What then is the literal meaning of Nam-myoho-renge-kyo? *Nam* is a verbal contraction of the Sanskrit word *namu* or *namas*, meaning "respect" or "devotion to." (When you finish a yoga class, the instructor will sometimes say, "Namaste." It's the same root word.) *Nam* is also an action word. It is placed in front of Myoho-renge-kyo, the title and first words of the Lotus Sutra, signifying "respect" for the Lotus Sutra. By praising our highest potential, our Buddha nature, we make it emerge. So that much is pretty straightforward.

The second word, *myoho*, means "mystic" or "mystic law." This is another way of saying "that which cannot be explained" or "those things which the mind cannot fathom." Even with all the advances of modern science, there are many things we cannot fully explain about life. For starters, what is life? Then there are the many inexplicable things that we see all around us. Why do bad things happen to good people? Why do sweet, wonderful children suffer from terrible diseases? Where does our energy or "life force" go when we die? Do blondes really have more fun? It might seem like a copout to say that things that we cannot explain should be designated "mystic." A few thousand years ago, pregnancy might have been considered a miracle or a mystical occurrence. (In some cultures, of course, it still is.) Now we know the phenomenon so completely we can control it quite elaborately in a high-tech hospital birthing room. From a strictly rational perspective, science will eventually explain most of the phenomena we even now consider unfathomable. But from the Buddhist perspective, the traditional distinction between religion and science is a distinction without a difference.

To illustrate this point, let's take a further look at *myoho*. The word can be split into two words: *myo*, signifying that which is beyond description, or the ultimate reality of life; and *ho*, meaning "all phenomena." As Nichiren himself put it in a famous passage:

> What does *myo* signify? It is simply the mysterious nature of our life from moment to moment, which the mind cannot comprehend or words express. When we look into our own mind at any moment, we perceive neither color nor form to verify that it exists. Yet we still cannot say it does not exist, for many differing thoughts continually occur. The mind cannot be considered either to exist

or not to exist. Life is indeed an elusive reality that transcends both the words and concepts of existence and nonexistence. It is neither existence nor nonexistence, yet exhibits qualities of both. It is the mystic entity of the Middle Way that is the ultimate reality. *Myo* is the name given to the mystic nature of life, and *ho* to its manifestations.[3]

So *myoho* signifies that the mystic realm and the phenomenal world are actually one. There are many examples of this. Consider the phenomenon of music. We can say that the essential nature of music is *myo* because it is so difficult to explain music's curious power to touch our emotions and move our spirits.[4] What is it about Schubert's "Wanderer Fantasy" that makes our hearts soar? It is a mystery or *myo*. But the actual sounds of the notes are absolutely real and tangible, even measurable, and thus are *ho*. Music therefore is both mystical and phenomenal. An entire book could be written about *myoho*, but let's move on to the next word.

Renge literally means "lotus flower." The lotus is a powerful symbol in Buddhist thought and culture, and it is no accident that the Buddha's supreme teaching takes its title from it. While the pure white lotus blooms on the surface of a pond, its roots issue forth from the muddy depths of the swamp, thus symbolizing the emergence of our Buddha nature amid the worries and impurities of daily life. Suffering and difficulties are normal. They come with the territory. It is not necessary to live in a pure land, a perfect environment, in order to seek or gain enlightenment. It is best to start right where you are, just as you are.

The lotus flower is also somewhat unique in nature because it seeds and flowers at the same time. Since both cause and effect occur simultaneously—symbolized in the blossom itself—the lotus, or *renge*, can be translated as "cause and effect." The law of causality governs the physical world and is the basis for scientific inquiry. Acceptance of this fundamental principle marked the transition from superstitious, magical societies to rational ones. Ancient peoples thought lightning and thunder were expressions of angry gods; now we know

The Buddha in Your Rearview Mirror

them to be manifestations of atmospheric electricity. We have a certain faith in the principle of cause and effect. Even if we do not know how some natural phenomena occur, we generally assume that scientists someday will find the cause. For example, we do not fully understand cancer, but we are working assiduously to discover its causes and mitigate its effects. We do not know how the universe came into being, but working our way backward from the faintly observable effects of the "big bang," the incredible explosion some twenty billion years ago that give birth to all the billions of galaxies in our physical universe, we are systematically studying a chain of cause and effect to find out. Indeed, as noted earlier, the big bang theory itself is a beautiful example of the simultaneity of cause and effect (*renge*), since the universe began to expand at the very moment it came into being.[5]

According to Buddhism, everything in the universe—including you—is ruled by the law of cause and effect. If something has happened in your life, it has to do with cause and effect. Notice we didn't say, "If something has happened *to* you." In Buddhism generally we do not stress the effect of the environment on the individual. We are not so interested in things over which we don't have much control. We are very much interested in the one thing over which we do have a degree of control—ourselves. Buddhism tends to focus on the individual's role in shaping his or her destiny. Most of us underestimate the role of the causes we have made. We are willing to accept the law of cause and effect in some things—you turn the ignition key, the car comes on—but not in others. When it comes to family arguments or troubles on the job, for instance, many of us much more readily ascribe the source of the problem to others, while ignoring or downplaying any actions (or causes) we have made. This is human nature, of course, but it leads to confusion and misunderstanding. One might even say it leads to delusion about the actual facts, especially complex interpersonal facts, of a given situation.

To carry on with our discussion of *renge*, or cause and effect: if everything in the world is ruled by the laws of causality, then there is no such thing as luck or chance, at least not in the sense that human beings give to those terms. Causality applies to situations one might suppose were quite random or accidental. When the space shuttle *Challenger* burst into flame seventy-three seconds after takeoff in 1986, the immediate response was to call it a tragic accident. Some called it the inevitable price of our risky, pioneering ventures into space. However, after lengthy scientific analysis, including exhaustive forensic review of every aspect of the shuttle's manufacture, preparation, and launch, it become abundantly clear that the "accident" was caused by a relatively inexpensive gasket, or O-ring seal, manufactured by Morton Thiokol. The O-ring was predictably unreliable at low temperatures—temperatures that prevailed on the unseasonably cold morning of the launch. Given this knowledge, and the benefit of twenty-twenty hindsight, the disaster was eminently avoidable. It was most certainly not an "accident" in the pure sense of that word.

While none of us has the benefit of a committee of NASA scientists and physicists like the Nobel Prize–winner Richard Feynman to examine in detail the events of our lives, it remains true that seemingly unlucky occurrences are nonetheless the result of the iron laws of cause and effect. Say you are a hit by a car. This is a kind of "accident," to use the conventional terminology. In nearly every accident involving a vehicle and a pedestrian, the onus is on the operator of the vehicle. But from the perspective of Buddhism, one might reasonably ask: How did you happen to be walking on that busy street? Are you typically distracted or lost in thought when you walk? What causes did you make to be there? In other words, to what extent was it your *responsibility* that you were at that corner at that time, and perhaps less than mindful of oncoming traffic?

Now it could be that you share *almost* no responsibility for what happened. The driver was clearly at fault. However, it is indisputable that you chose to be at that place at that time. Crossing the street entails a certain risk—minimal as it may be—that you may be hit by a car. In that limited sense, you were responsible for being there, for crossing the street, for not reacting quickly enough to get out of the way. That does not mean that it was your *fault*. The Buddhist view of responsibility is quite different from conventional notions of blame. Blame and guilt do not play significant roles in Buddhist discourse. As mentioned earlier, Buddhism is not so much about right and wrong as about winning and losing. In any event, it was your *karma* to be there—all the causes and effects you have ever made somehow led you to that moment and place. Much of what we normally perceive as "chance" or "accident" is just a function of causes and effects that we are unable to see.

This does not mean that Buddhists sit around endlessly examining past causes. Buddhism is not psychoanalysis. In order to make progress in life, you cannot live with a backward attitude, always dwelling on the past. Buddhism simply states that we should acknowledge that all reality stems from the underlying law of cause and effect. This is the law of life. This law is eternal and unchanging and it is called Nam-myoho-renge-kyo.

The last word in the phrase, *kyo*, means "sutra" or "teaching." Since Shakyamuni Buddha used the method of preaching to instruct the people and his teachings were orally transmitted, *kyo* is also defined as "sound." The sutras are chanted in many schools of Buddhism and in many different languages. Nam-myoho-renge-kyo, however, which is based on Sanskrit, the primordial language of ancient India and Hinduism, is recited the same way in every language. The vibration of our voice, or *kyo*, is very important in Nichiren's Buddhism. That is why we chant Nam-myoho-renge-kyo aloud, instead of silently meditating. It is a wavelike rhythm, like the underlying rhythm of the reality that surrounds us. Remember that Buddhist philosophy has long propounded the notion that matter is not a solid entity with absolute existence. This insight is referred to as *nonsubstantiality*. As we have said, this corresponds to the famous uncertainty principle of the German physicist Werner Heisenberg, who showed that subatomic particles behaved variably—sometimes as waves, sometimes as particles—depending on the conditions under which they were measured or observed. Ultimately, reality is not reducible to things but to waves and potentials. This is both the Buddhistic and the scientific view.

For too long, human beings have continuously looked under and behind things, searching for the meaning of life when it is right in front of them. According to Buddhism, in reality itself lies the ultimate meaning of life. As Daisaku Ikeda has written:

> In the eye of Buddhism, the true entity of all the movements in the universe is Myoho-renge-kyo. Common mortals see nothing but the trees waving in the wind, yet the Buddha sees the mystic rhythm of Myoho-renge-kyo pulsing within. . . . We can therefore say that every aspect of life is made up according to the supreme Law and that we always act in rhythm with it.[6]

When we consider possible English translations of the phrase Nam-myoho-renge-kyo, for instance, *Respect for the wondrous law of cause and effect through sound,* we might begin to sense its profundity. Even so, we are only scratching the surface. For now, it is enough simply to chant, without getting hung up on what the words mean. Earnest prayer becomes the rhythm of one's life and enables one to fuse with the rhythm of the universe.

How much should you chant? A saying goes, "once is enough and a million is not enough." In other words, it's up to you. (By the way, it takes about a year of chanting one hour per day to accomplish a million daimoku, or repeating Nam-myoho-renge-kyo a million times.) Two things affect the amount of chanting you will want to do: 1) your busy daily schedule, and 2) the depth of your problems and the height of your goals. In the beginning of your practice, try for five minutes in the morning, plus five minutes in the evening. It is best to practice chanting both in the morning and the evening at roughly the same hour, since in addition to the compelling rhythm of the words themselves, there is a definite rhythm to your day when you chant at regular intervals. You may find that you can chant for more than five minutes at a time; do so. Chant to your heart's content, and chant wholeheartedly.

As you meet other practicing Buddhists and they share their experiences with you, various strategies for chanting more effectively will become clear. You will find that both the quantity and the quality of your chanting affect the results. It's good to chant a lot, and it's good to chant with intensity and even passion. You can even imagine yourself at times appropriating the vocal enthusiasm of a favorite singer, one who knows how to "push" a lyric from deep within the heart. (See "Chant Like Judy Garland," p. 106.) Although the idea of chanting in this manner at the outset of your practice, when your mind is still swirling with doubt, might not seem feasible, try it anyway. Put some *oomph* into your chanting. Summoning forth this kind of intensity, in itself, will bring your Buddha nature gushing forth.

Effort is required. Think of your Buddha nature as a precious jewel, hidden in your life somewhere, neglected, obscured by layers of tarnish accumulated over a lifetime of various causes (thoughts, words, deeds) you have made. To polish that inner diamond, to buff it until it shines brightly, you must bear down and rub hard. Nichiren Daishonin used the symbol of a jewel-like mirror to explain how the chanting process dispels human illusion and replaces it with a new kind of awareness:

> When deluded, one is called an ordinary being, but when enlightened, one is called a Buddha. This is similar to a tarnished mirror that will shine like a jewel when polished. A mind now clouded by the illusions of the innate darkness of life is like a tarnished mirror, but when polished, it is sure to become like a clear mirror, reflecting the essential nature of all phenomena and the true aspect of reality. Arouse deep faith, and diligently polish your mirror day and night. How should you polish it? Only by chanting Nam-myoho-renge-kyo.[7]

This passage makes clear that there is essentially no difference between the life of a Buddha and an ordinary person. The one is a hidden potential of the other. But we must purify our lives of illusion and ignorance through practice. Chanting Nam-myoho-renge-kyo is like polishing your inner self. Some technique is involved. This is not to say that your first sincere, tentative efforts to practice will not produce stunning effects. Like rubbing a cloudy mirror with a moist cloth, your initial practice can bring forth brilliant results.

Chant Like Judy Garland

The sort of voice you chant with matters. It should be strong and vibrant but not necessarily loud. Inner determination shows in the voice and overflows into daily life. A firm, courageous voice results in firm, courageous action. There is no way to demonstrate on the written page what this means exactly, except perhaps by analogy with popular song. Take, for example, Judy Garland as a model (choose your own favorite singer). Garland was 4'11" but she sang her heart out. There are many wonderful recordings of Garland's signature songs—"Dear Mr. Gable (You Made Me Love You)," "Over the Rainbow," and so on—but the one that stands out to me, that seems to show her tremendous inward determination, is a rendition of the George Gershwin song "Swanee," before a live audience in 1961. In this verison, Garland sends every word to the balcony, drawing out the final three notes ("Swaneeeeeeeeee shore") with great vivacity and power. This is not to suggest that you should singsong while chanting—all the words get the same emphasis—but do put some zing in your chanting. Singers are sometimes encouraged to "push" a particular lyric in a song, which means to contract the diaphragm, or lower abdominal muscles, to project the words more forcefully. This applies to the discipline of chanting, where it sometimes becomes such a rote daily ritual we can almost fall asleep doing it. When chanting Nam-myoho-renge-kyo, push a little.

What to Chant For

You can chant for anything. Nothing is too small or too big. You can chant for a parking space, and you can chant to become enlightened.

The ultimate goal of enlightenment, while noble, may seem far off. Enlightenment actually means elevating one's life condition to that of a Buddha. It refers to the Buddha's ability to perceive and understand the law of the universe, while exercising wisdom to take action based upon that law. But this may not seem especially relevant or meaningful to someone suffering the pain of loneliness, the agony of serious illness, or the prospect of financial ruin. People with serious problems need practical solutions. It is not easy to aspire to enlightenment when you cannot pay the rent.

Therefore, newer practitioners are encouraged to chant for tangible results. You can chant for a promotion or a raise in salary, and you can chant simply to have a fulfilling job. You can chant to find an apartment, and you can chant for the money to buy a house. You can chant to have a loving relationship with someone, and you can chant for a suffocating relationship to end. You can chant for your child to do better in school, and you can chant for the strength to care for an aging parent. People need practical answers to life's problems. Although the long-range goal may be enlightenment—and with enough enlightened people, world peace—our quest for this goal requires that we develop on a step-by-step basis. These individual steps are measured in terms of benefits. Each new benefit provides evidence, or actual proof, that the practice works. When you see that the practice works, you will want to continue. That is faith. Faith, as we have said, equals practice. Buddhist faith is a matter of challenge and experience, never blind belief.

To offer another automotive analogy, faith is like the battery in your car. It is dependent on use to remain charged. You have to drive regularly in order for the mechanical action of the engine to recharge the battery. If you leave the car unused for long periods of time, especially in cold weather, then the battery becomes weak or unable to start the car at all. We can liken the motion of the car to Buddhist practice and cold weather to personal difficulties or obstacles that keep you from practicing. Both the car and Buddhist practice are like continuous feedback loops. When one practices consistently, every day, the charge of faith stays strong.

A pianist is no longer a pianist if he stops practicing. A baseball player can no longer be regarded as such if he neglects his batting practice and physical training. When you are chanting, you are a Buddhist, and the benefits follow. When you are not, well, you become more of a nightstand Buddhist again.

So, what we chant for, essentially, is benefits, whatever they may be. If you have health problems, you chant to overcome them. If you have serious financial difficulties, you chant about resolving them. If you have trouble sustaining relationships, or even finding one, you need to chant to change that aspect of your life. Why, you may wonder, do plenty of people have robust health, plenty of money, and great relationships *without* chanting? If you can get these benefits without practicing Buddhism, why bother?

A Buddhist saying goes: you cannot make a penny from counting another person's fortune. From the perspective of Buddhism, the key thing is not how beautiful, wealthy, or well-loved other people are. The important thing is where *you* are, what your life condition is, and what you are going to do about it. Good fortune and social rewards are benefits that may come to anybody conscientious enough to work or study for them. These are not special phenomena reserved for Nichiren Buddhists. While the Buddhist concept of benefit includes tangible results, it is primarily concerned with deep life changes that take place beneath the surface. These changes arise through continuous, day-by-day struggle in practice. When the benefits come, because the effort used to generate them was so great, they are that much sweeter.

Let's use a hypothetical example to illustrate this point. Say there are two very successful lawyers. Both are married to beautiful, loving wives. Both have healthy children, nice homes outside the city, and luxury cars in the driveway. However, the first lawyer slipped into his situation quite naturally, because he came from an affluent home, had two stable parents, went to all the best prep schools and an elite college, and, once out of school, benefited from family connections. On the whole, he never had to struggle much in life. By contrast, the second lawyer had to struggle every step of the way, beginning with his dysfunctional family; his father was an alcoholic, and his parents divorced when he was young. Later, he spent long nights working at a restaurant so he could put himself through law school. On paper, these two men may have similar qualifications, legal training, and so on. But beneath the surface, they are vastly different people.

Just as an individual using Buddhism to improve his life may struggle against adversity to awaken his higher potential and change for the better, another person, already in a comfortable position, may just want to coast, enjoy life, and not undergo any major changes.

He goes with the flow. The question becomes: how will each react to a crisis or a situation that requires guts to adapt to? The chances are good that the man with all the advantages, who is not used to fighting for his dreams, will undergo a difficult, if not shattering, experience. The other man, whose character has been forged by a lifetime of obstacles, will most likely take a dramatic upheaval or setback in stride and summon the inner drive to overcome it.

This, then, is a major benefit of practicing Buddhism—the ability to challenge and overcome adversity. No one would practice Buddhism or recommend it to others if it did not bring benefit into his or her life. What would be the point? The reason we practice is precisely to get benefits, concrete results. These can be seen in every sphere of human existence: health, career, relationships, finances, and, of course, personal wisdom. The benefits can be material improvements in your life, which we call "conspicuous" benefits, or they can be more subtle, gradual internal improvements, or "inconspicuous" benefits, like becoming more patient and understanding in raising your children. Of course, benefits of practice often tend to be both material and spiritual at the same time, mutually reinforcing each other, as in the following story, an experience from my early Buddhist days, when my practice was at a crossroads.

How I Started Chanting

The woman who introduced me to Buddhism, Kezia Keeble, used to tell me to chant to make my dreams come true. But what if I didn't have any dreams (aside from playing center field for the New York Yankees)? She told me I should pick something concrete and achievable in everyday life and chant to make it happen. She told me to use it as an empirical test of the validity of the practice. In essence, she was instructing me in how to create a Buddhist "experience."

In the fall of 1975, I was working for an Indian bicycle importer in Manhattan, selling a wholesale line of bicycles and accessories out of a van. I was an indifferent salesman, to say the least. I drove around the city and the suburbs in a beat-up old Ford Econoline with my various samples, selling a few dozen bikes here and there to various retailers. I was a fairly rebellious, antiestablishment, post-graduate type who refused to kowtow to authority. I was twenty-five years old. I had attended, somewhat reluctantly, a couple of Buddhist meetings, listened carefully to what was said, and even chanted a bit on my own. Most of all, I enjoyed the people and looked forward to hearing their experiences. But I remained unconvinced.

Kezia suggested that I chant for something very specific, like a sales goal, something quite tangible and measurable. I had an upcoming meeting at the most prestigious bike store in Manhattan, called Conrad's, which hitherto had been impervious to my charms. Kezia said to chant like crazy to make a big sale, and to keep chanting every available moment, even at the wheel of the truck, as I went on my appointment.

Conrad's was on the East Side near the United Nations, where many of the hard-core bicycle aficionados shopped, a place where I never had been able to sell the owner more than a few rolls of handlebar tape. The eponymous proprietor, Conrad, was an imperious fellow who wore a beret and sported a dark handlebar mustache; everyone in the bicycle world knew him by the one name. On previous sales calls, he had barely acknowledged my presence. Most of his stock was very high end—handmade bicycle frames from France, Italy, and Great Britain—and he turned up his nose at the Indian-made products I had on offer. I also sold a line of French bikes called Paris Sport and a line of Yamaha-made racing bikes with lugless frames, before lugless frames became popular (like today's mountain bikes). He never ordered a single one.

Kezia advised me to chant as strongly as possible, to focus on making a big sale, and to chant "to make a personal connection" with Conrad. I didn't know what that meant, but, as I say, I was not much of a salesman. I told her it would all be futile, that this guy would never buy my stuff. She said, "Okay, then just do as I say to prove me wrong, to show how the practice *doesn't* work. But please do it exactly as I say."

On the day of the appointment, I chanted early and hard. On the way to the store, I chanted as I drove. When I got there, Conrad, per usual, barely took notice of me. "You'll have to wait," he said. "I'm really busy." Meanwhile, he appeared to be just puttering around and chatting with a few bicycle racers in expensive Lycra tights and jerseys.

Hey, I thought to myself, *we had an appointment!* However, I tried to suppress my prideful annoyance and fought the urge to turn on my heel and walk away. I just smiled and continued chanting Nam-myoho-renge-kyo under my breath. My smile was actually genuine, a Cheshire cat smile, because I felt I had a secret weapon in our little tête-à-tête. Meanwhile, he made me wait . . . and wait . . . and wait. I was there a good forty-five minutes, carefully checking out his stock, admiring his displays, and so on, all the while chanting silently and biding my time. When he finally came over to talk to me, I was still smiling.

I couldn't really think of what to do to "make a personal connection," as Kezia had suggested. My mind was a blank. So I settled for making lots of eye contact. (I guess I had never, up to this point, known that a good salesman looks the customer right in the eye.) I spoke to him a bit about his wonderful store. I had gained some knowledge of his layout and stock while cooling my heels. Then I began to pitch my wholesale lines, being careful to point out that, while cheaply made, many of my models satisfied a need in his store because of their lower price point (which even to me seemed a bit ridiculous, since everything he carried was beautiful and well made).

Yet, for the first time, Conrad seemed not to consider my line or my approach ridiculous. In fact, he asked to see my various price lists. I thought, *this is it, he's going to order two dozen roles of handlebar tape and I'm out of here.* Instead, he asked a few questions and then began methodically ordering bicycles. Not just my cheap Indian three-speeds, but fairly expensive Paris Sport 10-speed touring machines and top-of-the-line Yamaha racers. He ordered in every color and every size and from every product line. He ordered dozens of each model, more than $10,000 worth of bicycles. In the end, he even ordered a bunch of handlebar tape.

To put this in context, I had never, ever sold more than a thousand dollars' worth of bicycles in my life. This was, by many degrees of magnitude, the largest sale I had ever made. When I called Kezia, I really had no choice but to admit that the practice in this instance had worked. I was exultant, but what was more interesting, Kezia clearly was, too. Despite all her own high-level challenges—she had her own fashion-related business and dealt with many big clients and famous designers—she was overjoyed for me. She was, if anything, more incredibly happy about my tiny, nuts-and-bolts triumph than I was.

Now certain identifiable hallmarks of the classic Buddhist experience can be seen here. Permit me to highlight a few of them. First, I clearly had elevated my "life condition," that inner state of feeling or being that we all experience throughout the day. Let's call it the average or mean of all the moods you undergo in a given time period. Usually, my inner world was like some sort of emotional roller coaster, utterly dependent on subtle little cues from the environment to send it surging upward or tumbling down. I got angry a lot. My upbeat mood that day was consistently even and quite unshakable. I had not been easily deflated. I had refused to be deterred. I would not be swayed.

Second, I was more *determined* than usual. I seemed to be more focused on the moment, on the goal at hand, and on what causes I needed to make to achieve my aim, as trivial as my bicycle sales may now seem to the reader (or to me, thirty years later). Inside, I had burned with a white-hot intensity, like a blowtorch, to make that sale. Previously, one might say, I had burned with a lukewarm intensity, like a match flickering in the breeze, easily snuffed out. This time when obstacles arose, I was not discouraged; I persevered. (Perseverance, by the way, is one of the six *paramitas*, or traditional practices for the bodhisattva, one who aspires to be enlightened, in most schools of Mahayana Buddhism.) But where had this inner determination come from?

The only thing I had done differently, really, was to chant.

Third, I was able to touch or connect with the life of another person. Whether I knew it or not, the advice I had been given to "make a personal connection" with the shop owner was comparable to making an extra effort to recognize or salute his humanity, which, in a way, was to tacitly acknowledge his Buddhahood. It's kind of like a tip of the hat—almost invisible, but unmistakable—to the inestimable value and preciousness of another person. This was not something that came naturally to me then, as I was a brooding, self-centered sort of person, pretty much engaged 24/7 in an unending inner monologue about myself and my struggles with the world. This, I think, is quite typical of people in their twenties, old enough to have a conception of how life works but too young to hear the wisdom in anyone's ideas but their own. But for that period when I was chanting for my goal, I was curtailing or temporarily abating this brooding, discursive inner chat (the stream of my consciousness) and allowing my larger self, or Buddha nature, to part the curtains and make a brief appearance on stage.

Finally, my experience represents a very clear-cut example of the master-disciple relationship at work, as discussed in Chapter 2, on Nichiren and his samurai follower, Shijo Kingo. In contemporary society, many people are skeptical of words like *master* and *disciple*, because they seem to imply traditional hierarchy or even some sort of intellectual slavery. So more and more we define this relationship as "mentor -disciple" or even "teacher-student." It is indispensable. If one is learning some art or advanced technique or pursuing a higher academic degree, one must put oneself under the tutelage of an expert to make genuine progress. For example, most doctoral candidates have a "thesis adviser." How much more necessary it is for one to have such a mentor when one is pursuing the practice of Buddhism, which one might call the art or science of being a human being!

In carrying out the kind of revolution in one's inner and outer self that we are talking about, the mentor-disciple relationship assumes the utmost importance. Without someone to guide you, particularly in the early stages of this Buddhism, it is very difficult to progress. Despite the popular view that Buddhism is a monastic pursuit, it is actually difficult to practice in isolation. Initially, the person who introduces you to Buddhism often becomes your mentor. That person's strength of will, or determination, can be decisive.

The person who introduced me to Buddhism, Kezia Keeble, was like a character out of fiction–Dickens, maybe, or Trollope. Fast-talking, pretty, eccentric, she was both caring and dynamic, a rare combination. She had worked for a number of years under the legendary fashion editor Diana Vreeland, and, like her, Kezia had style, vision, and a propensity for making incredible, faintly ludicrous pronouncements that later turned out to be true. She was also quite persistent, even relentless, when she really wanted something. She used to call me almost daily after we first met, inviting me to Buddhist meetings, encouraging me to chant, and otherwise just batting the breeze. She had this sort of obsession for me to wake up and lead a more fulfilling life. For all her success in business, she actually cared about *me*. I couldn't figure out where this caring attitude came from, or how she would have the energy for me and my little problems after taking care of her own affairs. I didn't realize then that this personal power of hers came directly from Buddhism. I sometimes wonder where I would be today if I had never met her.

So where did that mysterious energy, what we in Buddhism call abundant "life force," come from? Now is a good time to examine the Buddhist concept of *ichinen*, or moment-to-moment determination, which is central to understanding how the practice actually works.

Ichinen or "Life Moment"

When an individual begins chanting, the important thing is just to chant. No particular thought pattern must be maintained, no changes in lifestyle are required, no commandments or beliefs are imposed. All one needs is an open mind and a willingness to experiment.

After chanting for a few days or weeks, as surely as the sun rises in the east, one notices things: odd things, coincidences, fortuitous events. Whatever you call them, these occur within a short period of time to nearly everyone who chants. It may be an unexpected phone call from a long-lost friend. It could be a check that seems to arrive in the mail out of nowhere. Or it might just be some interesting confluence of events in which you happen to be exactly in the right place at the right time. We frequently chalk up such events, unexplained cool things, as "mystic coincidences," or *myoho*, to use the jargon of Buddhist practitioners.

Many new practitioners also report another common side effect of chanting that is much less mystical and actually quite mundane: a sort of restless energy to accomplish things, especially housework. This applies to both men and women. It might include cleaning the house or apartment, reorganizing the office, paying a stack of bills that have piled up, or washing and waxing the car. While these minor activities in themselves may not suggest instant enlightenment, they are symptoms of something. After you hear hundreds of such experiences over the years—of people chanting then washing the windows in their house or clearing decades of junk out of the basement—a common thread begins to emerge. Pulling at this single, loose thread, we may be able to unravel a core principle of Buddhism.

We call that restless impulse to do something, to take positive action *ichinen* (EACH-i-nen), a Japanese word that Buddhists tend to use in a slang manner, as in, "I have tremendous *ichinen* to do this right," or, "I barely had enough *ichinen* to show up for work." The word *ichinen* in these contexts means something like "energy" or "willpower" and, as we have said, it also can be defined as "determination." Whether or not you are victorious in life depends on your ichinen. How we apply ourselves in any endeavor is of the utmost significance. Indeed, the difference between winning and losing in our very competitive society is often very small. To take a negative example, this explains why even extremely talented athletes resort to performance-enhancing drugs like steroids. They feel they need a competitive edge. With pitchers now throwing 100-mile-per-hour fastballs, small differences in "bat speed," the sine qua non of success for a modern slugger, can add up to big performance increases. As players reach their thirties and their bats begin to decelerate, the temptation to take steroids to increase quickness becomes great.

Likewise, in our ever-competitive world—where a one-bedroom apartment can cost a million dollars in some cities—even a small increase in your ichinen, your life force, can make a huge difference in your daily endeavors. But the power you gain, and the good results you obtain, will be absolutely genuine and hard won. Using Buddhism to increase your own ichinen is entirely legal and natural. It will help with everything, from athletics to relationships. Those who practice Buddhism enthusiastically, with a clear-cut goal and strong determination in their heart, will produce a clear-cut result or actual proof. Naturally, in the beginning of one's practice, it is enough just to practice. One's individual ichinen will increase by itself. However, as time goes on, one's frame of mind, one's attitude in practicing Buddhism, becomes more important and will be reflected in the progress made.

The concept of ichinen pervades all life. It is nothing less than your orientation toward the universe and life itself. It is the moment-to-moment determinant of life's course. What can this mysterious concept mean? To help unpack it, let's compare it to the realm of mathematics known as calculus. (Keep in mind that the following explanation is a mere suggestion of how ichinen works.) Calculus was devised by Sir Isaac Newton to describe the seemingly irregular orbits of planets (not, as popularly believed, to torment generations of college students). In his time there already existed comparatively simple formulae to account for circles, ellipses, and other regular orbits. Calculus sounds and looks complicated—especially its system of notation—but it is a fairly straightforward means of analyzing curves. I studied it for years and never really understood it, until I began to practice Buddhism. The basic assumptions, when seen from the point of view of Buddhism, are actually quite simple:

Imagine you could look at a curve through an infinitely powered microscope. The smooth curved surface would not appear smooth. If enough magnification were available, you could see atoms or perhaps even smaller particles lined up next to one another. But they would not be in a curve. At this level of magnification, they would appear to be lined up in short, jerky angles to one another, more like links in a chain. So the curve, any curve, is really composed of an infinite number of points that are set at a small angle to one another. In calculus, that angle is called the "differential," thus the term *differential calculus*. (I won't even begin to try to explain *integral* calculus.)

In terms of a person's life, this differential, or ichinen, might be seen as one's instantaneous attitude or inclination. If at each point in time we are really trying to accomplish something, then over time, say, a year, we will see a certain kind of result. If at each point in time, we are not ceaselessly striving toward our goal, we will see a very different kind of result. Two students enter a university with the same desire to get ahead in life. But one buries his head in books, while the other looks up every few moments to stare out the window. After four years of college, the difference between the two students will be profound. By observing the first student's ichinen on the first day of class, we might have predicted the outcome of his college career. This is to take an almost empirical, scientific view of life. We are making causes each instant of our lives and the effects are being concretely determined in the same instant. Each moment is called "now," and each now is simultaneously the effect of previous causes and the cause for successive events. The pattern of this endless chain of events is determined by our ichinen.

When you begin to practice Buddhism, all the infinitesimal angles of inclination—all the ways you relate to the universe—subtly change. You are positioned differently in life. The way you look at things, and the direction in which you stand in relation to things, changes. This ichinen or moment-to-moment determination, which comes bubbling up inside you when you chant, seeks a direction or an object or a goal, just as water seeks its own level. Beginning early in your practice, there are five steps to take to ensure that your ichinen is channeled in a positive direction:

1) **Chant with courage.**
2) **Make a strong determination or vow.**
3) **Develop a concrete goal or goals.**
4) **Offer resolute prayer.**
5) **Take action until you see clear actual proof.**

When we chant Nam-myoho-renge-kyo morning and evening with a certain amount of determination or intention in our prayer, we get a certain result. In the morning, before the dramas of the day begin, it is a good idea to chant for the specific goals you want to accomplish that day, as well as the specific causes or actions you want to take in order to achieve those goals. So the day begins with determinations.

In the evening, you should take stock of how the day went. Did you make the causes you set out to make? Did you accomplish the goals you set for yourself? Report back to yourself on how well you did in terms of making your determinations come true. If some of the goals were not clearly achieved, perhaps only partially realized, then you should *re*-determine to accomplish them tomorrow. Each morning, *make* determinations and chant *with* determination. Each evening, *re*-determine to do what you need to do. When you do this over and over again, day after day—determining and re-determining to achieve your dreams—you become, in essence, *a more determined person*! Just as an athlete might do push-ups and sit-ups every morning to strengthen the body, a Buddhist practitioner uses the practice to strengthen his or her inner core. The process of chanting itself is virtually guaranteed to make you a more determined person. In this complex, tumultuous society of ours, that can be a very good thing. It's a little bit like having an extra dash of chutzpah in the hurly-burly of contemporary existence.

When you summon the inner will or ichinen to accomplish an objective, everything about you shifts in the direction of that goal. It is as if the "differential" of your entire being has been altered or moved a degree or so. This change in orientation, which you may not even realize yourself, can be compared to the way a backyard astronomer views the stars. Amateur astronomers often employ a circular star chart to assist in locating the various constellations and planets in the heavens. This two-sided map, or planisphere, shows the northern sky on one side, the southern sky on the other. An inner wheel allows the user to rotate the map and fix the hour and day of the calendar when the star watching is taking place. If you look north, you must hold one side of the chart above eye level and match it to the umbrella of stars you are seeing; if south, the other side of the planisphere chart is used. In order to change between them, the viewer is obliged, naturally, to turn his body 180 degrees and face in the opposite direction.

To apply this example to the practice of Buddhism, when you begin to polish your ichinen and strive toward clear objectives in life, it is not just a simple linear 180-degree turn in your fortunes and perspective. You are not required to change who you are, or how you dress, or even what you enjoy. But it does involve a turnaround subtler and deeper than that. From the standpoint of the stars, it is as if you were to *lie down in the grass*, perhaps in a clear meadow like the one in front of my house. You would thus be able to see the entire sky at once, both north and south, without having to change your perspective. You could flip the star chart at will (or better yet, get a whole-sky star map). You are now in the center of the oscillating light show overhead. You are the fixed center, an earthbound counterpart of Polaris, the North Star, around which the heavens seem continuously to rotate. You have only moved 90 degrees from your original position—from upright to prone—but the increase in perspective is enormous. Now you can see everything at once: all the stars and planets and their relationship to one another.

This is similar to the power of ichinen to change your perspective, the very position you occupy vis-à-vis the ever-changing universe we live in. The direction you have moved in is the direction in which you want to go. As Daisaku Ikeda has said, "One thing is certain: the power of belief, the power of thought, will move reality in the direction of your belief. If you really believe you can do something, you can. That is a fact."[8]

When people attend a Buddhist meeting for the first time, they often have difficulty connecting the concept of ichinen and other effects of chanting with the idea of religion. Through their experiences in other faiths, they have come to regard religion as a means to peace of mind, spiritual tranquility, or moral behavior. Beginning Buddhists are typically encouraged to chant for specific things, bearing in mind, as mentioned earlier, that certain material benefits, or the satisfaction of basic desires, can often free them to aspire to higher things. Gradually, as they begin to realize that Nichiren Buddhism is different from anything they have experienced, they seriously focus on the attainment of clear, concrete objectives. Through the realization of tangible benefits, new practitioners will find that their whole frame of reference is starting to change. Those impossible childhood dreams that had faded into distant memory now become very real goals.

The Needle in a Haystack

What do you want to *be* in life? For most of us, this is a very important question. We want to pursue a career of some sort, one that will best utilize our talents and offer us creative fulfillment, while paying the rent—or better. But finding the right job can be a daunting process. It's like looking for a needle in a haystack. Whether you feel stuck in your career or are not working at all, the prospect of looking for a job or searching for the right career path can bring out all the anxiety and inertia the human mind can bear. It's a cold world out there, especially when you have your hat in hand.

In Buddhism, we look at this dilemma somewhat differently. Yes, looking for a great job (or the ideal mate, or the perfect apartment) is a bit like searching for a needle in a haystack. But in Buddhism we try to magnetize our lives first, and then make solid causes in the direction of our search. In this way we are able to attract the benefit (the needle) toward us, even as we are grasping for it.

Central to Nichiren Buddhist practice is the human experience in faith, because we are not especially interested in lofty ideas that do not work in the everyday world. We want actual proof of something.

As I have said, when I first began seriously practicing Buddhism, I was a brooder, distrustful of authority in general and quite skeptical about the business world. It was 1975, after all. I was very much a product of the sixties and seventies counterculture. I saw working in the bicycle field as a kind of protest against the pollution and congestion wrought by the internal combustion engine. Meanwhile, I had a B.A. from a prestigious college but wasn't making much money. I most certainly was not utilizing my full potential. People used to tell me that I frowned often. I was probably angry a lot. Of course, if asked, I would say that I was perfectly happy.

I received my Gohonzon, the scroll or mandala that signifies one's membership in the Buddhist organization, on October 12, 1975. That was a very significant date, because Nichiren inscribed the original Gohonzon, known as the Dai-Gohonzon (or "great" Gohonzon) on October 12, 1279. In Buddhism, anniversaries of this kind are considered fortuitous or mystic. In any case, with winter coming on, I was beginning to dread another season of semi-employment in the bicycle trade, which tends to slow, if not shut down, during the cold months. My mentor, Kezia Keeble, had told me to chant for my dreams, but if I didn't have one, to chant to *have* a dream. When I tried to do that, certain things did begin to emerge, wispy and diffuse, as if from a fog from the unremembered past. I had always nurtured a dream about working around books. I loved books. Maybe I could write. Kezia suggested I establish the goal of getting a job in publishing and, further, that I treat the process of obtaining this job as a nine-to-five job itself.

That meant getting up early each morning, dressing in a suit, and going to my first appointment by 9 a.m. I was to continue searching for work until 5 p.m. each day, no matter what. That is an interesting phrase in the context of Buddhism: *no matter what.* At this time, I was chanting regularly, attending Buddhist meetings, and reading about the practice. Kezia suggested that, as part of my new regime, I chant each morning and evening at exactly the same time. I settled on 6:30 a.m. and 6:30 p.m. So each morning, no matter what, I would arise and ring the bell signifying the beginning of gongyo, or the chanting practice. I would chant Nam-myoho-renge-kyo for a half hour, then recite the sutra for a half hour, and then chant some more before dressing and hitting the street. This might seem overly regimented, but it offered me a powerful new rhythm: there was the rhythm of the chanting itself, plus the regular, almost circadian rhythm of practicing at the same time morning and evening. Many people lead unrhythmical, somewhat undisciplined lives. The rhythms they have—jobs, school, family responsibilities—are more a function of what their environment dictates than what they themselves impose on their world. Without realizing it, simply by the action I was taking, I was becoming a more disciplined person. It only takes a small change in discipline to enact a great change in the human being.

The quest began on a Monday morning. I had torn out the pages of the Yellow Pages phone directory under the heading "Publishing." Starting with the letter *A*, I began visiting the offices of every publisher in New York, working my way through the alphabet. I would just present myself at the personnel department, ask to be interviewed for any available openings, and fill out an application. None of them had any openings. Several granted me short, on-the-spot informational interviews. At the end of the day, I would return home to my apartment and, at exactly 6:30 p.m., ring the bell to do my evening prayer. Invariably, I would talk with Kezia. She would ask how it went and so on. When I told her about the various pro forma interviews, she emphasized the importance of excelling in those interviews, which didn't seem logical to me, since there were no openings. She stressed that sooner or later I would walk into an office where there *was* an opening, and I couldn't afford to blow the chance. She also encouraged me to "eshofuni" everyone I met.

This is a slang usage of the Buddhist concept of "oneness of man and environment." (As explained earlier, *esho* is a Japanese contraction of *shoho,* for "man," and *eho,* for "environment." *Funi* means "two but not two.") If one's inner life is essentially one with the environment, then, in a sense, the outside world mirrors the inner life condition of the person. If you are gloomy, even a sunny day seems gray. A bright, cheerful person lights up a room. So when Kezia encouraged me to "eshofuni" everyone I met, including the elevator man and the receptionist, she meant to be so full of smiling, cheerful, vibrant life force that I would bowl people over.

In personal terms, eshofuni is another iteration of one's ichinen. Since the average job hunter approaches every glass office door with a mixture of anxiety and dread, it is no easy task to convey confident high spirits. In fact, it is a small act of courage just to go through those doors. On Monday I chanted to have the highest possible life condition, and there I was on Tuesday, ascending elevators and knocking on doors. As the week went by I hit every book house, magazine company, and newspaper listed in the phone book. I also scanned the *New York Times* classified and answered every ad under "Editorial," "Writer," and "Publishing" that seemed interesting. I managed to obtain a courtesy interview at a science magazine, through a friend of a friend, but there was nothing. By the end of the day Friday, I had covered everything from *A* to *Z*, and while I had many little interviews and encounters, I had no job. There had been no openings and no big leads. I took off my suit and performed my evening gongyo, chanting for the strength to continue. I was determined not to give up, no matter what.

One thing I had accomplished, in addition to wearing out the soles of my shoes, was losing some of the nervousness and jitters that typically accompany interviews. When you go on dozens of interviews, especially meaningless ones, you eventually get pretty adept at relaxing and presenting yourself in an appealing manner: no sweaty palms, wavering voice, or trembling uncertainty. I had become a fairly breezy and confident interview subject. We can classify this under the category of inconspicuous benefits.

When I finished that Friday after one whole week of pounding the pavement, I decided to take a walk up to Columbia University, which was in my neighborhood. I was determined not to give up entirely on my job hunt. I decided to make one last "cause" before heading over to the West End bar for a beer. I stopped in the Columbia job center. Believe it or not, I had found out about my first bicycle mechanic's job there; it had been a summer listing posted on the bulletin board. So this time I examined the board again; nothing. But before I turned to go, I noticed several students going up a stairway to the left of the job board.

Curious, I followed them. At the top of the stairs was a grad student checking ID's. I didn't have a Columbia ID, so I took another picture ID out of my wallet, held my fingers over the letters, and briefly flashed it at the attendant. He let me in. I found myself in the actual job-placement office, a different level of sophistication from the bulletin board area downstairs. There were folders with job categories written on the covers. I picked up the one labeled Publishing and quickly found a listing that intrigued me: Book Jacket Copywriter/mass-market paperback publisher. They were looking for a junior writer to compose the blurbs that appear on the covers of their books. That sounded good, like something I could do. Even better, it was *an actual job*–the needle in the haystack!

I could have tramped all over Manhattan for months and never found that job opening; indeed, I had been already to Hearst Magazines, of which Avon Books was a part, where they told me they had no openings. The only way I could have found that job was by somehow magnetizing my life. You might say that there's nothing mystical about it, that my energetic efforts were bound to pay off. Of course, this is precisely so. But where did I get the energy?

Any dispassionate observer might concede at this point that my individual ichinen, or persistence, had somehow brought me, through various twists and turns and struggles, to the needle in the haystack. I had had a tantalizing glimpse of it, but it was still up to me to land the job.

My personal narrative is similar in plot and outcome to thousands of others recounted by Buddhists across the country. The extraordinary commonality and specificity of these experiences suggest an underlying principle, one we have already touched upon but which needs to be explored much more deeply. Although you don't need to know *how* this practice can work in your life, most people want to know anyway. The following discussion involves a good bit of theory and may challenge the reader's forbearance (fortunately, there will be no test at the end).

First, back to the word *ichinen*. It is actually part of a longer term, *ichinen sanzen* (or "three thousand worlds in a single life moment"). This is a phrase that has major significance in the philosophical evolution of Mahayana Buddhism (or northern Buddhism), the one we are talking about, whose ideas spread over the centuries along the trade routes, from India to Nepal to China and Korea, and eventually to Japan. To really grasp the meaning of ichinen and how it functions, we have to go way back and delve deeply into the early theory and practice of Chinese Buddhism in the centuries after Shakyamuni's passing.

In the modern age, we are aware that the universe consists of many worlds—innumerable solar systems, uncountable galaxies, and billions of stars—as well as submicroscopic worlds at the molecular, atomic, and subatomic levels. The ancient Chinese, who were ardent astronomers, also looked deep within the life of human beings and again saw many worlds—worlds within worlds within worlds.

The Ten Worlds

Fundamental to Buddhism is the concept of the Ten Worlds, a component principle of ichinen sanzen (or three thousand worlds). Traditionally Buddhism divided the multiplicity of human existence into Ten Worlds, or life conditions, that we all experience from moment to moment. They are: Hell, Hunger, Animality, Anger, Tranquility, Rapture, Learning, Realization, Aspiration (for enlightenment), and Enlightenment (Buddhahood).

Originally, these ten referred to the states of life into which one was born. They were considered fixed or predestined conditions, like a spiritual caste system, and, therefore, immutable. One could escape only by extraordinarily virtuous living, followed by death and rebirth in a slightly higher world. Generally, one was condemned to repeat one's state of life, according to one's karma, over and over again, existence after existence, through vast epochs of time, thus the traditional metaphor of a wheel, constantly turning and returning to the same place. But the great Chinese Buddhist philosophers and later Nichiren were convinced that the Buddha, in elucidating the Ten Worlds, had meant something else entirely, particularly in the Lotus Sutra. Here, in a sharp departure from Hindu thought, which had emphasized the role of destiny or fate, Shakyamuni made it clear that the Ten Worlds were far from fixed. They were the ever-changing subjective states of life within each human being that we experience from moment to moment every day. In the course of a day, everyone experiences different emotional states or psychological worlds, both positive and negative, as part of our interaction with the environment. In addition, each of us has one or more states to which we are strongly inclined. It is the world to which we gravitate when there is not much going on. This world is called our *basic life tendency*.

Therefore, Hell in Buddhism is not a place consumed by fire, but a condition of pure misery or absolute despair within the human heart. The key characteristic of this vision of Hell is hopelessness; that is, you cannot comprehend the *causes* of your suffering and, therefore, you see no possible way out. The kind of bottomless mental depression that afflicts some people in our society on a regular basis can be compared to the world of Hell.

The second world, Hunger, describes a state in which a person is overwhelmed by desire. This can be for many things—food, profit, pleasure, power—and even if you obtain them, you will soon be unsatisfied. You always want more. The fact that we have desires is not in itself wrong or bad. Most of civilization's greatest achievements were driven by some sort of desire. The problem is when desires manifest excessively or become greed. When a person eats obsessively, even when not hungry—as many Americans do—this is a literal example of the world of Hunger.

In the third world, Animality, as the word suggests, we are dominated or controlled by our instincts and are easily dominated by others. Many examples of this can be drawn from the business world, where executives and workers often act as if governed by the law of the jungle. People get so caught up in their immediate circumstances that reason and morality go out the window. A classic portrait of Animality would be the villainous character Uriah Heep in Charles Dickens' *David Copperfield*. He is mean but fawning. He secretly insinuates himself into a respectable law practice in order to fleece the senior partner and seduce his patron's daughter—all the while rubbing his bony hands together and proclaiming to everyone his humility or "umbleness." Confronted by Copperfield about his evil designs, he reveals his animal nature:

> "Ah, but you know we're so very umble," [Heep] returned. "And having such a knowledge of our own umbleness, we must really take care that we're not pushed to the wall by them as isn't umble. All stratagems are fair in love, sir."
>
> Raising his great hands until they touched his chin, he rubbed them softly, and softly chuckled: looking as like a malevelont baboon, I thought, as anything human could look.

Since Animality is a world of instinctive, animal-like behavior, people in this state act totally without scruple, as Heep does. They fear the strong but prey upon the weak.

The next world, Anger, is a state characterized by pride, arrogance, and sometimes even rage toward others. The person in the world of Anger needs to feel superior to others and, concomitantly, is inwardly gnawed by insecurity. What elevates Anger above the previous three, however, is a degree of self-awareness, or ego. It is preeminently a world of the ego-centered self. In modern middle-class America, that often amounts to a constant craving for status, a restless need to feel better off than others. Perfect literary examples of this type would be the arrogant bond traders, or "masters of the universe," in the Tom Wolfe novel about Wall Street, *The Bonfire of the Vanities*, or the swaggering college basketball stars in his more recent *I Am Charlotte Simmons*. In a 2006 newspaper profile, Wolfe said, "I think every living moment of a human being's life, unless the person is starving or in immediate danger of death in some other way, is controlled by a concern for status." In other words, once a person has transcended for the moment the worlds of Hunger and Animality, the next naturally sequential world is Anger (defined as "status"). The article went on to state succinctly that "status pours the foundation for our innermost lives."[9] From the Buddhist perspective, then, the next step after you have managed to climb out of Hell, Hunger, and Animality—as the vast bulk of our educated, bourgeois society has—is the ego-centered world of Anger.

The fifth world, Tranquility, is a kind of neutral state, when you are neither angry nor sad, and your inner life is controlled by the higher faculties of the human mind, those qualities that distinguish us from animals (which is why this world is sometimes called Humanity). You might be at rest or at leisure. You are in the world of Tranquility when you spend time at home with your family, sit quietly reading a good book, or take a walk in the country. Followers of some philosophies, especially self-help and semireligious approaches that seek to reduce stress and help you maintain a calmer state, often practice to reach this condition as a final goal. Tranquility marks an improvement over the first four worlds, which are known in Buddhism as the Four Evil Paths, but Tranquility often is characterized by passivity and laziness. Of course, the mere jangle of a telephone or the slamming of a door can wrench us out of it in an instant.

The sixth world, Rapture, refers to the gratification of a great desire—physical, material, or emotional—and it is the state in which a lot of us would like to spend most of our time (it is also called Heaven). Getting a raise, falling in love, overcoming an illness, buying a new car—all of these can lift us into the world of Rapture. But the joy of Rapture is ephemeral. It is contingent on the lasting fulfillment of desire. Like the taste of something sweet, Rapture soon fades. Your first bite of a chocolate sundae tastes wonderful, but by the sixth or seventh mouthful the pleasure turns to mere contentment and, when you are finished, sometimes guilt. The first time you drive a shiny new car you may feel exalted, but after a year of meeting the high monthly payments, the sense of fun and excitement may be gone. When we lose what made us happy, we typically descend into the Four Evil Paths (Anger, Animality, Hunger, and Hell). The more we depend on a given thing to make us happy, the deeper we fall into these lower worlds. Yet American society seems to be predicated on the notion that Rapture is the ultimate goal of existence, hence our culture's emphasis on material comfort, consumerism, celebrity, and romantic love.

The notion of love, especially, is often conflated with Rapture or Heaven as the purpose of life. We speak of "undying love" and

TEN WORLDS		JIKKAI
	十界	
Enlightenment	佛	Hotoke (Butsu)
Bodhisattva	菩薩	Bosatsu
Realization	縁覚	Engaku
Learning	声聞	Shomon
Rapture	天	Ten
Tranquility	人	Nin
Anger	修羅	Shura
Animality	畜生	Chikusho
Hunger	餓鬼	Gaki
Hell	地獄	Jigoku

The Ten Worlds or "life conditions" that we experience moment to moment throughout the day represent a concept fundamental to Buddhism.

How to Practice

celebrate passions that transcend cultural and religious differences. As the British Buddhist Richard Causton has perceptively written: "The desire for romantic love is so strong in our society that it could be seen as having displaced religion as the main source of 'spiritual' fulfillment and, indeed, almost displaced it as the means to personal salvation."[10] Thus a man can be "saved by the love of a good woman" and so on. Unfortunately, as everyone knows, love tends to be turbulent, unstable, and frequently short-lived. This in no way is to suggest that good relationships are not important ingredients in a happy life, but we must be aware that they are not necessarily permanent and that basing our whole lives on them is asking for a fall. The same is certainly true of fame, which can be fleeting, and of material wealth, which is transient. Great suffering goes on behind the walls of mansions.

Lower Worlds, Higher Worlds

The six worlds described so far—Hell, Hunger, Animality, Anger, Tranquility, Rapture—are known in Buddhism as the Six Paths or six lower worlds. In each, the individual is at the mercy of his or her own desires and external circumstances. You can certainly take action (make causes) in pursuit of your desires, but your happiness is contingent on the attainment of them and, furthermore, on that very attainment giving you lasting satisfaction. But it is in the nature of the case that it will not. Most of us spend our time bouncing back and forth among these six lower worlds or life states, sometimes caroming from one to another in a split second. One harsh word can doom a shaky relationship. A notice in the mail from the Internal Revenue Service can signal a looming financial crisis. Similarly, an unexpected bonus or a flirtatious smile can instantly make our spirits soar. The important thing, from a Buddhist perspective, is that in these six worlds where most of us live out our lives day to day, we are at the whim of our environment. Our happiness depends on outside events and our reactions to those events.

Perhaps a close-up portrait of a life shuttling among these worlds will illustrate the moment-to-moment reality of our lives as we move from one to another. Let's imagine a young woman we shall call

Maya (the name, by the way, of the Buddha's mother). Maya wakes up early, prepares a pot of Earl Grey, and sits calmly reading the newspaper. Her cat Sid (for Siddhartha) curls up in her lap. She is in the world of Tranquility, one of her favorite places to be. A thin, fragile beauty, Maya really hates to leave the cocoonlike comfort of her apartment, because, well, out there in the world, she is often reduced to a frazzle. She dons her coat and heads for the subway. An express train soon pulls in.

When the doors open, two opposing rivers of humanity try to squeeze through the opening—those exiting the train and those wanting to get on. Maya, who is physically slight, finds herself being buffeted right and left, tummy-bumped from behind, and stepped on by aggressive commuters. She pushes back frantically, her heart for a moment seized with anxiety. She is in the world of Animality, as characterized by her instinctive timidity and fear, if only for a few seconds, until she manages to squeeze through an opening in the mass of bodies and board the car. Whew! She dashes for a place to sit, and just then a chic young woman, all in black, slips into the last remaining seat, flashing a small but noticeable smile of triumph. "Look at her," Maya thinks to herself, "dressed head-to-toe in Prada, doesn't bat an eyelash at brazenly stealing *my* seat, and probably works at a cosmetics counter in a department store." Just for an instant, and not for the only time today, Maya will be in the world of Anger. But it soon passes, and within a few stops she gets off and walks on to her office building.

Arriving at work, she finds an urgent message to see her boss, a brusque, intimidating older woman. Again, with a mixture of apprehension and dread, Maya makes her way to the corner office, where her boss greets her warmly and tells her how much she appreciates Maya's recent hard work. She gets right to the point: she wants Maya to take full responsibility for the company's new, very prestigious, very lucrative account. Maya can't believe her good fortune. She returns to her office on a cloud. This is everything she has been working toward. She is in the world of Rapture or Heaven. She is so happy she could sing out loud. This calls for a celebratory lunch.

Maya and a friend pick a fancy midtown restaurant with cozy patent leather banquettes. They laugh and talk and even order cocktails. Suddenly, out of the corner of her eye, her companion sees something, like an incoming missile on radar. "Hey, isn't that your friend Rob?" she says, nodding toward a tall, dark-haired fellow hurriedly retrieving two coats from the check window. Maya turns to look over her shoulder. Sure enough, it is Rob, a guy she has been dating and, well, pretty much dreaming about all the time. But he hasn't called lately. "And who's that pretty blonde he's with, eh?" her friend asks. Maya, her heart sinking like a rock, doesn't answer. She has no idea.

By the time she returns to her little apartment that evening, Maya is beyond tired and slightly hung over from her cocktails. She is also flat depressed. She has never felt so lonely in all her life. For years now, she suddenly realizes, she has been burying herself in her work to compensate for the nonexistent meaningful relationships in her life. This is the final straw. So what if she got the new account? Her boss didn't say anything about a raise, and it just means tons of work, longer hours, and even less hope of ever meeting the right person. At this point, Maya is in Hell, a state in which one's predicament seems inescapable. She feels an anxiety attack coming on, like the kind she used to have in high school. She begins doing the breathing exercises that her therapist taught her. . . .

By observing the various ups and downs in Maya's day, one can readily see that she is a unique (albeit imaginary) individual but also a bit like all of us. She has her moments of rapture, tranquility, anger, and even occasional despair, whether justified or not. She also has a basic tendency, a world to which her life naturally moves. In her case, it is to be a bit timid and anxious about things. One could say that the fictional Maya's life tendency is to be in the worlds of either Animality or Tranquility, the latter being a typical refuge from the former. This is absolutely nothing to be ashamed of; it is the lot of human beings living in our complex times. We spend a great deal of time ricocheting around in the six lower worlds, generally hoping to ascend, at best, to Tranquility or Rapture. The four highest worlds—Learning, Realization, Aspiration, Enlightenment—known in

Buddhism as the Four Noble Paths, seem beyond reach. To us, involved in the rush-rush of everyday existence, they are pretty much unknown lands.

The six lower worlds resemble an ice hockey game in which your team is unable to move the puck out of its own zone. Even when you are able to make a good pass, another skater appears to check your team's progress up the ice. While some of your efforts and strategies may be good, you are never able to get the puck across your own blue line. If we let the opponent's net symbolize the goal of enlightenment, the situation is thus: you are unable even to get within the zone where you can take a decent shot at it. This is what life is like in the six lower worlds. When you see a hockey game like that, as a fan sitting up high in the stands, you may wish that the overmatched, bottled-up team could somehow get an aerial view, so the players could look down and see the way the opposing team is executing its "trap." It would be great if they could just elevate themselves to a "higher" life condition, so they could look down on their problems. Then perhaps they could find a strategy to make their way out of their own zone. This is exactly what Buddhism does. It enables us to raise our life condition so we can look *down* on our problems.

Being trapped in the six lower worlds (as most of us tend to be) includes being unaware of the reason why we are trapped, which is fundamentally that the desires and goals in those worlds are transient things. All happiness in these worlds is conditional. Once we recognize this and begin to aspire to something different, the search for lasting happiness—Buddhist seeking—begins. For the purpose of Buddhist practice is to establish an indestructible happiness, deep within our lives, that cannot be destroyed by changing external circumstances.

The quest begins in the next two worlds, Learning and Realization, which are known in Buddhism as the "two vehicles." These were the teachings expounded by Shakyamuni Buddha as "vehicles" to carry one to a higher life condition, where one could look down on the lower worlds and begin to bring the highest world, Buddhahood, into view. Originally, Shakyamuni trained his disciples, who often came from wealthy Brahman (upper caste) families, to give up worldly goods and position, and practice certain disciplines and austerities, in order to attain a partial state of enlightenment called *arhat*. But these pupils, however advanced they were intellectually, tended to become overconfident and attached to their own limited understanding. They thought they could achieve Buddhahood through reason alone. While Buddhism does not reject the power of reason—in fact, it venerates it—the door to enlightenment cannot be opened by reason alone.

The seventh world, Learning, describes that condition of life in which we seek knowledge about life from someone else—a teacher, a book, or a lecture. In Japanese the world of Learning is translated as *shomon*, for "voice hearers," a reference to those who originally listened to the voice of the Buddha preaching. In modern terms, Learning can refer to serious study about the nature of life, even in a non-Buddhist context, provided that it has to do with recognition of the true nature of reality (cause and effect) and self-improvement. It could be a research project in which you are involved or even a dialogue in which you are engaged in your community. But the key feature of Learning is that you acquire your knowledge from others.

By contrast, in Realization, the eighth world, you acquire your knowledge about the true nature of reality through your own perception. The Japanese word for Realization is *engaku*, for "cause-awakened ones," meaning those who have awakened to the truth of cause and effect. Realization is insight or self-enlightenment. Realization is achieved largely through your own efforts. Examples in history of people who have made great individual realizations include Beethoven, who by the age of twenty-two had composed three piano concertos, two symphonies, and two string quartets; and Madame Curie, the discoverer of radium and the only woman ever to win two Nobel Prizes.

Clearly, the two worlds of Learning and Realization are closely related. Scholars, scientists, philosophers, and writers spend a good deal of time in these worlds. It might be said that musicians, poets, and other artists tend to be in the world of Realization, which is sometimes called Absorption, since it is characteristic of people in these fields to become quite absorbed in understanding and conceptualizing the true nature of the phenomenal world. While these are relatively high life conditions, the drawback is that those in these worlds commonly seek the truth for its own sake, or for their own sake, rather than for the sake of others. Indeed, people who spend a great deal of time in these worlds have a tendency to become arrogant, to descend into the world of Anger, and to show disdain for others. It is perhaps enough to say that people who are capable of great absorption in their work often are self-absorbed as well.

The ninth world, the one just before Buddhahood, is called Aspiration or Bodhisattva (a Sanskrit word consisting of *bodhi,* or "enlightenment," and *sattva,* or "being"). Here one aspires to achieve enlightenment and is determined to help others reach that state. Aspiration is characterized by selfless compassion and altruistic behavior. In history, Florence Nightingale would be an excellent non-Buddhist symbol of this life condition. Nichiren said that ordinary humans can manifest this world by placing less importance on themselves and greater importance on others, even to the point of bringing evil upon themselves in order to impart goodness to others. (An example of this might be the relative poverty and material hardships often suffered by those who sincerely make sacrifices to help others.) However, a distinction must be made between those who pursue ultimate truth for the sake of others, and those who desire to seek spiritual truth purely on their own, for their own sake, causing them to ignore the realities of their own daily lives (perhaps neglecting their families). Self-denial and self-abnegation of this sort are not features of the Buddhism we are discussing. A true bodhisattva is not solely concerned with his or her own enlightenment. As Buddhist scholar Yasuji Kirimura puts it:

> If efforts are directed only to self-improvement, any truth obtained will never be more than partial. Each form of life is inseparably linked with all other beings and things in the universe because the ultimate reality of life which supports them all is one with the life

of the universe. Consequently, in the attempt to grasp an overall and complete view of life's truth, one must first realize that he cannot live apart from other living beings, and then he must identify with the pain of others to the point that he exerts himself fully to relieve those around him of their sufferings.[11]

The world of Aspiration or Bodhisattva, in which you freely exert yourself for the enlightenment of others, is the gateway to Buddhahood. But is it really feasible to feel and act in this way when you are mired in the lower worlds? In this regard, Shakyamuni Buddha and Nichiren Daishonin both made it clear that our own enlightenment is inextricably linked to the enlightenment of others. The key to understanding how an ordinary human being, amid all the daily challenges of existence, can somehow become a bodhisattva lies in grasping a rather complex point: each of the Ten Worlds individually contains the potential of all the others. This is known as the *mutual possession* of the Ten Worlds. Nichiren put it this way:

> The fact that all things in this world are transient is perfectly clear to us. Is this not because the worlds of the two vehicles [Learning and Realization] are present in the human world [Tranquility]? Even a heartless villain loves his wife and children. He too has a portion of the bodhisattva world within him.[12]

As we have seen, the Ten Worlds concept depicts the variability of our own minds. Our inner world is like a kaleidoscope, whirling and changing in response to the environment. Our various life conditions—anger, sadness, joy, ease—arise and overlap one another from moment to moment. We have also seen that one life condition or world tends to define us or become our dominant life tendency. Each of us has an overall tendency to be in one world more than in others. If you frequently lose your temper or find yourself constantly striving to assert your superiority over others, your dominant world or life state may be Anger. If you are an anxious, timid person, who instinctively recoils from conflict and controversy, perhaps Animality is your life tendency. That does not mean you are *always* in that world; it's just a place you end up in a lot. Naturally, at any given moment, each of us possesses the *potential* for all ten, and, indeed, we pass through many of them quite rapidly during the course of a typical day. A person's life condition can soar from Hunger to Rapture in an instant—a starving person is presented with a rich banquet. It can descend back to, say, Anger, just as quickly—the person is presented with a huge check for the meal—depending on changing external circumstances.

The notion that these worlds mutually possess one another, that each world *contains* the other nine inherent within it as a potential, may seem obscure or needlessly complicated, but it is the only conclusion one can draw on close examination of the facts of human life. For example, though we may have a tendency to be passive and sedentary (Tranquility), certain events may cause us to spring into action. If we are very, very lazy, it will take a big stimulus from the environment to get us into action. One could say that when we are in the state of Tranquility, the other nine worlds are just dormant.

In fact, in its detailed description of how life changes from moment to moment, the Ten Worlds rivals anything modern psychology has produced. Yet Nichiren knew that the concept of mutual possession of the Ten Worlds would be hard to convey. He wrote: "The possession of the Ten Worlds is as difficult to believe as fire existing in a stone or flowers within a tree. Yet under the right conditions such phenomena occur and can be believed."[13] To cite just two examples: coal is a stone that can be burned, and the jacaranda tree blooms with beautiful blue flowers. You may not think that you have the condition of Buddhahood within you, but under the right circumstances it will surely manifest itself.

Enlightenment or Buddhahood

At last we come to the world of Enlightenment or Buddhahood, the highest of the Ten Worlds, a state of absolute happiness. This life condition exists within everyone as a potential. The pre–Lotus Sutra teachings suggested that the Buddha was an extraordinary being, to be worshipped from afar. When the word *buddha* comes up in many contemporary contexts, it still conjures an image of a static figure, seated in meditation, a saint or a prophet, someone who is not really of this world—but beyond it. However, according to the principle of the mutual possession of the Ten Worlds, the world of Buddhahood contains the other nine, and all nine contain it. It is not necessary to obliterate or extinguish the lower nine worlds in order to dwell in Buddhahood. To do so would be to renounce your humanity along with your desire. Therefore common people (you and I) are capable of attaining this noble and happy state.

Shakyamuni's highest teaching, the Lotus Sutra, propounded the notion that regular people, including women, could become Buddhas. In the "Devadatta" or twelfth chapter of the Lotus Sutra, he tells the story of the dragon king's daughter, who achieves enlightenment in a single moment without changing her dragon form. This was a revolutionary idea in ancient India, both because it suggested a female was capable of enlightenment and because she was able to do so exactly as she was. Nichiren emphasized this parable in his own time. The notion that we can attain Buddhahood in our present form, just as we are, is at the heart of contemporary Nichiren Buddhism.

Nichiren realized that describing the state of enlightenment, convincing people that it even existed, would not be easy. He wrote:

> Buddhahood is the most difficult to demonstrate. But since you possess the other nine worlds, you should believe that you have Buddhahood as well. Do not permit yourself to have doubts. Expounding on the human world, the Lotus Sutra says, "The Buddhas wish to open the door of Buddha wisdom to all living beings.". . . That ordinary people born in the latter age can believe in the Lotus Sutra is due to the fact that the world of Buddhahood is present in the human world.[14]

While it is the highest state of life, Buddhahood does not imply a transcendental state, involving mystic powers, levitation, time travel, or any other superhuman qualities. Shakyamuni Buddha was not a supernatural being but a man. Let us revisit his great moment of realization. His enlightenment was achieved after years of strenuous effort. He had practiced various austerities—fasting, temporary suspension of the breath, and various forms of meditation and mind control—all aimed at extinguishing desire and attachment. Ultimately, he rejected these processes of self-mortification and renunciation. After recovering his strength (in legend he was fed milk curds offered by a village girl named Sujata) he began the final, prolonged meditation that resulted in his enlightenment. It is said that he awakened to the eternal truth, the law of life that permeates the universe and the human being. Shakyamuni saw that desires and obsessive attachments were problematic, that they could blind people to this law. When one regards himself as supreme, he will invariably view the world egocentrically. Instead, a Buddha recognizes that one's own life and the cosmic life are inseparable. Through his enlightenment he was able to solve the fundamental human dilemmas that motivated his quest—the four sufferings of birth, old age, sickness, and death—as expressions of the unending cycles of disintegration and rebirth which sustain life and the universe. This is the true aspect of all things. At the same time, he realized his mission to release all people from these sufferings. After his enlightenment, Shakyamuni traveled throughout India for five decades teaching the people, according to their level of understanding, the secret of his enlightenment.

While Shakyamuni's achievement was glorious and world changing, it should not be regarded as otherwordly or exclusive, nor should it be seen as reserved for Buddhists. Many thinkers have suggested that enlightenment, or at least a degree of enlightenment, is common to various spiritual traditions and cultures, and that, since it is a human potential, it can manifest itself almost spontaneously in certain circumstances. As Ikeda writes in his interpretive biography of Shakyamuni, *The Living Buddha:*

> We may go further and say that many great thinkers and men of genius have probably experienced enlightenment of one kind or another. Descartes, for example, on November 10, 1619, when he

was absorbed in thought in a village on the Rhine, had a sudden flash of inspiration, according to his biographers, that revealed to him a "wonderful discovery" and a "marvelous science." The nineteenth-century existentialist philosopher Kierkegaard, while walking along lost in thought, is said to have had a sudden violent flash of understanding that shook his whole being. In the West, such flashes of understanding are known as revelation and are traditionally believed to be imparted by a God who is absolute and omniscient. In terms of Buddhist philosophy, men like Descartes and Kierkegaard would be regarded as belonging to the category of *pratyeka-buddha*, the level of existence just below that of Buddha and bodhisattva.[15]

To be fully enlightened is to perceive the true nature of life and to realize one's highest potential. There are all kinds of poetic descriptions of Buddhahood, many of them emphasizing a kind of otherworldly gloriousness. What does it mean for today? Ikeda defines it this way:

> Manifesting our Buddhahood does not mean we become special human beings. We still continue working to defeat the negative functions of life and to transform all difficulties into causes for further development. Buddhahood is a state of complete access to the boundless wisdom, compassion, courage and other qualities inherent in life. . . . To give an analogy, if we liken dwelling in the nine worlds to being cooped up in a room, then dwelling in the world of Buddhahood would be like basking outdoors in the clear, bright sunshine.[16]

The important thing is not to regard enlightenment as something alien to ordinary human consciousness. It is a natural part of the Ten Worlds and integral to each of them.

Why ten? It would seem that several of the worlds overlap a bit. For instance, a person who is just mildly bemused or sarcastic might be in a kind of in-between state of Anger and Tranquility. In a sense, then, ten does not seem to depict fully the myriad states of mind and emotion—the subtleties, the shadings that we experience from moment to moment. In fact, in the Buddhist philosophical system, the Ten Worlds is really just a template or model, albeit a powerful one, to facilitate understanding. We live every day in the nine worlds, but with strong Buddhist practice, we realize the possibility of living in the tenth world of Enlightenment. The more we practice, the more our life tendency becomes Buddhahood, instead of, for example, Hunger, Animality, or Anger. Since the Ten Worlds mutually possess one another, the radiant glow of Buddhahood begins to transform the lower worlds. When we get depressed (Hell), the depression will not be as deep. Increasingly, you will not be swayed by the Eight Winds.

This happens automatically, without you even thinking about it. We do not need to go around trying to figure out which world we are in at each given moment. Such "mindfulness" could be counter-productive in the real world. If you are angry at times, perhaps it can't be helped. Sometimes you will desire something that you cannot have. Other times, you will lose something you have cherished. The pain of suffering and the anguish of loss cannot be entirely avoided without renouncing the world. As Nichiren wrote, "Suffer what there is to suffer and enjoy what there is to enjoy." This marvelously blunt statement summarizes the Buddhist attitude. In the midst of suffering, one can still be free and relatively strong. You can be yourself. You don't have to smile and frolic around while a disaster is happening. We are going to struggle at times. The difference is you don't face your obstacles or problems with a feeling of profound resignation; rather, you have a spirit of hopeful challenge.

In trying to convey the essence of his enlightenment, the Buddha initially despaired of ever being able to do so. Eventually he resorted to parables and metaphors, including the rich imagery and verse of the Lotus Sutra. It was from this latter part of the Buddha's writing that the Chinese derived their theory of *ichinen sanzen*, or three thousand worlds.

Three Thousand Worlds

To explain the state of Buddhahood, the Chinese philosopher known as T'ien-t'ai developed and used the theory of *ichinen sanzen*. We have mentioned earlier that Nichiren Daishonin studied at a monastery of the Tendai School in Japan. This particular school based its teachings on the Lotus Sutra, as interpreted by the Chinese monk and Buddhist scholar Chih-i (538–597), more commonly known as T'ien-t'ai (named for the mountain range where he retired to study and meditate, hence also Tendai School). Many Japanese schools of Buddhism, including Zen, trace their direct lineage to Chinese monks and scholars. The Buddhism of all these schools, therefore, has a distinctly Chinese flavor. Ikeda has written:

> The religion of Shakyamuni, when it was transmitted from India to other countries with very different languages and cultures, naturally did not remain unchanged. Though the philosophical core of the religion stayed the same, various adaptations in matters of custom and procedure and various shifts of doctrinal emphasis took place in the new environments . . . so that in time China, for example, developed its own distinctive Chinese Buddhism, and the same process was repeated in Japan.[17]

Nichiren considered the sixth-century Chinese scholar T'ien-t'ai to be a great Buddha, in fact, *the* Buddha of the Zoho period, which is the name used to describe the second thousand-year span following the death of Shakyamuni. (As discussed, the age we live in is known in Buddhist tradition as Mappo.) It may seem surprising, but the works of T'ien-t'ai are still intensively studied by the Buddhist community in the People's Republic of China.[18] Like other Chinese thinkers, T'ien-t'ai was a phenomenologist, very much interested in the relationship between the natural or phenomenal world (the world of things and events) and people's apprehension of it, especially the workings of human consciousness.

He was also a great classifier of things, including the sutras, which he listed systematically in the order of their importance, with the Lotus Sutra at the top. In his works, T'ien-t'ai likened the other sutras or teachings of Shakyamuni Buddha to streams and rivers. The Lotus Sutra was the ocean. The many waters that made up the teachings of Buddhism flowed from all directions without losing a single drop into the great ocean of Myoho-renge-kyo, the daimoku or title of the Lotus Sutra.[19]

According to scholars, T'ien-t'ai, the son of a leading government official, first encountered the Lotus Sutra at the age of six, when he came upon a temple where monks were reciting chapter twenty-five (the "Kannon" chapter). He immediately committed it to memory, revealing himself to be both a precocious intellect and a prodigal seeker of Buddhist truth. He soon became an expert on this sutra; indeed, he devoted his entire life to it.

He was especially fascinated by the Hoben ("Expedient Means") and Juryo ("Life Span") chapters of the Lotus Sutra, which, we have said, are chanted or recited daily by Nichiren Buddhists. T'ien-t'ai expounded the principle of ichinen sanzen, which means "three thousand realms in a single moment of life." *Ichinen* literally means "life moment," and *sanzen* means "three thousand." This figure is the product of the Ten Worlds, their mutual possession, the ten factors, and the three realms.

The ten factors or aspects are: 1) appearance, 2) nature, 3) entity, 4) power, 5) influence, 6) cause, 7) relationship, 8) effect, 9) reward, and 10) their consistency from beginning to end. These ten factors are based upon the Ten Worlds and further depict how they function. The aspects (or factors) of an individual do not exist apart from his or her life condition (or world). For example, if the world of Hunger rules your life, your activities and dealings with other people will be colored by this basic condition. If you are in the state of Hell, then your *appearance* (1) will reflect that, as will the *causes* (6) you make and the *effects* (8) you receive. Finally, regardless of what world a person is dwelling in, that life condition will show a certain *consistency* (10) throughout the individual's ten factors. Therefore, a person in the world of Tranquility will most likely have a low energy level (*power*), have an easygoing manner (*nature*), and perhaps be reluctant to take action in life (*cause* and *reward*).

In the verse portion of the Lotus Sutra that Nichiren Buddhists recite daily, the ten factors are introduced by the words *Shoho jisso sho* (see illustration, p. 145), which mean literally "the true aspect of

all phenomena" (the ten factors are *Nyoze-so, nyoze-sho, nyoze-tai.
. . and so on*). A Buddha understands the true aspect of all phenomena, but this is not an intellectual process. We can spend our
whole lives studying and chanting about ichinen sanzen. The key
point of this almost mathematical approach to life philosophy is that
by chanting Nam-myoho-renge-kyo, you will inevitably manifest the
true aspect of enlightenment throughout the ten factors—in your
appearance, nature, power, relationships, the causes you make, and
so on. If this does not seem self-evident to you, keep in mind that
this is the very same passage in which the Buddha declared, "the true
aspect of all phenomena can only be understood and shared between
Buddhas." It is a difficult thing to comprehend.

The final element of ichinen sanzen is the three realms. These
are: 1) the realm of the five components (form, perception, conception, volition, and consciousness), 2) the realm of living beings (individual human beings and the social environment they interact with),
and 3) the realm of the environment (the land and its insentient life
forms). These are merely the various realms where the drama and
interplay of the Ten Worlds and ten factors unfold. Now, to do the
math: since we have said that each of the Ten Worlds mutually possesses one another, that is 10x10=100. Multiply that by the ten factors, and you get 1,000. Finally, multiply by the three realms to get
3,000 worlds—or human possibilities in a single moment of existence.
It may seem enough to make your head spin, but it is really no more
than a very precise phenomenological approach to cataloguing or
systematizing all the various emotions or life states an individual can
experience at any given moment. Each potential life moment or
experience is treated as a phenomenon, a measurable event. T'ien-
t'ai said there were three thousand.

You might even say that there are just so many moods or
thoughts a human being can experience during the course of the day.
We do not require the eye of a scientist to discern them. We typically
read these moods in our friends and colleagues by the expressions on
their faces. You can obtain a pretty acccurate snapshot of what people
are feeling by a quick look at their faces. Even in a smiling face, the

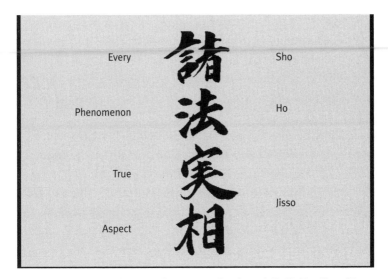

	諸	
Every		Sho
Phenomenon	法	Ho
True	実	
		Jisso
Aspect	相	

Buddhism teaches that every phenomenon has ten aspects, based upon the Ten Worlds or life conditions. By chanting Nam-myoho-renge-kyo to the Gohonzon, a person will manifest the true aspect of enlightenment. Theoretically one's enlightenment or Buddha nature is inherent in every phenomenon. Whether it is activated or not is up to the individual's strength of prayer.

tiniest little sign—a movement of the lips or eyes—can suggest something else entirely, perhaps a lack of sincerity or an attempt to put on a brave front. Your true ichinen, or attitude at each moment, is invariably reflected in your face (unless you are a very good actor). Generally, the face tells a true story of the life within. In fact, Buddhists sometimes refer, somewhat slangily, to "the ichinen in your face." This can mean something as unextraordinary as observing that you look, say, stern in a moment when you are concentrating on a difficult task, or that you perhaps are glowing after a great meeting. Nevertheless, the ichinen of one's face is a very important indicator of one's life condition.

None of this is particularly provable. It seems to exist not in the realm of measurable phenomena but in some other region, the numenal world of life's suspected but unproven mysteries. It is in the area of things we think might be true but have no empirical way of knowing for sure. But T'ien-t'ai and Nichiren insisted that these are actual phenomena, true facts of existence, and, furthermore, manifestations of the ultimate truth.

Now let us turn to the book *Blink*, by the *New Yorker* writer Malcolm Gladwell. In this durable bestseller, the author examines many phenomena of contemporary life to build his thesis that a startling amount of human knowledge is acquired in a brief instant of time, in a blink, so to speak, of an eye. He calls this "the power of thinking without thinking." Eventually he meets a pair of brilliant research psychologists, Paul Ekman and Silvan Tomkins, who work out of a laboratory in a Victorian mansion at the University of California, San Francisco, where Ekman is a professor. Beginning in the 1960s, their main field of study has been the human face. Specifically, they have set out to chart a common set of rules governing the facial expressions of human beings—to create a taxonomy of facial expressions. They have traveled all over the world, from the cities of Europe and Asia to the jungles of the Amazon, taking and analyzing photographs of men and women making a stunning variety of faces. They then carefully outlined the facial muscles and bones, and every distinct movement the parts of a face could make. There were 43 such movements, each of which they labeled an "action unit" (A.U.). These movements, in their various combinations, could be inextricably linked with underlying thoughts and emotions, even expressions that were hiding something else, like dishonesty or fear. The face does not lie. Here is Ekman, demonstrating the technique:

> He flashed a smile, activating his zygomatic major. The inner parts of his eyebrows shot up. "That's A.U. one—distress, anguish." Then he used his frontalis, pars lateralis, to raise the outer half of his eyebrows. "That's A.U. two. It's also very hard, but it's worthless. It's not part of anything except Kabuki theater. Twenty-three is one of my favorites. It's the narrowing of the red margin of the lips. Very reliable anger sign. It's very hard to do voluntarily."[20]

Ekman and Tomkins can pinpoint what a person is experiencing inside—joy, suspicion, boredom, sarcasm, thinly disguised contempt—by observing carefully the expression on his or her face. They further claim, as author Gladwell puts it, "that the information on our face is not just a signal of what is going on inside our mind. In a certain sense, it *is* what is going on inside our mind."[21]

Ultimately, based on their empirical observations, they assembled the myriad facial expressions into a Facial Action Coding System, a five-hundred page document. Many of the possible facial combinations don't mean anything, but some of them almost certainly do. As Gladwell tells us, by working through each action-unit combination, the researchers eventually identified a number of them, a grand total, that were clearly significant. The number? *Three thousand.* In other words, closely parallelling the theory of ichinen sanzen, which states that human beings have the potential to experience any one of the three thousand worlds or life states at a given moment in time, Ekman and his modern-day colleagues catalogued the essential repertoire of human facial displays of emotion—and came up with three thousand!

It is enough to say that the cosmic-sounding theories of Buddhism often have clear, verifiable roots in the reality of everyday life. In developing the theory of three thousand worlds, the Chinese showed their inclination to view the universal in the light of the particular. In contrast, societies in which the concept of God is all-important tend to view the particular in the light of the universal. God directs the destiny of the world. The Chinese avoided the concept of God and attempted to extract underlying principles of universal validity directly from reality itself.

The ultimate aim of Buddhism is enlightenment, or happiness. This might entail many things: a purposeful career, satisfying relationships, good health, a feeling of joy, perhaps merely rejoicing at the laughter of a child or contemplating the snow peacefully falling on a beautiful garden. Other schools of Buddhism preach a kind of "mindfulness" that is ever present, that guides one through the day. In Nichiren Buddhism we say "chant and take action." It is imperative to take positive action (to make good causes) in your life. So the chant itself is active, and once it is finished, further action is required. Just what kind of action? Well, that is entirely up to you. First, chant for the wisdom and courage to make the right causes throughout the day, then go out and try to make them.

How do you know which causes (or life decisions) are the right ones? You don't really. While you are chanting there is no lightbulb that goes off in your head, no flashing sign telling you: *I need to go in today and quit my job!* Or: *I have to ask so-and-so out on a date.* Or even: *I should buy the Ford, not the Honda.* What you must do is chant vigorously, sincerely, and courageously to make the right decisions. You are already making the highest possible cause for your individual happiness: you are chanting Nam-myoho-renge-kyo. Then arise, close the *butsudan* (the box housing the Gohonzon, if you have one), and go out and live. You will find that more and more, as your practice deepens, you will make the right calls—the right causes in your life. Many religions address the issue of suffering and enlightenment, but Nichiren's Buddhism answers the question from the strict point of view of cause and effect.

Enlightenment is an effect. The question is: what is the right cause to attain it? Buddhism would have us never forget that our own human lives are themselves the eternal, unchanging force in the universe, the force that we call Nam-myoho-renge-kyo. It is joy in a bottle. When we chant this phrase, we call up our own Buddha nature. But Nichiren knew that eventually, for great numbers of people to chant and gain enlightenment, the people would need an object. So he created a marvelous tool for bringing out the individual's highest potential, the Gohonzon, the subject of the next chapter.

Practice for Oneself and for Others

Buddhism for Buddhism's sake has no meaning at all. Buddhism exists to show the way to live a happy and meaningful life in this world. This is why we say that faith is manifested in daily life and Buddhism in society. The statement, "No affairs of life or work are in any way different from the ultimate reality," indicates that Buddhism is the wellspring of success and fortune in all human endeavors. It goes without saying that those who have faith in Buddhism will not be indifferent to social matters.

In Buddhism there are two ways of practice, *jigyo* and *keta*, which mean "practice for oneself" and "practice for others," respectively.

The jigyo aspect, or practice for oneself, involves chanting Nam-myoho-renge-kyo, doing morning and evening gongyo (sutra recitation), and studying. Practice for the sake of others, keta, does not imply altruistic practices associated with other religions. An altruistic person typically sacrifices his own happiness or subordinates his own desires for another human being. Altruism is living for the sake of other people. While there may be something beautiful in altruism, it is still a denial of the self. In Buddhism, practicing for others does indeed benefit other people, but at the same time the person carrying out this practice receives benefits. Simply attending a monthly Buddhist meeting, encouraging others in their chanting, or teaching another person the sutra book constitute strong elements of keta, or practice for others.

It is shallow to practice to the Gohonzon solely for the purpose of making things easier for oneself in life. The point of practice is to change oneself into a more effective individual. There is really no sacrifice in Buddhism. Desires and dreams, though seemingly discarded in the quest for *Kosen-rufu*, or world peace, are actually elevated and enriched.

Practicing both for oneself and for others can be compared to the Earth's rotation on its axis and its revolution around the sun. Our practice for ourselves and others accords with the principles of nature.

Notes on Chapter 3

1. In Japanese, the *Hoben* and *Juryo* chapters.
2. Ikeda, *Unlocking the Mysteries of Birth & Death*, 17.
3. *The Writings of Nichiren Daishonin*, 4.
4. Richard Causton, *The Buddha in Daily Life* (London: Ride Books, 1988), 101.
5. Ikeda, *Unlocking the Mysteries of Birth & Death*, 179.
6. Cris Roman, "Buddhism and the Western Philosophical Tradition," *Seikyo Times* (November 1978), 45.
7. *The Writings of Nichiren Daishonin*, 4.
8. Daisaku Ikeda, *Faith into Action* (Inglewood, CA: World Tribune Press, 1999), 9.
9. Joseph Rago, "Status Reporter," *The Wall Street Journal* (March 11, 2006), 8.
10. Causton, *The Buddha in Daily Life*, 59.
11. Yasuji Kirimura, *Fundamentals of Buddhism* (Tokyo: NSIC, 1981), 109.
12. *The Writings of Nichiren Daishonin*, 358.
13. Ibid., 387.
14. Ibid., 358.
15. Daisaku Ikeda, *The Living Buddha* (New York: John Weatherhill, 1976), 62–3.
16. Ikeda, *Unlocking the Mysteries of Birth & Death*, 121–2.
17. Daisaku Ikeda, *The Flower of Chinese Buddhism*, trans. Burton Watson (New York: John Weatherhill, 1986), 4.
18. Ibid., 104.
19. Ibid., 111.
20. Malcolm Gladwell, *Blink* (New York: Little, Brown, 2005), 203.
21. Ibid., 206.

4

THE OBJECT OF DEVOTION

For the Observation of One's Mind

EVERY RELIGION HAS ITS OBJECTS OF VENERATION, focal points for prayer, and other forms of devotion. In Catholicism, images of Jesus Christ on a cross are the dominant symbol, but worshipers also offer prayers and make oblations to the Blessed Virgin, the saints, and the stages of Christ's passion, as illustrated, often in magnificent stained glass, in the stations of the cross. Protestant faiths tend to be more austere, but the cross as a symbol still predominates. People of Jewish faith revere the five books of Moses, the Torah, and Islam regards the Koran as sacred.

Even people who practice no formal religion often have certain things they turn to for self-improvement or spiritual satisfaction that border on the sacred—the yoga mat, the barbell rack, the rose garden, the gourmet kitchen, the artist's easel, the violin, the actor's stage. These objects provide a central focus on which people can concentrate their dreams and ambitions. In Buddhism, we term such things *honzon*, or "objects of fundamental respect or worship." A honzon can be many things in life. For the financier on Wall Street, money or "growth" can be a honzon. For the aging celebrity, it can be air time or applause. For people in late adolescence, another human being—a love object—often becomes a kind of honzon. The external objects we worship tell a lot about us and have a profound effect on every aspect of our lives.

Some schools of Buddhism worship images of the historical Buddha, Shakyamuni, often in the form of bronze statues—standing, lying, and sitting Buddhas—displayed in homes or in temples. Throughout southern Asia, Buddhists have erected fantastic monuments, or *stupas*, said to contain his bones, hair, or other remains. Nichiren was against all this. He believed that the essence of the Buddha's teaching was contained in the law, a law that was absolute and unchanging, eternally existing throughout the universe and therefore predating any historical Buddhas or other religious figures. He called this law Nam-myoho-renge-kyo and encouraged his followers to put this teaching, not the teacher, at the center of their lives. As mentioned, in his middle years Nichiren began inscribing scrolls with this law and various other characters in sumi ink, a very black ink used in calligraphy, and bestowed them on believers, including Shijo Kingo and his wife, Nichigen-nyo. These scrolls he called Gohonzon or "objects of worship" (*go* is an honorary prefix; note that the plural form of Gohonzon is the same as the singular). As he wrote to one woman who received a Gohonzon: "I, Nichiren, have inscribed my life in sumi ink, so believe in the Gohonzon with all your heart. The will of the Buddha is the Lotus Sutra, but the soul of Nichiren is nothing other than Nam-myoho-renge-kyo."[1]

Such personal Gohonzon inscribed by Nichiren himself are called "Gohonzon of specific receptivity and relatedness" and were given to those who were devout and rather well-versed in Buddhist doctrine. Realizing that these paper mandalas were perishable, and recognizing the natural human need for an object of devotion, Nichiren resolved to create a more enduring symbol of his enlightenment, one that could be transmitted to future generations. On October 12, 1279, worried that he might be killed or die from natural causes before achieving his mission, Nichiren inscribed the Dai-Gohonzon (*dai* means "great") on a large block of wood. This original Dai-Gohonzon—a large black-lacquered rectangle, inches thick and as tall as a man, with gold characters beautifully etched into its surface as in a woodblock—still exists (the author made a pilgrimage and chanted to the Dai-Gohonzon in 1991). Nichiren thus had achieved his mission of expressing his enlightenment in physical form so that future generations might attain Buddhahood as well.

Within a few weeks or months of starting to practice Buddhism, Nichiren believers around the world receive their own Gohonzon, a silk-screened transcription of the original. These are enshrined in their homes and kept safely inside a wooden box called a *butsudan* ("house of the Buddha"). Some people have elaborate (and expensive) butsudans constructed to keep their Gohonzon protected and to provide a centerpiece in the home for their Buddhist practice. However, it is not necessary to make a palace for your Gohonzon, especially at the outset. In the early stages of practice, a good cardboard box will suffice. At one time in New York, the most common beginning butsudan was a good, stiff shirt box from Saks Fifth Avenue (others preferred the slightly larger bathrobe box from Bloomingdale's). Nowadays, relatively inexpensive wooden ones can be purchased by mail order or online. Many people make their own. It basically just needs to be sturdy, clean, and large enough to hang the Gohonzon (roughly 8 inches by 16 inches), with a cover or door to close on the scroll when a chanting session is over. In time, as one begins sincerely to respect the Gohonzon and sense its power, more durable and refined arrangements can be made. The important thing is one's sincerity in protecting the scroll and one's seeking spirit in putting it to work.

The Gohonzon is, first of all, a marvelously effective tool. It gives you something to focus on while chanting. Since Nichiren Buddhists do not practice silent meditation, the Gohonzon provides a place to direct the chanted words and helps keep the attention from wandering. But the Gohonzon is significant not just because it is *there* but also for what it *says*. Down the center in large Chinese characters are the words Nam myoho renge kyo. Then it says, "I, Nichiren, place my seal." (See diagram of the Gohonzon, pp. 154–5.) It is signed by Nichiren, signifying in graphic form the oneness of the person and the law. Symbolically, this is the very same oneness you will try to achieve through practice—you and the law as one.

THE GOHONZON: TREASURE MAP OF LIFE

Schematic Diagram of the Gohonzon Enshrined in Practitioners' Homes

With phonetic original, English translation, and Sanskrit of characters on the Gohonzon

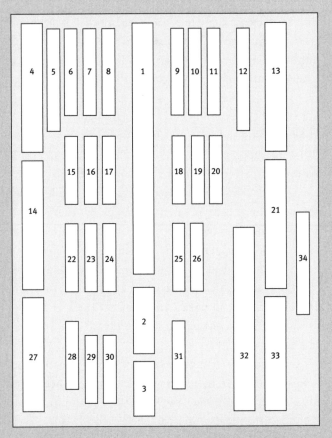

1. **Nam-myoho-renge-kyo**

2. **Nichiren**

3. **Zai gohan**—This is Nichiren Daishonin's personal seal.

4. **Dai Bishamon-tenno**—Great Heavenly King Vaishravana (Skt.), also called Tamon-ten (Hearer of Many Teachings).

5. **U kuyo sha fuku ka jugo**—Those who make offerings will gain good fortune surpassing the ten honorable titles [of the Buddha].
NOTE: In Buddhism, making offerings has a broad meaning; here it means to respect and praise.

6. **Namu Anryugyo Bosatsu**—Bodhisattva Firmly Established Practices (Skt. Supratishthacharitra). **NOTE:** The word *namu* is added to some names in the Gohonzon as a sign of great respect.

7. **Namu Jyogyo Bosatsu**—Bodhisattva Pure Practices (Skt. Vishuddhacharitra).

8. **Namu Shakyamuni-butsu**—Shakyamuni Buddha.

9. **Namu Taho Nyorai**—Many Treasures Thus Come One (Skt. Prabhutaratna Tathagata).

10. **Namu Jogyo Bosatsu**—Bodhisattva Superior Practices (Skt. Vishishtacharitra).

11. **Namu Muhengyo Bosatsu**—Bodhisattva Boundless Practices (Skt. Anantacharitra).

12. **Nyaku noran sha zu ha shichibun**—Those who vex and trouble [the practitioners of the Law] will have their heads split into seven pieces.

13. **Dai Jikoku-tenno**—Great Heavenly King Upholder of the Nation (Skt. Dhritarashtra).

14. **Aizen-myo'o**—Wisdom King Craving-Filled (Skt. Ragaraja). **NOTE:** The name is written in Siddham, a medieval Sanskrit orthography.

15. **Dai Myojo-tenno**—Great Heavenly King Stars, or the god of the stars.

16. **Dai Gattenno**—Great Heavenly King Moon, or the god of the moon.

17. **Taishaku-tenno**—Heavenly King Shakra (also known as Heavenly King Indra).

18. **Dai Bontenno**—Great Heavenly King Brahma.

19. **Dai Rokuten no Mao**—Devil King of the Sixth Heaven.

20. **Dai Nittenno**—Great Heavenly King Sun, or the god of the sun.

21. **Fudo-myo'o**—Wisdom King Immovable (Skt. Achala). **NOTE:** The name is written in Siddham, a medieval Sanskrit orthography.

22. **Hachi Dairyuo**—Eight Great Dragon Kings.

23. **Dengyo Daishi**—Great Teacher Dengyo.

24. **Jurasetsunyo**—Ten Demon Daughters (Skt. Rakshasi).

25. **Kishimojin**—Mother of Demon Children (Skt. Hariti).

26. **Tendai Daishi**—Great Teacher T'ien-t'ai.

27. **Dai Zojo-tenno**—Great Heavenly King Increase and Growth (Skt. Virudhaka).

28. **Hachiman Dai Bosatsu**—Great Bodhisattva Hachiman.

29. **Kore o shosha shi tatematsuru**—I respectfully transcribed this.

30. **Nichikan, personal seal**—Signature of the high priest who transcribed this Gohonzon, in this case, Nichikan, consisting of his name and personal seal.

31. **Tensho-daijin**—Sun Goddess.

32. **Butsumetsugo ni-sen ni-hyaku san-ju yo nen no aida ichienbudai no uchi mizou no daimandara nari**—Never in 2,230-some years since the passing of the Buddha has this great mandala appeared in the world.

33. **Dai Komoku-tenno**—Great Heavenly King Wide-Eyed (Skt. Virupaksha).

34. **Kyoho go-nen roku-gatsu jusan-nichi**—The 13th day of the sixth month in the fifth year of Kyoho [1720], cyclical sign *kanoe-ne*.

Naturally, since you are chanting Nam-myoho-renge-kyo and at the same time gazing at the characters for Nam-myoho-renge-kyo, you and the law literally *are one*. This is a vivid and unique experience, and it is the prime point of everything else in Buddhist practice. Nichiren said, "Embracing the Gohonzon is itself enlightenment."

To dispel any illusions surrounding this key concept, let us return to a general observation made at the beginning of this book: Many of us intellectually acknowledge the concept of "the oneness of the person and the universe" whether we are Buddhists or not. We now find many modern expressions and practical applications of this principle in the fields of ecology and medicine. This oneness or dynamic harmony between the person and the environment follows from–is a necessary corollary of–the principle of "dependent origination," as explained earlier. This is the idea that everything in the universe is interrelated through a complex web of cause and effect. This was a core truth the Buddha realized for himself beneath the bodhi tree and then preached to his followers for the remainder of his life. The inseparability of human beings and their environment, as well as the interconnection of all things, is nowadays something we accept as valid and empirical science has verified. However, merely *thinking* this and knowing it in our minds is not especially useful. It is just an intellectual abstraction. One must *experience* it. When you chant Nam-myoho-renge-kyo to the Gohonzon, which has Nam-myoho-renge-kyo inscribed down the center, you are fusing your own subjective wisdom with the objective reality of the universe. It is like a self-directed laboratory experiment in the oneness of subject and object. The current of Nam-myoho-renge-kyo within you (microcosm) harmonizes with the universal rhythm (macrocosm). This is exactly as Shakyamuni taught, T'ien-t'ai theorized, and Nichiren demonstrated for all time. When we chant Nam-myoho-renge-kyo, we also *manifest* the law of Nam-myoho-renge-kyo within ourselves.

Here, again, Asian categories struggle to stretch and then break through the membrane of Western thought. How can a person fuse with a paper scroll, which is necessarily, to our way of thinking, outside of the person? It is a paradigm of the age-old dichotomy between subject and object. For centuries Western philosophers debated the nature of man's knowledge of the world. Is there an objective world out there? Or is what we see, hear, taste, smell, and touch inevitably colored and transformed by our own subjective impressions? Does the color-blind person observe the same scarlet rose that others see? Can reality exist independently of the observer? These questions were summed up in the famous conundrum: if a tree falls in a forest and no one is there to hear it, does it make a sound?

The answer to all these questions can be found in the Gohonzon, that is, in chanting to the Gohonzon. The phenomenal world (objective reality) and the individual human being (subjective wisdom) are both permeated by the same law of life. This law functions, by definition, both within you and without you. In Buddhist terms, the two—subject and object—are also *not two*. The world that we see outside of us appears to be external and different in kind from the interior world of thoughts and emotions that we experience from moment to moment. To a limited extent, this division seems real and may even be helpful to us in an everyday way, in terms of processing information that is beneficial to our immediate comforts and ultimate survival. We tend to function as "ghosts" inside a machine, or body, only because this delusion helps us to get along. It's a fiction based on adaptation that allows us to cope with what the world throws at us. However, as Shakyamuni Buddha realized during his prolonged meditation—and the Chinese philosopher T'ien-t'ai declared in his theory of ichinen sanzen—the life of the universe is one with our own, and the law that permeates the universe also courses through our bodies. Every thought and emotion is a manifestation of this unchanging law.

When we chant and fix our gaze steadfastly on the Gohonzon, focusing our attention on the bold characters of Nam-myoho-renge-kyo down the center, we begin to close the perceptual gap between the words on the scroll and the words in our mind. The realm or optical gulf between scroll and mind begins to blur, diminish, and grow indistinct. To some, it's almost a physical sensation. To others, it's more of a mental thing. The Japanese term for this harmonious fusion of subject and object is *kyochi myogo (kyo* for "subject," *chi* for "object," and *myogo* for "harmonious fusion"). When we are seated in front of the Gohonzon chanting, we can achieve this fusion regularly, or just from time to time, depending on our moment-to-moment determination, or, to reintroduce a favorite term, our ichinen. When you chant with terrific ichinen, you will experience the fusion of your subjective wisdom with objective reality (Gohonzon) on a regular basis. In fact, after a particularly intense chanting session, when you close the butsudan and go out into the world, you will probably note that some things—colors, sounds, architectural details—seem more vivid than usual. This is because your subjective self is more attuned to the objective reality of the world. The "dust on your eyes," to borrow a phrase from the ancient sutra, will have been blown off. More important, you may also note that certain complex interpersonal situations—say, a difficult relationship with a coworker or a longstanding rift with a parent—can now be seen in sharper relief. You might realize, for example, that the coworker you have always seen as a ruthless, manipulative rival is fundamentally jealous, insecure, and fearful of you, and that you really need to take positive action to allay his or her underlying insecurity. You might understand for the first time that your parent, who seems to be continually judging you, actually is full of regret about his own life, sincerely wants you to avoid his mistakes, and is desperate for you to show your appreciation and approval of *him*. One becomes in a sense a detective of human affairs, making excellent deductions about the reality of the situation—a reality that is perhaps only grasped clearly for the first time. (See "The Most Excellent Buddhist Detectives," pp. 160–61.)

The ability to see deeply into complex interpersonal situations is a concrete result of aligning your subjective mind with objective reality. It is substituting wisdom—a correct understanding of the true nature of things—for delusion. With respect to human relationships, this process is not just a sideshow in Buddhism. It is the main event. Indeed, the Buddha himself never intended to solve the mysteries of the universe for purely scientific or speculative reasons. His purpose was to bring an end to human suffering.

A Picture of Enlightenment

Now let's continue with our description of the Gohonzon itself. Since we cannot supply a photograph or an exact drawing of it (the Gohonzon is considered sacred in Nichiren Buddhism), we must rely on words (and a general diagram). You may think it superstitious to regard an inanimate object as so sacred it cannot be photographed or reproduced, or to invest in it a kind of power empirical science could not confirm. The Gohonzon is, after all, a scroll of paper. But consider this: paper has different meaning in our culture depending on what is written on it and what value we assign to it. A love letter can bring great joy, whereas a foreclosure notice can plunge a person into despair. A bill of U.S. currency with a picture of Abraham Lincoln ($5) has a different value than one with the image of Benjamin Franklin ($100). Whatever you may think of the relative merits of Lincoln or Franklin, we *assign* more value to the note bearing Franklin's visage. In this sense, the Gohonzon has inestimable value because we *regard* it as being precious, even sacred. Indeed, we treat the Gohonzon *as if* it were our life itself. It represents our enlightened life. Like a flawless mirror, it reflects the Buddhahood within us. It's a billion-dollar bill.

Naturally Buddhists treat the Gohonzon with tremendous respect. The way a person responds to an object of worship, the response that object elicits, depends on the life condition of the person and the nature of the object. As the British writer Richard Causton observes:

> A golden statue of Shakyamuni Buddha, for example, could reflect the state of Hunger, the desire for material wealth in the person making it, while a statue of Christ on the Cross might well reflect the anguish and guilt, the state of Hell, subconsciously experienced by the sculptor. In worshipping these objects, then, one could be unknowingly strengthening in oneself a tendency toward one of the lower conditions of life, despite the sincere effort one may be making to appreciate, say, the Buddha's wisdom or Christ's compassion. In contrast, the Gohonzon was inscribed by Nichiren Daishonin himself, desiring nothing other than the happiness of all human beings, and therefore reflects *his* life state.[2]

THE MOST EXCELLENT BUDDHIST DETECTIVES

Buddhists see things in a fresh and accurate way, especially the complex webs of interpersonal relationships—like excellent detectives of human life. Many of the great fictional detectives have been portrayed as Buddhalike. Sherlock Holmes was depicted as spending long interludes with eyes closed, feet crossed beneath him, contemplating the facts of a case in profound, uninterruptible meditation. Hercule Poirot, the little Belgian sleuth of the Agatha Christie books, was also drawn as a kind of deductive monk, closing his eyes for long periods to allow "the little gray cells" to work. Nero Wolfe, the corpulent protagonist of the Rex Stout novels, had many Buddha qualities, including his monastic reclusiveness and impassivity. Several more recent crime-fiction creations have had explicit Buddhist connections. The hero of Howard Fast's mystery novels, Masao Masuda, is a Nisei detective in Beverly Hills who uses Buddhist serenity and unwavering focus to unravel cases. Similar heroes turn up in the novels of Dutch writer Janwillem van de Wetering and the more recent *Bangkok 8* and *Bangkok Tattoo* by John Burdett, featuring Thai detective

When we chant to the Gohonzon, which is a pure expression of Nichiren's enlightenment, unmediated by any other hand, we continually develop and strengthen the highest life condition, Buddhahood. No priests, gurus, or other intermediaries are required in this process. The relationship between you and the Gohonzon is naked and matter-of-fact. The unfolding drama of one's Buddhist practice is none other than one's personal struggle in front of the Gohonzon.

Nichiren called the Gohonzon "the object of devotion for observing one's mind." Observing one's mind, he added, was "to find the Ten Worlds in it." All of the Ten Worlds are pictured in various ways on the scroll, but viewed as a whole the Gohonzon is really a portrait of the tenth. As previously explained, Nichiren was confident that people could grasp the reality of the first nine worlds (Hunger, Anger, Rapture, etc.) because these could be readily demonstrated with examples from everyday life. But he knew that convincing them of the existence of the tenth world, Buddhahood,

Sonchai Jitleecheep, who is at once a Buddhist and a part-time owner of a Bangkok brothel.

But our choice for the most excellent Buddhist detective may seem an unlikely one: Miss Jane Marple, the aging spinster in the tiny town of St. Mary Mead, as created by Agatha Christie (and played to perfection in the BBC series by Joan Hickson). With her sensible tweed suits, black lace mittens, and knitting needles, Miss Marple is so self-effacing that it is easy to underestimate her. "I am afraid I am not very clever myself," says she, "but living all these years in St. Mary Mead does give one an insight into human nature." In her many cases, she seldom examines a footprint or searches for clues. Instead, she uses her "comprehensive knowledge of the facts of rural life" and her talent for viewing human behavior "microscopically." She understands life with a capital L. Her inferences and her methods are purely deductive, in that she solves the specifics of a crime based on her enlightenment to the laws of life as applied to human beings. More than any other sleuth, she embodies the wisdom of the Buddha.

would be much more difficult. In Buddhism, the essence of faith is believing in the existence of this Buddha nature within your own life.

Nichiren believed that one could not see the tenth world without the mirror of the Gohonzon any more than one could see one's own face without looking into a physical mirror. By inscribing the Gohonzon he sought to give all people a concrete reminder of this highest life condition. He made a distinction between the theoretical teaching of the Ten Worlds and the actual embodiment of the concept, on the Gohonzon itself.

As explained, down the center of the scroll are the words "Nam myoho renge kyo, Nichiren," indicating Buddhahood. At the sides, the nine worlds are depicted in subsidiary positions, indicating their proper relation; enlightenment should be at the center of your life. To the left and right, respectively, of the central inscription are written the names of Shakyamuni Buddha and Taho (*Nyorai*), a legendary Buddha. In this scheme, Shakyamuni represents subjective wisdom (*kyo*) and Taho symbolizes objective reality (*chi*). Also along the sides are the four leaders of the Bodhisattvas, learned leaders (*shomon*), gods, human beings, and others—a diverse cast of real and symbolic figures as described in the exotic Ceremony in the Air passages in the Lotus Sutra.

In this sublime and consequential section of the Lotus Sutra (chapters 11–22), Shakyamuni expresses his enlightenment to the fundamental law of life in symbolic terms—as a splendid Ceremony in the Air, a miraculous convocation in which all Buddhas from throughout the universe assemble to hear his words. In this dazzling parable, a metaphorical Treasure Tower, encrusted with jewels, rises from within the earth and Shakyamuni, seated upon it beside Taho, begins to preach. He tells of the difficulty of teaching his enlightenment to others, warns of the arrogance of priests, and prophesies a time two thousand years in the future when a supreme teacher will come forward to teach the law. In reproducing the Ceremony in the Air on the Gohonzon, Nichiren captured this most cosmic moment in Shakyamuni's most important teaching.

Living in an age when the many schools of Buddhism were at war with one another and the historical Buddha's teachings were becoming obscured, Nichiren wanted to make things perfectly clear. His intention was literally to allow us to enter the Treasure Tower of the Gohonzon, to enter the world of Buddhahood. In this regard, an interesting fact about the Gohonzon should be mentioned. The Gohonzon is inscribed on paper or wood, so it appears to be flat. However, in describing the Ceremony in the Air, it is three-dimensional. As we sit facing the Gohonzon, the figures of the Buddhas Shakyamuni and Taho are facing outward, toward us, while the Bodhisattvas and other figures representing the nine worlds are facing away, in the same direction as we are facing. In a sense, then, we are taking part in the ceremony with them, face to face with enlightenment, our negative functions and karma facing toward (seeking guidance from) wisdom and the ultimate truth.

Nichiren also wanted to stress the idea that the enlightenment portrayed on the Gohonzon was not just an airy, fantastic metaphor, but that it directly pertained to the physical person who contemplated it. So some figures he drew on the mandala also symbolize earth (*chi*), wind (*fu*), water (*sui*), and fire (*ka*). In addition, he included the heavenly bodies—the sun, moon, and stars—which symbolize the rhythm of the universe and are harmonious with the rhythm of our own lives. These celestial bodies were personified on the Gohonzon by various Bodhisattvas and mythical beings, just as they are in our own constellations. To explain why he equated a metaphysical idea (enlightenment or Buddhahood) with the physical elements—and also to bring the metaphor of the Treasure Tower down to earth—Nichiren wrote the following in a letter to a native of Sado Island named Abutsu-bo:

> At the present the entire body of the Honorable Abutsu is composed of the five elements of earth, water, fire, wind, and space. These five elements are also the five characters of the daimoku [Nam-myoho-renge-kyo]. Abutsu-bo is therefore the Treasure Tower itself, and the Treasure Tower is Abutsu-bo himself. No other knowledge is purposeful. It is the treasure tower adorned with the seven types of treasures—hearing the correct teaching, believing it, keeping the precepts, engaging in meditation, practicing assiduously, renouncing one's attachments, and reflecting on oneself.[3]

In other words, the mystic law of Nam-myoho-renge-kyo is contained in our physical bodies and the potential for happiness within each human life—the jeweled Treasure Tower—is coextensive with the infinite cosmos. Our bodies are expressions of this mystic law.[4] Additionally, Nichiren contends, practicing to the Gohonzon encompasses and includes all traditional forms of Buddhist practice.

In the same letter, Nichiren makes a further statement about the relationship of this metaphorical tower rising into the air and its significance to his lay supporters:

> No Treasure Tower exists other than the figures of the men and women who embrace the Lotus Sutra. It follows therefore, that whether high or low, those who chant Nam-myoho-renge-kyo are themselves the Treasure Tower, and likewise, the Thus Come One Many Treasures.[5]

"Thus Come One Many Treasures" refers to a Buddha called Many Treasures, who is also represented on the Gohonzon. In characteristic fashion, Nichiren here is suggesting that the common people are themselves Buddhas (or at least potential ones), and that the Treasure Tower imagery is simply a device to point them in the right direction.

✳

Among the other characters depicted on the Gohonzon are: Ryunyo, the eight-year-old Dragon King's daughter (who achieved enlightenment in her present form); King Bimbasara, a real-life monarch who ascended to the throne of India and first established Buddhism as the state religion; Devadatta, a malicious cousin of Shakyamuni who despite his efforts to undermine and kill the Buddha was still said to be capable of enlightenment (symbolizes the notion that even a heartless criminal has the seed of enlightenment within); Asura, a demon who represents the world of Anger; and Tensho Daijin, a heavenly figure in the traditional Shinto folklore of Japan. It has been said that if Nichiren had been familiar with the teachings of Jesus Christ (he wasn't), he would have inscribed him on the Gohonzon, too.

Obviously, Nichiren sought to be comprehensive and exquisitely nuanced in his rendering on the Gohonzon all the various qualities and phenomena pertaining to enlightenment. This was indeed the enlightenment poetically described by the historical Buddha in the Lotus Sutra and made even more explicit by the Chinese master T'ien-t'ai. So he included characters for T'ien-t'ai and for Dengyo, the founder of the Japanese Tendai sect, on the Gohonzon. One might even say that, in addition to depicting the Ceremony in the Air, the key moment in Shakyamuni's most momentous work, Nichiren also graphically represented the theory of ichinen sanzen itself on the Gohonzon.

The principle of three thousand worlds in a single moment of life, as discussed earlier, is a comprehensive view of life that clarifies the interpenetration of the ultimate reality and the phenomenal world. It accounts for everything we think and feel, and explains the relationship between the individual mind and the reality of life unfolding within and without. T'ien-t'ai was considered a great Buddha himself (he is sometimes referred to as "The Buddha of the Middle Day of the Law," that is, in the second millennium following Shakyamuni's death). But his teaching was difficult to grasp and practice. Meditating with the aim of internalizing the principle of ichinen sanzen was the focus of the T'ien-t'ai school. The various techniques he employed were known as the "meditation on the ten objects," meditation on "the region of the unfathomable," the twenty-five preparatory exercises (which included observing precepts, eating certain foods and wearing certain clothes, and suppressing one's desires), and the "threefold contemplation in a single mind." In general, these practices were forms of introspection that delved deeper and deeper into one's own mind until the truth of ichinen sanzen became clear.

One should not underestimate the profundity of T'ien-t'ai's wisdom or his enlightenment. However, this comprehensive meditation entailed substantial intellectual ability, great powers of concentration, and, of course, lots of time. A clue to the demands of his methodology is contained in the title of his last and most important treatise, which detailed his views on devotional practice: *Great Concentration and Insight*. Not everyone comes to Buddhism with a talent for great concentration and insight. These qualities are often what they hope Buddhism will provide. Needless to say, T'ien-t'ai's comprehensive meditation was not an easy practice for the layman to adopt. His was a theoretical breakthrough that left out the practical part. Like so many forms of Buddhism that emanated from mountain monasteries, it was too high and rarefied for the people. It could only be practiced by those with a lot of knowledge and a great deal of time—the elite. And for centuries that is who practiced it: monks, aristocrats, and scholars. It remained for Nichiren to embody the principle of ichinen sanzen on the Gohonzon, so that everyone could attain Buddhahood as well. With deft brushstrokes, he swept away a multitude of arcane meditations, renunciations, and ascetic practices, and established a sure way for the common person to connect to his or her higher self. In the Gohonzon, Nichiren did not formulate some new system or theory. He translated what had been purely theoretical into the realm of actuality.

One can compare the Gohonzon to a schematic diagram. Like the electrical wiring grid for a computer's motherboard or an engineer's drawings for the interior of an office building, the Gohonzon is a very precise map or schematic diagram of enlightenment. It is a picture of your Buddha nature. It also precisely defines the relationship of the world of enlightenment to the other nine worlds. The Gohonzon, Nichiren said, is the concise expression of the Lotus Sutra's statement that "all phenomena reveal the true entity." The Gohonzon is the embodiment of ichinen sanzen, and, as such, a perfect mandala, using as one's object of meditation the truth inherent in one's own life.

As beautiful and extraordinary as the Gohonzon is, it is not especially significant without the person—you. The Gohonzon gains its power in relationship to a person.

Receiving and Caring for the Gohonzon

Anyone can receive a Gohonzon. It is necessary only to have a seeking spirit and a determination to practice Nichiren Daishonin's Buddhism. Typically, one attends several Buddhist meetings over the course of weeks or months, learning about the practice and taking the first steps to practice on one's own. As one's daily practice of chanting without the Gohonzon progresses, it is natural to ask other Nichiren Buddhists about obtaining the Gohonzon. If you have never been to a Buddhist meeting and would like to attend one, go to the SGI website (www.sgi-usa.org) and click on "SGI," then use the map to find a meeting place near you. Buddhist discussion meetings, in which the fundamentals of practice, the history of Buddhism, and the experiences of practitioners are presented and discussed, take place once a month, often on the third Thursday of each month, in the homes of Nichiren followers. They are lively, fun, and refreshing.

When a person decides to receive the Gohonzon, a simple application is filled out and a conferral ceremony is planned. The conferral of the Gohonzon can take place in the private home where meetings are held, but it can also be done at one of the various SGI community centers located around the country (again, visit the SGI website for locations). The Gohonzon conferral ceremony is simple but meaningful. It usually lasts about five or ten minutes, depending on how many people are receiving the scroll. Well-wishers, both Buddhist and non-Buddhist, especially friends and family members, can be invited. This is a joyous occasion, marking the beginning of a new life.

Once the Gohonzon is safely home, great care must be taken to protect it and enshrine it properly. Within a few days after receiving the Gohonzon, the practitioner will have it enshrined, or placed inside the small altar, or butsudan. This is a very important event in a Buddhist's life. It is like welcoming the enlightened life of Nichiren Daishonin into your home. The person who introduced you to the practice and an appropriate leader, that is, someone who is experienced in Buddhist faith, will preside and help with the details. If you live with nonpracticing family members or friends, their understanding and support should be graciously encouraged. While the butsudan may be modest, it should reflect the person's respect for the Gohonzon. Everything is based on this attitude of fundamental respect. For example, the people who help with the enshrinement will be sure to avoid touching the white area of the scroll. They will unroll the Gohonzon by carefully holding it at the ends of the two wooden bars that secure it at the top and bottom. The new Gohonzon may curl forward slightly at the bottom when hanging, but after a few days will straighten itself out through its own weight. One may be initially surprised to see that those who are enshrining the scroll also take measures to avoid breathing directly on it. They may place a leaf, a piece of paper, or a stick of incense between their lips. This gesture of respect is traditional in Buddhism. It may seem superstitious, but the idea of demonstrating utmost respect for the Gohonzon, which is symbolic of your own highest self, begins to make sense over time.

One might compare the Gohonzon to an "objective correlative," a literary term that refers to events or actions in a work of literature that objectify a particular emotion and are used to evoke a desired emotional response. The Gohonzon is the objective correlative of your Buddha nature. You want to bring this nature out and into the forefront of your life. Many of us, prior to receiving the Gohonzon, are prone to letting certain negative emotions shadow our lives and sway us from our goals. Let us say, without getting too psychoanalytical, that we all have various strategies for achieving happiness, but some of them in the long run prove to be self-defeating. With the Gohonzon, one gains a powerful tool for moving the negative, self-destructive forces in our lives to the side, and placing Buddhahood (Nam-myoho-renge-kyo) down the center.

With the Gohonzon safely enshrined, the practitioner can chant to his or her heart's content. You can spend as many minutes or hours as you like chanting Nam-myoho-renge-kyo to your own Gohonzon. It is there when you need it. When you are chanting, it is recommended that you focus on the character *myo* (third from the top, in the center line). Your Gohonzon should be positioned at the proper height to ensure that your natural eye level is slightly below the character of *myo*. You should be looking up slightly at the Gohonzon's focal point. If your attention wanders from this point, try to bring it back. But do not worry. There is no strict rule regarding what part of the Gohonzon to look at, but it is a good idea to train your eye on the scroll as much as possible. If nothing else, this is an exercise in one-pointedness of mind. It helps you to train your focus, laserlike, on things that matter. Think of those youthful experiments that kids play with a magnifying glass, trying to use the sun's rays to burn a hole in a leaf. Practicing to the Gohonzon is like that; it brings your faculties into a sharp, red-hot focus. You can then apply this intensity to your everyday life. Everything you learn and every skill you develop from the Gohonzon will overflow into your life.

During the first few months, one should also strive to master gongyo—the recitation of two excerpts of the Lotus Sutra that constitutes the secondary practice. (Chanting daimoku, or Nam-myoho-renge-kyo, is the primary practice.) Regularly performing morning and evening gongyo, in a resonant and clear voice, will result in tremendous results. In the early days of practice, if time and circumstances do not allow, it is not necessary to perform the entire gongyo at every sitting. However, as time goes on, the people who practice Buddhism correctly are the ones who do morning and evening gongyo consistently throughout their lives.

Initially, Buddhism, like any other important activity, presents time-structuring problems. Chanting to the Gohonzon twice a day clearly subtracts two chunks of time from your busy schedule. Where can you fit this in? It's not that hard. Actually, practicing to the Gohonzon seems to result in a net increase in time for people to accomplish things. You will find that Buddhist practice, because it focuses the attention and energizes you about your goals, actually *frees* up time in the rest of the day. You become more productive, not less. Countless practitioners' experiences refer to the Gohonzon's ability to help them prioritize their lives. The more you chant, the more you begin to attack life's challenges in the correct *order* in which they can be best resolved. When you undertake projects, you accomplish them quickly and more easily. You waste less time pursuing dead ends. You begin to know what you want to accomplish and what actions you must take in order to do it. Practice to the Gohonzon has been compared to heating a knife before cutting into ice-cold butter. Things in life that hitherto appeared unyielding suddenly give way to your efforts.

Life with Gohonzon

When you chant to the Gohonzon, you can make your dreams a reality. The Gohonzon is utterly reliable. Even if you cannot chant at various times because of your busy schedule, the Gohonzon will always be there for you. You can chant to the Gohonzon as much as you want, for anything you want: health, happiness, career, and relationships. Nothing is too large or too small. In fact, it is important to test the Gohonzon with your biggest desires, problems, and challenges.

Even if you have no particular dreams or challenges right now—as if your life were stuck in neutral—you can chant to the Gohonzon to get going again. Since it mirrors the deepest wisdom within your own life, the Gohonzon has a way of bringing forward exactly what you need, exactly when you need it. That is why Nichiren called it "a wish-granting jewel."

Yes, the Gohonzon is the second mysterious object, along with "joy in a bottle," referred to at the beginning of this book. It definitely has the power to help you achieve your wishes right here in this life. However, we need to make a firm distinction straightaway regarding the word *wish*. As a matter of both spiritual attitude and technique, it is better not to wish to or beseech the Gohonzon. It is perfectly all right to *have* wishes, dreams, and desires, and to chant to make them come true. This accords with the principle of "earthly desires are enlightenment," as discussed. But, ideally, the attitude of one's prayer, one's chanting to the Gohonzon, should not be in the form of wishing. It should be more like vowing or determining. Instead of "I wish," we say, "I will." You will definitely have many wishes to bring before the Gohonzon, but you should first tamp them down a bit, like tamping down tobacco in a pipe. Then your sincere chanting will light a match to them. In this Buddhism, we use our desires as fuel for achieving enlightenment.

Therefore it is better not to chant with thoughts like: "Oh, I wish I had a new job," or "I really need a hundred thousand dollars." A more effective prayer would be: "I will definitely search for and find the right job for me," or "I will change my financial karma so that I can pay off all my debts and have a hundred thousand dollars in the bank." Like Aladdin's lamp, the Gohonzon will not function fully as a wish-granting jewel if you rub it the wrong way.

Yet you need not feel guilty or inadequate about wishing a bit or not chanting with an ideal attitude. We are human, after all, and the habit of imploring something or someone exterior to ourselves for the things we want is deeply ingrained. At the beginning of one's practice, a certain amount of begging to the Gohonzon is to be expected. Even a prayer directed to the Gohonzon in a wishful way can be beneficial. The important thing is simply to chant. As one gains experience with the Gohonzon, one's inward desires and resolute prayers will automatically be purified and unexpected benefits will accrue. Chief among them is the sense that you are in control of your destiny, that your hands are on the controls. For the first time on the road of life, you actually feel as if you have your hands on the steering wheel and your foot on the pedals.

You begin to take responsibility for everything that happens to you. This can be very empowering, even exhilarating. Where once you blamed your circumstances and other people for life's problems, now you are looking first to yourself. "The fault, dear Brutus, is not in our stars but in ourselves," wrote Shakespeare in *Julius Caesar*. As one becomes more and more rigorous in viewing one's destiny as a product of one's own actions or causes, one regards external events less and less as the shaper of happiness. In parallel to this change in attitude, practitioners come to view the Gohonzon less and less as an external thing—an object outside themselves—but more as a mirror or reflection of their inner lives. In one of his most famous passages, Nichiren wrote: "Never seek this Gohonzon outside yourself. The Gohonzon exists only within the mortal flesh of us ordinary people who embrace the Lotus Sutra and chant Nam-myoho-renge-kyo."[6]

Now, each day, morning and evening, as one fuses with the enlightened life condition portrayed on the Gohonzon, one's own life condition is elevated. The life condition of Buddhahood begins to permeate each of the other Ten Worlds. The lower worlds still exist, as potentials, but increasingly one begins to tend toward the higher, especially the world of enlightenment, as a sunflower bends toward the sun. Viewed this way, enlightenment can be seen as an incremental process. When a person correctly chants to the Gohonzon, that is enlightenment. (Remember Nichiren's words "embracing the Gohonzon is itself enlightenment.") As a person chants regularly, twice a day, for years and years, that person becomes more and more enlightened. Like the rose-fingered dawn creeping over a mountain, one's potential for enlightenment begins gradually to glimmer, then glow more brightly, until it becomes a radiance.

There does not have to be a single "eureka" moment, like Archimedes making a discovery or Sir Isaac Newton getting bonked on the head by a piece of fruit. Nor does it have to be some sort of blissful, ecstatic, all-at-once experience. One does not have to become "the fool on the hill," retreating from life, feeling above it all, and treating "unenlightened" friends with the condescension that emanates from a superior being. Nonetheless, sitting in front of the Gohonzon, there will definitely be moments of deep insight, as we draw forth our own Buddha nature, again and again, and reflect on the underlying causes that are shaping our lives and propelling us among the various lower worlds. By consistently chanting to the Gohonzon, we gradually make Buddhahood the dominant karmic tendency.

Enlightenment in Nichiren Buddhism is something for regular people to experience in their everyday existence. It is not an escape to some transcendental place or realm, but an immersion in the joyful possibilities of daily life right where you are, as you are.

NOTES ON CHAPTER 4

[1] *The Writings of Nichiren Daishonin*, 412.

[2] Causton, *The Buddha in Daily Life*, 229–30.

[3] *The Writings of Nichiren Daishonin*, 299.

[4] Ikeda, *Unlocking the Mysteries of Birth & Death*, 185–6.

[5] *The Writings of Nichiren Daishonin*, 299.

[6] Ibid., 832.

QUESTIONS & ANSWERS

About Buddhist Practice

FOR SOME OF HIS MOST IMPORTANT TREATISES and letters Nichiren Daishonin used the question-and-answer format, in the form of an imagined dialogue with a skeptic or critic, to illuminate profound issues of Buddhist doctrine. In this way he was able to address the dilemmas that arose in his disciples' minds and also to submit himself to the doubts of nonbelievers and government officials. The questions ranged from penetrating critiques of his own ideas to blunt queries about seeming contradictions between his life and his philosophy. (For example, "If Nichiren is so great, why is he suffering from persecutions?") The following questions and answers are offered in the spirit of that tradition.

Q: Isn't Buddhism, as you have described it, just a form of "positive thinking"?

A: This is one of the classic questions people ask after hearing about Buddhism. Chanting for tangible goals, for the things you need in life—and determining deep within your life to make them happen—does involve a fresh, optimistic attitude. It is very difficult to remain a pessimist when you are striving hard, taking action, and the benefits are rolling in. This newfound optimism, which is reinforced by the results one sees on a daily basis from practicing, is inextricably tied to the Buddhist concept of faith described throughout this book. However, when it comes to the idea that Buddhism is "just a form of positive thinking," we would like the reader to consider the converse of that statement: *Positive thinking is a form of Buddhism.* This is very different. Without pretending to know much about Norman Vincent Peale and his actual philosophy of positive thinking, we can state with confidence that positive thinking is perhaps a very small element or ingredient in the larger truth that is Buddhism. To the degree that positive thinking enhances life, Buddhism includes and embraces it. But Buddhism is much more than just having a positive attitude. One might say that positive thinking is an *effect*, not a cause, of Buddhist practice. On its own, positive thinking would be a very partial, rudimentary kind of practice. There are many, many inspirational books, self-help programs, and New Age disciplines that encourage you to maintain a positive attitude, to form positive mental images of yourself succeeding in various endeavors, etc. All well and good, as long as you realize that picturing yourself being successful, without any underlying practice or discipline to improve yourself from within, is like daydreaming or fantasizing.

Being negative makes no sense as an approach to life (dazzling wits like Fran Lebowitz notwithstanding), but what good is the injunction to "think positive"—an intellectual notion—when things actually go wrong, when a crisis looms? One quickly reverts to the old patterns and negative responses, based on one's karma. This is the essence of the theory of the Ten Worlds. When we are in the lower worlds, we are at the mercy of our circumstances, buffeted by Hamlet's "slings and arrows of outrageous fortune," and we react as we would tend to, according to our well-established karma. We can never completely prevent the slings and arrows from raining down on us. Obstacles arise. Challenges keep coming. The solution is to use one's Buddhist practice to elevate one's life condition in general. When we chant Nam-myoho-renge-kyo to the Gohonzon, day in day out, we begin to engrave the life condition of Buddhahood deep within our lives, and this higher state begins to permeate and elevate all the other worlds, all the experiences we have. Unlike the effort to "think positively," the process whereby our lives become one with Buddhahood or enlightenment happens automatically, without our even having to think about it. It is the natural and inevitable byproduct of the fusion of our subjective wisdom with the ultimate reality of the law.

The practice of Buddhism provides the means whereby a more positive spirit can be generated from within, leading to the wisdom to transform all negative situations. So by all means, maintain a positive attitude, and even "think positive," but continue to practice Buddhism.

Q: I chanted about a very specific goal, and it didn't happen. So where is my benefit?

A: Progress in your Buddhist practice leads to changes within you. This must happen, ineluctably, because the act of chanting itself, and the alterations you make in your routine and mental outlook to do this, are themselves significant changes to you. These changes are always marked by concurrent changes in your environment, which mirrors your inner life. This is cause and effect. Effecting noticeable changes in our surroundings, based on those taking place within, however, is not as simple an instance of cause-effect as, say, flicking a light switch, so there frequently is a time lag between them. It is only natural to become impatient. But you must be confident that if there are changes taking place inside, external changes are inevitable. This is in accord with the principle of oneness of person and environment.

Some benefits are instant, some take time. But the intrinsic benefits of chanting are immediate, if often unseen. According to the principle of simultaneity of cause and effect (in Japanese, *inga guji*), when you make the right cause, that is, chanting to the Gohonzon, the effect is assured. It is like planting. Once the cause of putting the seed in the ground is made, the effect is already *inherent* in the seed. Or to use another example, it is like writing a check. It may be awhile before you can cash it, but the effect, the cash, will surely manifest eventually under the right circumstances (e.g., a bank).

The important thing is that you have undertaken a process by which you can change your life. Therein lies the first benefit. It is a major one. Particularly in today's world, where the individual often feels that circumstances are beyond his or her control, the power of Buddhist practice becomes increasingly apparent. The most valuable change is a measure of control over our destiny. The extent to which we can direct our lives, shape our fate, is to a large extent the measure of our enjoyment in life. When you are chanting for your goals, your attitude becomes transformed. You are fixed on the future, on the attainment of your goals, and you are achieving a kind of one-pointedness of mind. You face problems rather than retreat from them. You advance with a spirit of hopeful challenge rather than one of resignation. When you are able to face up to and deal with obstacles, even if they cannot be surmounted immediately, your capability as a person is increased. If you have a heavy suitcase to carry, the added strength you gain is the benefit. Searching for lighter luggage is an escape.

Perhaps the exact benefit you are seeking, some conspicuous benefit in your environment, is unyielding, but other equally significant benefits are accruing to you without your knowing it. This is quite normal and is to be expected.

Nichiren Daishonin described four types of prayer and benefit (or response):

1. Conspicuous prayer and conspicuous response. This means a clearly formulated wish or praying with a particular goal in mind. For instance, in a medical or financial crisis, one might pray to the Gohonzon with special urgency. That type of all-out, focused daimoku typically yields a quick, clear result. Conspicuous response means that an obvious benefit appears immediately in response to the prayer.

2. Conspicuous prayer and inconspicuous response. Sometimes in answer to a specific prayer we receive a benefit that we do not see. Instead, our desire is being fulfilled like the slow, imperceptible growth of a tree.

3. Inconspicuous prayer and inconspicuous response. When you practice Buddhism sincerely, day after day, you may not always see benefits, but your life is moving in exactly the direction of what you desire. When you look back at such a steady practice after a number of years, you will understand this principle.

4. Inconspicuous prayer and conspicuous response. You may not be chanting for anything particular, and nothing momentous may be happening. However, whether you are chanting for a particular benefit or not, the thing you need most in your life will suddenly turn up at the critical moment. In the meantime, your health, fortune, and family will be protected by your strong practice.

When you undertake to practice Buddhism, you stop looking for salvation outside of yourself. There is no one "up there" to help you, nobody to beseech. You have opted to take full responsibility for your own life. In that spirit, you may now begin to ask yourself this question: *to what extent is my own negative karma preventing me from gaining this goal or benefit?* Nichiren wrote that you can never hope to attain enlightenment unless you "perceive the nature of your own life." The benefits that are elusive, most difficult to grasp, are precisely the signposts pointing back to our own negative karma. The fact that you cannot get or achieve certain things indicates the areas of your life that you have to work on. Do not give up easily. Push on. Chant sincerely to overcome those negative points in your own karma, then the benefit, in time, will surely follow.

Finally, we must never be satisfied with small benefits. At some point, it becomes important to stop focusing exclusively on the personal and material and to chant for the larger goals of enlightenment and world peace.

Q: I believe I can already get what I want out of life purely through my own efforts—without Buddhism. Isn't chanting just a crutch?

A: Anyone who is willing to work hard can accomplish a lot, with or without Buddhism. That does not mean that Buddhism or the Gohonzon are some sort of crutch, or that you are better off without them.

Picture for a moment the phenomenon of "through hikers" on the Appalachian Trail, which snakes from Georgia to Maine. Some of the thousands of people on the Appalachian Trail each year undertake to walk its entire length—2,160 miles from Springer Mountain, Georgia, to Mount Katahdin, Maine—in a single year. It's quite a feat. But all kinds of people—grandmothers, retired businessmen, married couples, and college students, not just experienced outdoorsmen—make these bone-crunching treks. Out of necessity, through hikers carry the barest minimum in their backpacks to survive—just enough food, a lightweight tent, a compact stove, and so on. Anything that proves superfluous they will discard along the way. Yet almost all of them now take along a pair of ultralight walking sticks, called trekking poles, to assist them on the rocky, arduous paths. Similar to ski poles, these high-tech walking accessories feature cork handles, alloy shafts, and spring-tensioned carbide tips that cushion the shocks when they contact the ground. Over hundreds of miles of trail, the poles prove invaluable in helping backpackers keep their balance, especially descending steep slopes, where the poles can lessen the impact on the feet and joints. But when you see these hikers emerging from the woods, rhythmically poling along, you might think at first that they were using a pair of crutches. Of course, they may actually be limping a little bit from a hard day on the trail, but, as a group, through hikers develop above-average reservoirs of strength and determination to be able to traverse the country from bottom to top. It's laughable to think of them as needing crutches. Their trekking poles keep them focused on the path and add a new dimension to hiking. One might even guess that the poles make it possible for ordinary (even previously sedentary) people to accomplish treks unthinkable fifty years ago.

Similarly, true religion is not a crutch. It provides a challenge through which a person can maximize his own determination and resources, utilizing talents that might otherwise go undeveloped. Buddhism is definitely a challenge. When you meet its challenges, you will be able to meet those of life. Its object of worship, the Gohonzon, is an indispensable tool that helps us find the pathway of our Buddha nature, a path that anyone can walk, not just holy men, gurus, and priests.

Another way to think of the Gohonzon is as a compass, one that directs a person in the search for the Buddha nature within. One would never go out into the woods without a compass. Chanting to the Gohonzon gives direction to the dynamism and power inherent in human life.

Q: What is the point of chanting the sutra, or doing gongyo, in a language I do not understand?

A: Although translations of the Lotus Sutra are available, it is not necessary to understand the English meaning of the words you are chanting. You do not have to understand how your television works in order to be entertained by it, nor do you need to know how a computer works in order to get e-mail or surf the web. You should first master the rhythm and pronunciation of gongyo before trying to understand its literal meaning. Then you can read and study the English version printed in the back of your sutra book or obtain a copy of the entire Lotus Sutra in translation.[1] But there is no hurry. It is like appreciating a piece of symphonic music. First you make a personal connection to the music itself, simply immersing yourself in it, without analyzing it. Then you may want to begin listening to particular instruments, isolating certain motifs, as you continue to experience the different moods and feelings they generate. Or you may not. If a deep understanding of musical theory were required to appreciate music, then the way to enjoyment would be barred to substantial numbers of people. In the same way, if a profound knowledge of Buddhism were required before anyone could practice it, then it would be a religion for the elite.

Each word of the sutra that we recite in the morning and evening has profound meaning. Nichiren encouraged us to read it "with our lives." As we have seen in our discussion of the Ten Worlds and ichinen sanzen, because human beings are preoccupied with a thousand different thoughts and problems, large and small, our minds tend to be extremely variable, flitting from one thing to another. Our thoughts ebb and flow in a swirling stream of consciousness. When we do gongyo, the act of mastering the words momentarily halts that stream. It is sometimes difficult to learn the foreign-sounding pronunciations and keep up with the rhythms of gongyo. It takes effort and concentration. Particularly during those moments when we are most intently absorbed with learning the sutra, the normal stream of consciousness is effectively halted. The usual thoughts stop. The sutra touches and speaks to a different part of us, the part beyond or above the typical "I-me-mine" conversation that dominates inner life. That in itself is a benefit. By making sincere efforts to learn gongyo, we unlock the essence of the sutra from within our own lives. Gongyo may seem strange and foreign at first, but it soon becomes second nature. Many practitioners memorize the sutra passages completely within a few months and no longer need to read them. Daisaku Ikeda writes:

> In a sense there is no simpler practice than doing gongyo and chanting daimoku. We do not have to undertake strange austerities, as in some esoteric Buddhist traditions. The very superiority of [Nichiren] Daishonin's Buddhism enables us to tap the state of Buddhahood through this very simple practice. . . . The Daishonin has taught us that through gongyo and chanting daimoku we can reach an elevated state in which, while engaged in our daily lives, we travel throughout the entire universe. When you worship the Gohonzon, the door to your microcosm is opened to the entire universe, the macrocosm, and you experience a great, boundless joy as if you were looking out over the entire cosmos.[2]

While the practice of doing gongyo is relatively easy, doing it every day, morning and evening is difficult. If you are having trouble reciting gongyo on a regular basis, then this is exactly where you need to concentrate your efforts in order to change your karma rapidly. In other words, the practice of gongyo identifies our weakness. If you have been chanting for a long time, you might even want to look to the English translation to see which words you are stumbling over. Ponder those words deeply. The problems one encounters in gongyo can be very revealing, even mystic. Remember, in Buddhism there are no coincidences.

Q: I have been chanting for some time, but it is not convenient for me to receive the Gohonzon. I have no place to put it. Can I receive benefit just from chanting Nam-myoho-renge-kyo?

A: This is really two distinct questions. To take the second one first—yes, absolutely you will gain benefit from chanting Nam-myoho-renge-kyo, with or without the Gohonzon. In some countries, Nichiren Buddhists have had to wait for years to receive their Gohonzon. Fortunately in the United States it is relatively easy to receive one's own Gohonzon. It is our great benefit and a precious opportunity. So whatever your circumstances are, chant sincerely and determine deep within your life to receive the Gohonzon. In the meantime, you can always chant abundant daimoku without the scroll. You can even set up a temporary altar, including butsudan, water cup, candles, incense, and offerings of fruit and evergreens. While you chant, you can imagine the Gohonzon is there on your altar. You will definitely receive full benefit.

Perhaps your circumstances are such that you cannot even set up an altar, either because your living area is too small or the people you share your space with are opposed to your practice in some way. That is not unusual. Many people who know very little about Buddhism think it is weird or worse. If you come from a very devout

Christian family, for instance, and you still live at home, your parents may not approve of your Buddhist practice. In that case, you must take care not to disrupt the harmony of your home. If you chant at all, be certain to do so at a time and with a voice that will not disturb others. Eventually as an adult you will have to decide whether you should continue living in a place where you cannot practice your faith freely. In the meantime, chant sincere daimoku at meetings and at the homes of Buddhist friends. Seek out the guidance of your Buddhist leaders. These situations come up frequently and can be resolved with equal measures of wisdom and Buddhist mercy (jihi).

If, on the other hand, your situation is such that you do not wish to receive the Gohonzon merely because it is "inconvenient," then you need to take a close look at your life. Change can be daunting and the Gohonzon represents change. If you can't find a place for it, perhaps you need to reorganize your apartment or house. Sometimes reorganizing things in that way can change your whole life. In Buddhism, we view change as great. In fact, the world is constantly changing all around us, and we are continually changing, too. The question always is: what sort of changes are you making amid this ceaselessly changing world?

Some people hesitate to receive the Gohonzon primarily because a friend, roommate, or lover disapproves. They just can't visualize the Buddhist altar in their homes, because they are insecure about what people will say when they see it. It is not uncommon for people receiving Gohonzon to prefer initially that it be enshrined in the farthest corner of an unused room. Some people even try to enshrine their altars in a closet (no kidding). Just keep chanting. Before long you will realize that the Gohonzon should be at the center of your life. If it starts out in a back bedroom, it will soon find its way to the front of your home. The place where you enshrine your Gohonzon is important. How you take care of it is important, too. Talk with the person who introduced you to this practice about these matters.

Chanting for one's happiness without the Gohonzon can be compared to playing tennis alone. You can definitely improve your tennis game and practice all the strokes by hitting a ball against a wall. You can even simulate competition by deliberately directing the ball so that you have to run to hit it. Many people master the basic forehand and backhand strokes in this way. However, the full dimensions of tennis only reveal themselves to you on a court with a net and an opposing player on the other side.

Chanting with and without the Gohonzon brings benefit. But also realize that receiving the Gohonzon itself is a great benefit. Therefore, to fully enjoy and benefit from Nichiren Buddhism, chant to overcome any obstacles, internal or external, to receiving your own Gohonzon.

Notes on Chapter 5

[1] For an excellent translation of the Lotus Sutra, see Burton Watson's *Lotus Sutra* (New York: Columbia University Press, 1993).

[2] Ikeda, *Faith into Action*, 115, 118.

6

BUDDHISM & CHRISTIANITY

IN TRADITIONAL CHRISTIANITY, MAN CAN APPROACH GOD but can never become Him. By contrast, Buddhism teaches as its fundamental principle that everyone can become a Buddha.

In Buddhism there is neither creation nor a Creator. The universe always existed and always will. Your life is eternal and one with the eternal universe.

Buddhism is unique among the major religions in that it makes no claim to divine revelation. First and foremost, it is the teaching of a human being who, through his own efforts, awoke to the law of life within himself. The law is inherent in the universe and, therefore, available to all. It was not established by the Buddha or anyone else. In the Lotus Sutra, Shakyamuni states that other Buddhas had been enlightened to the same law or truth before him. The word *buddha* was a common noun used in Shakyamuni's day.

Most of us who live in the United States were raised to believe in God. Polls consistently show more than 90 percent of Americans believe in God or a supreme being, usually as articulated in some form of Christianity or Judaism. This does not mean that Americans can never practice Buddhism wholeheartedly or that we must give up our faith in order to learn more about Buddhism. Actually, most of the Buddhists practicing in America today are former Christians or Jews. Many have family members who are practicing Christians and Jews. There is no conflict. Indeed, you can begin your study and practice of Buddhism while you continue to attend church or synagogue. Buddhism only enhances and enriches the faith that you practice. Eventually, based on the concrete results you experience in your life, you may come to put more faith and effort into Buddhism, but this is entirely up to you.

In the rural area of Connecticut where I live, a place where small-town traditions survive and white clapboard churches abound, there is substantial cultural and theological interchange between the local Christian institutions and Buddhism. Just up the road at St. John's Episcopal Church in Salisbury, where my friend the Rev. John Carter is minister, they invite a delegation of Buddhist monks to visit each year. The monks make traditional sand paintings called mandalas, which are meticulously composed of various colored sands, and attend church services along with the rest of the congregation. Up on the hill above town, at the Salisbury School, a classic New England prep school with mandatory Christian chapel services, they too invite Buddhist monks to come stay for a period each year. The monks attend classes, dine with students, and conduct seminars on religious topics. Examples of this kind of cultural exchange are numerous across the country.

The Buddhism of Nichiren Daishonin does not regard Christianity or Judaism adversely. All great religions speak eloquently to intrinsic qualities of the human being, answer large questions posed by our existence, and generally are internally consistent. From the Buddhist point of view, they are valid, if not necessarily complete, teachings. They are worthy of respect. But in today's complex, scientifically oriented society, some old-fashioned faiths are losing their power, especially among the young.

Profound differences among religious traditions do not mean that they must be totally at odds with one another. In fact, there are many concordances between Buddhism and Christianity. Both Jesus and the Buddha had life-changing spiritual experiences around the age of thirty, when they realized a mission to preach a gospel of peace and love. Leaving aside the question of divinity, both men shared a message that has had enduring relevance for millions of people.

Jesus and the Buddha

The parallels between major religions are great, even between religions that are thought to be diametrically opposed. The first Catholic missionaries who encountered Buddhist priests in China were confounded by the similarities and thought the Buddhists had somehow learned about and were mocking their own sacred rites.[1] The tonsured Chinese monks or lamas used rosaries, prayed in an unknown tongue, kneeled before images, practiced celibacy, burned incense, and lighted candles. As one mid-nineteenth-century Portuguese missionary wrote:

> The cross, the miter, the [vestments] which the grand lamas wear
> on the journeys, or when they are performing some ceremony out
> of the temple—the service with double choirs, the psalmody, the
> exorcisms, the censer suspended from five chains, and which you
> can open or close at pleasure—the benedictions given by the lamas
> by extending the right hand over the heads of the faithful—the
> [headgear], ecclesiastical celibacy, religious retirement, the worship
> of the saints, the fasts, the processions, the litanies, the holy water—
> all these are analogies between the Buddhists and ourselves.[2]

Of course, then as now, some Buddhists had a sort of pope, the Dalai Lama, who is revered as a reincarnated Buddha.

While the forms of Buddhism strongly reminded missionaries of Catholicism, its theology was more redolent of Protestantism. Buddhism was a reaction to the prevailing Hindu creed of Brahmanism, just as Protestantism was a revolt against Catholicism. Both Brahmanism and Catholicism had made sacrifice the essence of their faith. The daily sacrifice of Mass is the defining feature of Roman Catholicism. Brahmanism is really a system of sacrifices. In place of sacrifice, Protestantism and Buddhism save the "soul" by teaching. In Catholicism, the sermon is subordinate to the Mass. In Protestantism and Buddhism, the sermons are the main event. Shakyamuni was essentially a traveling preacher.

That Buddhism and Christianity separately took similar approaches and shaped parallel messages of peace and love may not seem too surprising. Major religions speak to common human needs and aspirations. However, some scholars believe that early Christians clearly derived some of their principles and monastic institutions from Buddhism. While this view is difficult to prove conclusively, it is certainly intriguing. In a series of articles in *Living Buddhism*, a magazine published by the organization of Nichiren Buddhists in America (SGI-USA), the Buddhist writer Greg Martin, a coauthor of *The Buddha in Your Mirror*, takes an in-depth look at some startling parallels between Buddhism and Christianity. He concludes that there is little doubt that Buddhism had an important influence on Christianity, especially on the New Testament and the four Gospels.[3]

Since Shakyamuni Buddha predated Jesus, living and preaching about 500 years before Christ, it is eminently possible that some of his doctrines could have spread to the Middle East. Scholars have demonstrated that Buddhist teachings and stories were passed along by traders traveling the Silk Road from China to central Asia and on through Persia (Iran), Mesopotamia (Iraq), Syria, Palestine, and Egypt. The caravan cities along the Silk Road were filled with Buddhist followers, and traders journeying through what is now Afghanistan would have passed enormous Buddha images carved into cliffs (the very same images destroyed by the Taliban in 2001). These towering statues were an example of *gandhara*, a Buddhist visual art based on the Greco-Roman heroic style that was brought to northwest India by the Greeks.[4]

Interactions between India and the Middle East in the centuries before Jesus' birth are well-documented. The conquests of Alexander the Great, who invaded India in the third century before Christ, most certainly opened commercial and intellectual avenues of exchange between ancient India and the civilizations to the west. It was a two-way street. King Ashoka of India (272–232 B.C.), who made Buddhism the state religion under his reign, dispatched missionaries with the goal of spreading the Buddha's teachings westward. Evidence of Buddhist monastic activity has even been found in Alexandria, one of the capitals of early Christianity on the shores of the Mediterranean. Greek coins have been uncovered that were inscribed with the word *Buddha*. Martin writes: "It is most likely that

Buddhist teachings and teachers were known and perhaps even commonplace in the Jerusalem of Jesus' day and Buddhist influence upon Jesus and early Christianity is certainly plausible."[5] Some scholars believe that the authors of the gospels were directly influenced by ancient Pali texts of the Buddhist sutras, and even borrowed stories and language from them.

Similarities in the life stories of Jesus and the Buddha are quite striking:

- Both were born amid prophecies heralding the advent of a great spiritual teacher who would relieve the sufferings of the world. In the Gospel of Luke, an angel brings the message that a son of God is to be born on earth. His conception is immaculate, and he is born of Mary, the Blessed Virgin. He is destined to become "the light of the world" and fulfill his people's ardent wish for redemption. In Buddhist scripture, Brahmin soothsayers foretell the birth of a son to the queen of Kapilavastu, Maya, so named because her beauty is beyond belief (*maya* means "illusion"). She dreams of a white elephant that bears a silver lotus blossom in its trunk. The elephant circles three times around her bed. It strikes her once with its trunk, and she perceives this as entering her womb. This is her immaculate conception. She gives birth to Siddhartha ("fulfillment of every wish") and dies seven days (or months or years, depending on the version) later. The Brahmins say the boy, if he remains at home in the palace, will become a monarch, but if he chooses to venture outside, he will become a Buddha, the wisest of men.

- Both endured hardship and persecution to achieve their compassionate missions on earth before ascending into heaven, or in the Buddha's case, Nirvana.

- Both were said to have had the ability to walk on water.

- Both men were attacked for consorting with undesirable people: Jesus with sinners and whores, Buddha with murderers and thieves.

- Both faced great temptations: Jesus in the desert, where he was tempted by Satan, and Shakyamuni beneath the bodhi tree, where the god Mara tried to dissuade him from his final meditation and eventual enlightenment.

While prophets and saints might be expected to lead lives with similar histories and trajectories, the commonalities between Jesus and the Buddha also extend to the specifics of their messages. Jesus' Sermon on the Mount is an area where scholars have discerned convergence that seems beyond coincidence. Two phrases from the Beatitudes section echo and embody the Buddha's universal message of peace:

"Blessed are the meek: for they shall inherit the earth."

"Blessed are the peacemakers: for they shall be called the children of God."

Further on in the sermon, Jesus speaks to the crowd and tells them,

"If someone strikes you on the cheek, offer the other also."

This also contains an echo of the Buddha's words:

"If anyone should give you a blow with his hand, with a stick, or with a knife, you should abandon any desires and utter no evil words."

Martin suggests that the Sermon on the Mount is one of several Christian teachings that closely match the content and style of early Buddhist literature. "Various parables appearing in the Gospels are clearly adapted from Buddhist sutras," he writes, "including the Lotus Sutra, most notably the parable of the prodigal son."[6]

In linking the Gospels and the Lotus Sutra, Martin cites several other examples of convergence, including the expression "son of man," which is a variation of the Sanskrit *saddharma-pundarika*, the title of the Lotus Sutra (or Myoho-renge-kyo). He also notes that when the texts of the New Testament and the Lotus Sutra, both rendered in Indo-European languages, are compared side by side, there is a strong similarity between them. A good example is Jesus' explanation that it is easier "to pass through the eye of a needle than for a rich man to enter heaven" and the Buddhist parable of the tortoise, which says it would be easier for an ocean turtle to put its neck through a hole found in a board floating on the water than for a fool to be reborn as a human being. In addition, the word *cross*, or *stauron* in Greek, can be translated as sutra, or *sutram* in Sanskrit. Thus when Luke states in the Gospel that one should daily take up the cross (the symbol of Christ's sacrifice and salvation), it can also be interpreted from the Buddhist point of view as stating that one should take up the *sutra* daily (which is what we do when we chant and recite gongyo). In like manner, the story of the turtle, paralleled by the camel in Jesus/Luke, was intended to show how difficult it was to attain the level of the gods. In other words, concludes Martin, "To become perfect, one had to propagate the Lotus Sutra, the gospel of the son of man."[7]

Then there is the famous Golden Rule, as formulated by Jesus,

"Do unto others as you would have them do to you." (Luke 6:31)

This is almost identical to the Buddha's teaching,

"Consider others as yourself."

There are many other examples of the Gospels and Buddhist scriptures echoing each other. An entire book of such quotations, *Jesus & Buddha: The Parallel Sayings*, has been published. In his preface to that book, editor Marcus Borg, an Oxford University–educated Christian, notes that if Jesus and Buddha were to meet, "neither would try to convert the other."[8]

Borg points out that both Buddha and Jesus taught a philosophy of life based on the way less traveled. "'Way' or 'path' imagery is central to both bodies of teaching," he writes. "The way of the Buddha is enshrined in the four noble truths of Buddhism, the fourth of which is 'the eightfold path.' Jesus spoke regularly of 'the way.' Moreover, according to the book of Acts, the earliest name for the Jesus movement was 'the Way.' The Gospel of John thus only takes this image one step further in speaking of Jesus as the incarnation of 'the way.'"[9]

In the case of both teachers, "the way" is closely linked to a new way of seeing. As previously mentioned, one of Nichiren's most famous writings, "The Opening of the Eyes," told of a new way of seeing that involved looking inward and casting off one's transient identity in order to recognize one's Buddha nature. Writes Borg: "Sayings about seeing, sight, and light are central to Jesus' teaching. So also for the Buddha. . . . Both Jesus and the Buddha sought to bring about in their hearers a radical perceptual shift—a new way of seeing life. The familiar line from a Christian hymn expresses an emphasis common to both: 'I once was blind, but now I see.'"[10]

While that soulful line is quintessentially Christian, if not born-again Christian, it fits in very well with the Buddhist view of perceptual advancement. In a sense, a person beginning a Buddhist practice is like someone who has been blind all his or her life and suddenly is able to see. It can be compared to the developmental process of sight in infants. When an infant first begins to see, he or she does not perceive objects as such and does not comprehend what is in the field of vision. It takes a long time of relating vision to touch and body movement before a child learns how optical sensations relate to the surrounding environment. The beginning Buddhist practitioner experiences the same widened perspectives as that of an infant experiencing sight. He or she makes elementary steps on the way to mastery of the causality of human existence by changing negative karma (the cumulative effect of negative or self-destructive causes) and building fortune (positive effects gained through accumulation of life-enhancing causes). Eventually the practitioner's own life and karmic tendencies come into full view.

So was Jesus himself a Buddha? From the Buddhist perspective, he appears to fit the definition. He was very wise, extremely courageous, and most compassionate. He is sometimes said to ideally fulfill the concept of Bodhisattva, in the sense that he was an enlightened individual who voluntarily declined or postponed entry into Nirvana (or heaven, where he would "sit at the right hand of God"). Instead he chose to be made man, to live among the people and relieve their suffering. Comparing the enlightenment of Shakyamuni and Jesus, Daisaku Ikeda puts it this way:

> Jesus appears to have had a similar experience, though the level of enlightenment was perhaps different from that of Shakyamuni's. Christ's enlightenment gave him his sense of mission and there-fore, in Buddhist terms, it represents a merging of the universal state of bodhisattvahood with the state of bodhisattvahood within his own mind, for the bodhisattva, representing the state of existence just below that of Buddha, is the potential Buddha who vows to save all mankind before he himself shall enter Buddhahood.[11]

If Jesus Christ can be accepted by Buddhists as a kind of Buddha, it is not surprising that many modern Christians are moving toward a more personal, inward-dwelling definition of God.

"Personal" Christianity

In Tolstoy's final novel, *Resurrection*, the hero Nekhlyudov abruptly goes from a life of aristocratic privilege and moral dissipation to one of caring and compassion. Standing as a juror in a murder trial, he suddenly realizes that the defendant is a woman whom he had seduced and discarded years before. Seeing her, he undergoes a tumultuous inner upheaval, both moral and emotional, that leads to a flash of insight. He describes this revolutionary change as the beginning of "a conversation with myself, with that genuine, divine self, which lives in every man."

This is a resounding affirmation of a personal Christianity, wherein one has direct dialogue with God. From the standpoint of Buddhism, it touches on two fundamental points. First, Buddhist practice entails an unflinching conversation with one's self, a more real, more powerful, more loving self than we normally imagine. Second, it is axiomatic in Buddhism that all people have the seed of Buddhahood within them. This higher, enlightened self is typically dormant during our mundane, workaday existence, but it is always there, like a rosebush in winter, ready to bloom in the right conditions. It is just waiting for the right environmental stimulus to bring it out. In Nichiren Buddhism the correct stimulus is the Gohonzon. In Tolstoy's novel, it was the wrenching plight of a woman the hero had wronged.

Since there is no God in Buddhism, it's difficult for some Westerners to regard it even as a religion. Many Nichiren Buddhists refer to their faith simply as "the practice," although it surely is also a religion. Buddhism is largely a self-directed faith. This would seem to place it at odds with the more hierarchical strictures of Christianity and Judaism. But just as society is being subtly, almost invisibly transformed by Buddhist concepts, so the traditional faiths are coming around to more personal, inner-directed approaches. Tolstoy, who was a savage critic of the prevailing Russian Orthodox Church in his country, gravitated late in life toward a much more personal religion. This shift from top-down, catechismal-type religious experience to a more flexible, personal faith also characterizes the contemporary American landscape.

In his best-selling book *Bobos in Paradise*, the author and *New York Times* columnist David Brooks uses the word *flexidoxy* to sum up this new spiritual age as exemplified by the "bourgeois bohemians" of his title. Flexidoxy is defined as a hybrid mixture: a need for freedom and flexibility on the one hand, with a yearning for rigor and orthodoxy on the other. People inside traditional faiths are pushing and bending the bubble of belief. Brooks writes:

> Whereas earlier believers felt that, paradoxically, freedom was achieved through a total submission to God's will, blind obedience of that sort is just not in the Bobo mental repertoire. Among Jews, for example, there is a growing movement of young modern

Orthodox who know Hebrew, study the Torah, and observe the kosher laws. They are rigorous observers, but they also pick and choose, discarding those ancient rules that don't accord with their modern sensibilities—most any rule that restricts the role of women, for example. Furthermore, they pull back from biblical teachings whenever those teachings clash with pluralism—with any teaching that implies Judaism is the one true faith and that other faiths are inferior or in error. This is Orthodoxy without obedience—indeed, Flexidoxy.[12]

At times, the deep suspicion regarding authority and traditional organizations can lead to extremes of self-exploration and spiritual indulgence. Using your own personal tastes and philosophy to assemble a theology has its limits. Brooks cites the case of a young nurse named Sheila Larson, who describes her faith as "Sheilaism," her own custom religion, with God defined as "whatever filled her needs."

Buddhism is not sheer personalism or egotism. In fact, it is the opposite of those things. But it does combine the rigor of a traditional practice with the freedom and flexibility of a life philosophy based on the individual. Buddhism is essentially nonauthoritarian, democratic, and based on insights obtained primarily through individual efforts. As such, it suits the skeptics among us, who are less receptive to dogma than they are to firsthand experience. Modern Buddhism is also nonmoralistic. In a world characterized by a great diversity of peoples, cultures, and lifestyles, Buddhism does not suggest any one way of living. There are no commandments (except, perhaps, to chant). Buddhism derives its moral power from the inner transformation of the individual. This transformation, which we call Buddhahood, is not limited to monks and gurus who live on mountaintops, nor is it confined to Buddhists. This is perhaps why Buddhists are so remarkably tolerant of other faiths.

Often one of the first questions a visitor to a Buddhist meeting asks is: do I have to stop going to church in order to practice Buddhism? The answer, as we have indicated, is no. It is entirely possible to practice Buddhism and continue to observe Christian or Jewish services—even to remain faithful to those traditions. That is to say, *Buddhists* would not object to you temporarily practicing

Buddhism and Christianity side by side. (Your minister may have other ideas.) Eventually, of course, some people will find they get a better, more specific *result* from practicing Buddhism assiduously. Ultimately, the individual will have to make some sort of choice.

Many people of Jewish faith come to Buddhism and find it to be, initially at least, a supplement to their own religious practice. Certainly there has been a great deal of attention paid to more personal, mystical branches of Judaism, like Kabbalah. Again, the power of the Buddhist practice eventually should be measured by the results, or what we call "actual proof" of its efficacy in the various realms of everyday life.

Religion and Ecology

It has long been suggested that the Judeo-Christian world view, which places man at the apex of nature, has led invariably to the pillaging of our environment. Both Christian and Jewish faiths articulate an anthropomorphic concept of God and give rise to the view of man as apart from nature, taking from it what he needs so that he may multiply, and so forth. Chapter I of Genesis states that man was shaped in the image of God and was granted dominion over all creatures. According to this view, technology is just another expression of man's right to rule and exploit the living planet. Buddhism, on the other hand, holds it as axiomatic that the individual is connected to everything on the Earth and that all of life is interrelated in a complex web. Thus Buddhism has been said to provide a better spiritual and intellectual framework for environmental awareness.

While these views may be compelling—they were fashionable in the 1960s and '70s and still turn up with frequency in various Buddhist journals—they are not entirely true. We must be very cautious in generalizing about belief systems, particularly one as richly complex as the Judeo-Christian tradition. As the famed microbiologist and author Rene Dubos pointed out, "Erosion of the land, destruction of animal and plant species, excessive exploitation of natural resources, and ecological disasters are not peculiar to the Judeo-Christian tradition and to scientific technology."[13]

Even before the Bible was written, dramatic extinctions of mammals and birds took place during the Neolithic period, when humans first began systematic expansion of agriculture. In the ancient Egyptian and Assyrian empires, wholesale destruction of wild animal herds has been documented, in some cases leading to eradication of large animal species. The golden age of Greece, as Plato observed in *Critias*, was cut short by deforestation and overgrazing.

Nor were the nations of Asia, where Buddhist thought flourished, completely free of ecological depredation. The bare hills of central and northern China are thought to have been heavily forested in ancient times, before fire and overgrazing denuded them forever. Wildlife in modern Japan has been so ravaged that sparrows and swallows are the only types of birds that pass through Tokyo, compared to dozens of species only a century ago. Even aboriginal peoples, the objects of much dreamy ecological idealism, recklessly cleared forest lands and burned vast areas to facilitate hunting and agriculture. In Australia, fire-wielding aborigines set rangeland ablaze in already semiarid areas, destroying the vegetation, promoting erosion, and killing much of the native fauna. As Dr. Dubos writes:

> All over the globe and at all times in the past, men have pillaged nature and disturbed the ecological equilibrium, usually out of ignorance, but also because they have always been more concerned with immediate advantages than with long-range goals. . . . If men are more destructive now than they were in the past, it is because there are more of them and because they have at their command more powerful means of destruction, not because they have been influenced by the Bible. In fact, Judeo-Christian peoples were probably the first to develop on a large scale a pervasive concern for land management and an ethic of nature.[14]

Dubos cites Saint Francis of Assisi and the Benedictine monks as positive examples of Christian stewardship of the land. Saint Francis preached an absolute identification with nature and treated all living creatures as though they were his brothers and sisters. In our own times, animal shelters continue to be named in honor of Saint

Francis. The monastic order founded by Benedict of Nursia favors a harmonious relationship between man and nature. Saint Benedict insisted that his monks get their hands dirty in the fields, a tradition that continues. The Benedictines consider such labor a form of prayer, which is not much different from Nichiren's assertion that the affairs of life and work are themselves a form of Buddhist devotion. (Or as stated earlier: Faith equals daily life.) Buddhism and Christianity are quite different, but on some levels they are the same.

When it comes to Charles Darwin, however, Christianity seems to be in denial (not all Christians, surely, but the more fundamentalist ones who see the Bible as literal truth). In the United States, against all logic and common sense, the political quarrel over creationism versus evolution continues to rage. Darwin's thesis on the origin of the species challenges the idea that God made man out of whole cloth, that he made the Earth in a day, and that the Bible is literally true. It upends the creation myths not just of Judeo-Christianity, but also of nearly every religion in history. He was an equal opportunity upender.

Buddhism, of course, has no problem with Darwinian theory. A vivid example of a Christian thinker who embraced Darwinian evolution and used it as building block for an entirely new theological vision was the French scientist and philosopher Teilhard de Chardin. De Chardin was uniquely equipped to make a historic synthesis: he was both a Jesuit Father and a skilled paleontologist. He spent years in the field doing original paleontological research. In *The Phenomenon of Man*, written in 1955, De Chardin undertook to treat the evolution of man as a proper subject for both paleontological inquiry and theological speculation. He had studied the phylogenesis, the ancestral trees, of many species and had come to the conclusion that man's evolution was unique. This was because of the phenomenon of *reflection*, the power acquired by the consciousness, somewhere along the evolutionary trail, to turn upon itself, to take possession of itself, "no longer merely to know, but to know oneself; no longer merely to know, but to know what one knows." Animals may know things, but they cannot know that they know. Father

Teilhard also keenly felt what he termed the "irreversible coherence of all that exists," which he expressed rather cogently:

> The least molecule is, in nature and in position, a function of the whole sidereal process, and the least of the protozoa is structurally so knit into the web of life that its existence cannot be hypothetically annihilated without *ipso facto* undoing the whole network of the biosphere. The distribution, succession, and solidarity of objects are born from their concrescence in a common genesis. Time and space are organically joined again so as to weave, together, the stuff of the universe. That is the point we have reached and how we perceive things today.[15]

His eloquent analysis of the state of science was a gentle rebuke to members of his own order, as well as to scriptural literalists everywhere, who refused to accept the verdict of science. He was impatient at the sight of so many minds remaining closed to the idea of evolution. He wrote, "A truth once seen, even by a single mind, always ends up imposing itself on the totality of human consciousness."[16]

Father Teilhard decided that man held a special position in the Tree of Life in that he represented a new stage in which evolution became conscious of itself. He theorized that all evolution tended toward complexity, a process he called, inelegantly, *complexification*. Because evolution was irresistibly drawing men and women toward a higher and higher stage—facilitated by migration, cultural diversity, and advanced communications—he saw the eventual union of the whole human species into a single interthinking group, based on a common framework. He called this the *noosystem*. He also coined the word *noosphere*, which refers to a new layer or membrane on the earth's surface, a "thinking layer," floating above the biosphere. He considered the global unification of human awareness a prerequisite for the future progress of civilization. Now, a half century later, with the Internet linking billions of people in cross-cultural webs of unimaginable complexity, his ideas of a noosystem and noosphere hardly seem farfetched.

De Chardin also postulated that such cultural convergences could arouse fears of global uniformity and drab intellectual conformity. He offered instead the theory of "variety-in-unity," in which individuals, though interconnected and bound together by potent and rich art, culture, and information, would retain their intellectual independence. This is remarkably similar to the Buddhist concept of *itai doshin,* which means "many in body, one in mind," and has the same connotation, that of unity in diversity.

Although he was a devout Jesuit, the great de Chardin sounds more like a Buddhist than anything else.

Gods in Buddhism

The most important thing the Westerner needs to remember about Buddhism is that the Buddha was a man, a human being. Buddhism is not defined or limited by the concept of a savior. In place of worship of a supreme being, it teaches self-reliance and self-respect. Through our own power we can gain release from the sufferings of life. Therefore, Buddhism claims a unique ability to empower the individual in overcoming problems, right now, in the real world in which we live. As Daisaku Ikeda has written:

> The essence of Buddhism lies in developing oneself through one's own determination and tenacious effort—not by depending on anyone else. We don't need others' sympathy or sentimentality. We have to stand up and advance, even if there is no one to encourage us. We resolutely and cheerfully take responsibility to change ourselves, our surroundings, society, and the land where we live. That is the principle of ichinen sanzen, or three thousand realms in a single moment of life. . . . What Buddhism teaches is not abstract theory; it is not a weak-kneed way of life of constantly clinging to something for support. At the same time, neither is it to be confused with the egotism to arrogantly suppose, "I alone am correct and respectworthy."[17]

The historical Buddha was born in a land and during an era where myriad gods were worshipped and propitiated with primitive sacrifices. As Jawaharlal Nehru, India's first prime minister, once told the French writer André Malraux, "The genius of the Buddha has to do with the fact that he is a man . . . an accuser, vis-a-vis the teeming multitude of the gods." Nehru went on to explain why he thought Buddhism had died out in his native India, where Shakyamuni is still revered but is generally regarded as just another of the many Hindu gods. After Shakyamuni's death, according to Nehru, "[Buddha] became deified, he merged with that multitude, which closed round him."[18] In other words, the Buddha lost his humanity and became just another god.

The Buddhism of Nichiren Daishonin treats the Buddhas throughout history as human beings, but it is not completely devoid of gods and spirits. There are many mentions of various gods and goddesses in his letters and treatises—so many in fact that one might suspect that Nichiren believed in the power and influence of supernatural forces. How are we to explain them? In actuality, these references to gods and goddesses were expressions of the prevailing culture of the time. As it spread from region to region, Buddhism not only changed the hearts and minds of the people where it took root; Buddhism itself changed, as it absorbed elements of the background culture in which it was found.

The various Buddhist gods referred to in Nichiren's writings originated in Indian and Japanese folklore. Because Nichiren realized that Nam-myoho-renge-kyo suffused all things throughout the universe, he was comfortable incorporating the traditional gods of the culture in his teachings. When Nichiren spoke of the protection of "the prince of heaven" or "the sun god," he was referring to the notion that his life was in harmony with the universe. Since in Buddhism our lives and the surrounding environment are one, our environment mirrors our inward life condition. Buddhist "gods" are forces or phenomena in the universe that protect or aid human life. In terms of deities, Nichiren refuted all philosophies that force people to kowtow to religious authority and opened instead a way for ordinary people to discover the sacred life within themselves. It was for this reason that he suffered such persecutions. His was basically a struggle for human rights, the most essential right of all, to be true to one's highest self.

In the gosho "The True Entity of Life," Nichiren states: "The common mortal is the entity of the three properties, or the true Buddha." (The three properties may be defined as the dharma body or truth, wisdom or the capacity to realize the truth, and emancipation or freedom from suffering.) This means that the human being, the "common mortal," is equal to the Buddha. Every human being is therefore inestimably precious. About this, Ikeda has writtten, "I would like to interpret this as the ultimate declaration of the humanization of Buddhism. Nichiren Daishonin's Buddhism is a humanistic religion that will illuminate the third millennium, beginning with the twenty-first century."[19]

Sin and Karma

Another salient difference between Buddhism and Judeo-Christianity can be found in their approaches to the idea of sin or karma. Sin is central to the theology of Judaism and Christianity. Both religions have highly developed commandments, codes, and systems of moral behavior. Since the fall of Adam, according to the Christian doctrine of original sin, human beings have been in a state of sin. Even if you don't know Adam from Adam, you share a burden of responsibility for his sin. Like Kafka's Joseph K, we are all born guilty.

By contrast, Buddhism downplays sinfulness and guilt. Instead of dwelling obsessively on what good or bad deeds have been done in the past, Buddhism focuses on choosing the best actions for the future. Whether your behavior is right or wrong is less important than how your behavior will shape your future. This is a function of karma, a Sanskrit word that literally means "action." The concept of karma has been fundamental to Indian philosophy since the Upanishadic era, three hundred years before the historical Buddha's awakening. Your karma is the net result of every single cause you have ever made—every thought, word, and deed. You are creating karma (positive, perhaps) by reading this book. Karma includes everything you have ever done and everything you have impetuously set your heart on. It comprises all you have felt and all you have learned. Naturally it includes your hereditary inclinations, your DNA, all the medicines you have taken, all the cigarettes you have smoked, all the miles you have walked. It is like a scientific bank account of every thought, word, and deed one makes throughout a lifetime. It is scientific in the sense that it is based on the law of cause and effect. It would take a supercomputer to track and record all of these millions of mini-events in your life, but according to Buddhism your life itself is the storehouse.

There is no escaping who we are. If you think you can move to Hawaii or buy a bigger house to solve your problems, think again. According to Buddhism, we carry our karma with us, like a suitcase, everywhere we go. Everything in our existence is eternally etched at the deepest levels of our lives. This resembles the Christian concept of soul, but without the sin. If Buddhism were to have an equivalent to the idea of sin, it would be the notion of committing an unwholesome act—that is, something that would create bad karma. This is judged to be a transgression against the self. Therefore, correct behavior can be considered to have a strong element of self-interest.[20] Yes, there are good causes and bad causes. If you eat foods high in cholesterol, for instance, you may eventually have heart problems. If you treat people with respect and compassion, you will eventually enjoy the friendship and trust of others.

In addition, karma putatively encompasses the causes and effects of past lives. Since Buddhism teaches the eternity of life, the idea of rebirth or reincarnation is implicit. Taking the concepts of karma and rebirth together, we naturally reach the conclusion that even a newborn baby carries the effects of previous existences. This is somewhat analogous to what other religions call original sin. But Buddhism rejects the need for lifelong guilt. Buddhism maintains that karma is a natural outcome of the eternity of life and can be changed.

It is widely thought that Buddhism, and Asian religions in general, hold that humans are in the grip of destiny, enchained by their karma. Certainly we must concede that our thoughts, words, and deeds become engraved in our lives and create what might be called habits, or tendencies, that remain long after the actions that created them are over. As we have seen in our examination of the Ten Worlds, one's karmic tendency seems to coalesce around a single world, or life condition, which we tend to return to with thudding regularity. This could give rise to a pessimistic view. There really is no running away from one's karma. So Buddhism says, why not just face your karma squarely? Look it right in the eye, in front of the Gohonzon. Nichiren Buddhism encourages us to surmount these lower worlds built on negative karma by aspiring to the higher one of enlightenment.

If you think about it, karma actually entails a kind of radical freedom. If you are, essentially, a product of everything you have thought, said, and done, then with each new thought, deed, and action you are creating new karma. Buddhism makes it very clear that our destiny is a matter of our own creation, the effect of causes we have made. That is why it is imperative to practice Buddhism with the spirit of "from this moment on," generating positive wisdom from deep within life, in order to stop making negative causes and start making positive ones. This is the key to leading a winning life. Indeed, the key question for Buddhists is not *What have you done?* but *What are you doing right now?*

The Buddhist concept of morality as expressed in the law of karma has become part of our language and everyday consciousness and, as noted, is widely misused. It is roughly translated to mean "what goes around comes around," as in the Black Eyed Peas song "Karma." But strictly speaking, karma is not a kind of moral boomerang. It implies a radical responsibility. Your karma will not come back and hit you. It *is* you. You must take full responsibility for it. Unlike Brahmanism (or Hinduism), which postulated a caste system into which all sentient beings are born—and can never transcend in this lifetime—Buddhism views karma as a radical assertion of the self, a present-time free will. You are creating a karmic bank account every moment of your life.

How We Pray

While Buddhism gently coexists with other religions and life philosophies, it generally takes a sharply different approach to the power of
prayer. Since there is no "higher power" in Buddhism, it is therefore
senseless and unwise to appeal to something outside oneself for the
solution to one's problems. The sutra chanting that is the heart of
Buddhist practice differs from conventional Western concepts of
prayer in that a) it is spoken aloud, and b) it is inner-directed. Instead
of beseeching an outside force, the Buddhist musters his or her own
inner resources to meet the problem. One calls on one's own Buddha
nature, summoning the wisdom and courage that is within each of us.

If we are all essentially Buddhas, why do we need to pray? The
answer is that we have the Buddha nature, but it lies deep inside.
Chanting is like priming a pump, with the goal of bringing the
Buddha nature welling forth from the depths of life. When one
chants, a vow or determination is typically made. Instead of "Lord,
give me strength," or "Please, God, make this happen," the Buddhist's
prayer is more along the lines of: "I will have strength." Your prayer
includes the idea that it is up to you. In the end, it all depends on
you. Nothing more distinguishes modern Buddhism from traditional
Western religions than its emphasis on personal responsibility. There
is no guilt in Buddhism. Instead, there is responsibility.

It is liberating to take full responsibility for one's own actions
and leave the guilt behind. Guilt can be a paralyzing burden, making
positive action much more difficult. Since we create karma, positive
or negative, through our own actions, we thus have the power to
change. This is the promise offered by the practice of Buddhism.
While in theory all we have to do to succeed in life is to make the
best possible causes, in most cases we have little control over the
causes we make. Some of us (perhaps most of us) have some self-
destructive tendencies. We all tend to be caught up in the unbroken
chain of cause and effect that is our current karma. But when we
begin to practice Buddhism, we start to illuminate the negative
aspects of our karma (we see our own weakness vividly) and can then
take steps to change our destiny.

*

Buddha was not God, although certainly some Buddhist sects worshipped him as if this were so. When Shakyamuni Buddha died at the age of eighty (probably of dysentery), his last words were: "Decay is inherent in all composite things. Work out your own salvation with diligence." The key words are *work out your own salvation*. He was a man whose own efforts resulted in an amazing enlightenment. His message was, do the same.

Centuries later, Nichiren Daishonin realized and asserted his own Buddhahood. But he never asked his followers to worship him. In his gosho "Heritage of the Ultimate Law of Life," written when he was fifty-one and living in a ruined shrine on windswept Sado Island, Nichiren emphasized the importance of worshiping the law of the universe, as opposed to the prevailing Japanese worship of personages and shrines. In his own time, Nichiren excoriated the followers of other sects of Buddhism for using pictures of Buddhas and bodhisattvas as mandalas, or objects of worship. These images and beings were regarded as sacred. When Nichiren vigorously opposed such practices, as we have seen, he endured assassination attempts and various persecutions.

In order to express his own enlightenment, Nichiren inscribed a mandala, the Gohonzon, which was not a just symbol but also an embodiment of his enlightenment, with Nam-myoho-renge-kyo down the center, and signed "I, Nichiren," at the bottom, signifying oneness of the person and the law. Nichiren did not say that you could become a god, but you can inherit the law. He wrote: "Shakyamuni who attained enlightenment countless aeons ago, the Lotus Sutra which leads all people to Buddhahood, and we ordinary human beings are in no way different or separate from each other."[21]

This law of life is inherent in the universe. It was not established by Shakyamuni or any other Buddha. It is not the exclusive possession of anyone, including a cloistered, close-minded sect of priests. The Lotus Sutra was the expression of Shakyamuni's enlightenment to the law of life. Nam-myoho-renge-kyo actually is the law of life.

Religion Without Priests

All religions have their holy men and women, usually dressed in dark robes, often of black and white, symbolizing the moral poles of evil and purity. In some churches, the priests and ministers are more ornate; in others the approach is simple and spare. But in Nichiren Buddhism, there are none.

Though its founder was a priest, and many monks and priests preserved the purity of its lineage over the centuries, modern-day Nichiren Buddhism is primarily a religion with no clergy. It is unique in that sense. The SGI is an entirely lay organization. Thus, there are no doctrinal dicta handed down by robed men on high, no elaborate rituals with ornately dressed poohbahs and solemn sermons, and no moral scolds. It has been that way since 1991.

The history of the Nichiren priesthood issue is long and complex. Its origins go back to World War II, when the two founders of the Soka Gakkai (today, SGI), the lay organization, were jailed for refusing to cooperate with the war effort, which meant honoring the Shinto religion that was woven into the very fabric of the militaristic Japanese regime, ultimately including the Emperor himself, who under Shinto doctrine was considered divine. Under pressure, the priesthood of Nichiren Shoshu (orthodox school) gave in to the demands of the government and allowed their temples to display support for the Shinto-dominated military regime. Meanwhile, in jail and refusing to submit, Tsunesaburo Makiguchi, the first president of the Soka Gakkai, eventually died in 1944. Resentment over this issue festered for decades.

In 1991, the priesthood of Nichiren Shoshu denounced the lay leadership of the Soka Gakkai in Japan, declaring themselves the ultimate arbiters of truth in Buddhist doctrine and severing all ties with the laity. Among other things, the high priest accused the SGI and its president emeritus, Daisaku Ikeda, of committing heresy by allowing performances of Beethoven's Ninth Symphony, particularly the "Ode to Joy" chorale, at Buddhist meetings. To put this in broader context, the Japanese people love Beethoven's Ninth beyond anything a Westerner might imagine. It is performed, especially around

Christmastime, at thousands of concert halls, secondary schools, colleges, and community organizations. It is a Japanese holiday tradition as ubiquitous as "Silent Night" in our own country. Nevertheless, the priests condemned it, saying Schiller's lyrics refer to Christianity, and, therefore, singing it is to praise the Christian God.

Without getting too deeply into the merits of Beethoven's Ninth, a symphony whose noble spirit echoes with universal themes and is loved by people of all ages and cultures everywhere, the schism between priests and laypeople may be a symptom of our spiritual times. Today we have seen many examples of priests, men of the cloth of various faiths, who have shown themselves to be distinctly out of step with the norms and values of contemporary society. This is an unfortunate but true situation.

In an article in the *Seikyo Shimbun*, a Japanese daily newspaper, Ryosuke Inagaki, a non-Buddhist and professor of medieval Christian philosophy at Kyushu University, likened the Japanese priesthood's stance in this matter to the Vatican First Council of 1869, which declared the doctrine of papal infallibility in the Roman Catholic Church. "How could such an absurdity take place in these modern times?" he wondered. "It is clearly incorrect for the priesthood to self-righteously believe that its role in upholding the heritage of the law implies its superiority to lay believers. . . . I believe that a genuine religion should be open, vibrant, capable of coping with the trends of the times and society."[22]

The fact that Nichiren Buddhists must practice without priests to guide them may turn out to be a strength rather than a weakness in the long term.

A True World Religion

Buddhism has been called "the first world religion." This is not only because it was a religion that spread beyond its region (in fact, it owes its continued existence to its dissemination outside India). It is also a world religion because it gently tolerates and embraces other faiths, often absorbing some of their best points, then moving on to a new synthesis. It is like a carton of milk that absorbs some of the more piquant odors from other foods in your refrigerator.

The Buddhism of China was heavily influenced by Confucianism, particularly its notions about filial piety. Thus Nichiren Buddhism, which traces its lineage to China, contains many admonitions to respect one's parents and to repay "debts of gratitude" to one's parents, teachers, and sovereign. Buddhism in Japan was also influenced by Shintoism, which involves nature worship and veneration of the ruler, the emperor, as a god. References to Shinto ritual and symbolism, especially the cultlike worship of the sun gods and goddesses, crop up repeatedly in Nichiren's writings. But at a crucial moment in history, during World War II, as mentioned, the leaders of Nichiren Buddhism's lay organization, the Soka Gakkai, went to jail rather than submit to the Shinto faith and leadership.

In our own time, the Buddhism that is taking root in the United States has been influenced by its practitioners' prior faiths, notably Christianity and Judaism. You might say that Nichiren Buddhists in this country practice with varying degrees of guilt and awareness of their own sinfulness or shortcomings. If one misses gongyo, one's daily practice, in the morning, there is a tendency to feel guilty throughout the day. Although Buddhism teaches us not to harbor such guilt, people nonetheless do. It is unavoidable, given our backgrounds. Over time and with strong practice, Buddhists can largely overcome these feelings of guilt, and that is a liberating thing. In the meantime, we should not regard vestiges of Judeo-Christian upbringing and training in an invidious way.

Nichiren Buddhists do not take a refutational approach to traditional faiths, nor do they reject the social and economic institutions that these faiths fostered. Indeed, Daisaku Ikeda has written:

> Christianity is one of the bases of the development of Western civilization. Materialism is also the foundation of the prosperity of today's civilization. The Buddhism of Nichiren Daishonin does not regard Christianity or materialism adversely; rather it encom-

passes and leads them. Buddhism includes at once the spiritual and the material, and holds a total view of life.[23]

Buddhism tends to illuminate one's existing faith, not subvert it. Eventually, of course, some people will find they get a better, more specific *result* from practicing Buddhism assiduously. Again, the power of the Buddhist practice eventually comes to be measured by what we call "actual proof" in the realm of everyday life.

In a world where the choice seems to be between an almighty God and the emptiness of materialism, Buddhism steers the path of the Middle Way, between the philosophical extremes. Blazing such a path requires tremendous reserves of wisdom, courage, and compassion. But it is the path human civilization must take.

[1] James Freeman Clarke, *Ten Great Religions: An Essay in Comparative Theology* (New York: Houghton Mifflin, 1871), 139.

[2] Ibid., 140.

[3] Greg Martin, "Did Buddhism Influence Christianity?", *Living Buddhism*, Vol. IX, no. 2 (February 2005), 5.

[4] Mishra, *An End to Suffering*, 296.

[5] Martin, "Did Buddhism Influence Christianity?", 6.

[6] Ibid., 7.

[7] Ibid., 8.

[8] Marcus Borg, *Jesus & Buddha: The Parallel Sayings* (Berkeley, CA: Ulysses Press, 2002), 8.

[9] Ibid., 9.

[10] Ibid.

[11] Ikeda, *The Living Buddha*, 62.

[12] Brooks, *Bobos in Paradise*, 243.

[13] Rene Dubos, *A God Within* (New York: Scribner's, 1972), 158.

[14] Ibid., 161.

[15] Teilhard de Chardin, *The Phenomenon of Man* (New York: Harper Colophon, 1959), 218.

[16] Ibid., 218.

[17] Daisaku Ikeda, "Wisdom of the Lotus Sutra," *Living Buddhism*, Vol. II, no. 3 (March 1998), 27.

[18] André Malraux, *Anti-memoirs* (New York: Holt, Rhinehart and Winston, 1968), 228.

[19] Ikeda, "Wisdom of the Lotus Sutra," 41.

[20] Sin Yatomi, "The Lotus and the Cross: A Perspective on Sin and Karma," *Living Buddhism*, Vol. VIII, no. 9 (September 2004), 19–20.

[21] "Heritage of the Ultimate Law of Life," *Seikyo Times* (January 1990), 64.

[22] Ryosuke Inagaki, "Comparisons with the First Vatican Council," *Seikyo Shimbun* (January 31, 1991).

[23] Daisaku Ikeda, "Guidance Memo," *NSA Quarterly*, Vol. II, no. 3 (Summer 1974), 92.

7

PEACE
Kosen-Rufu

PEACE IS THE NOBLEST GOAL OF HUMAN BEINGS. Buddhism is always a peace movement, everywhere it exists. The collective goal of Nichiren Buddhist practitioners is world peace, or *kosen-rufu* in Japanese. Kosen-rufu means to widely teach Buddhism, thereby allowing its peaceful principles to transform the lives of the people from within.

Many people speak about world peace and love for all mankind, but when it comes to extending themselves in individual cases, even in their own families, they are not so interested. In the philosophy of Nichiren Daishonin, one comes to respect the dignity of the individual above all. Throughout human history, every revolution, every political movement, no matter how lofty and idealistic, ends up sacrificing the individual for the sake of the cause. The revolution started by Nichiren Daishonin and led today by Daisaku Ikeda is called "human revolution," because it starts with the individual and considers as its highest aim the cause of human happiness.

In his autobiographical novel, *The Human Revolution*, Ikeda writes, "The reformation within one man can transform not only his karma, but that of a nation and of all mankind as well." Buddhism holds that a transformation in the inner life of a single individual can spur and encourage positive change in others, which then extends and spreads throughout society, just as a pebble causes ripples in a pond. Therefore, a succinct way of stating the goal of kosen-rufu is "world peace through individual enlightenment." That means person to person, life to life, one by one by one. Although this may seem like an arduous, slow process, it is still the sure way to create peace in the world.

When we take a closer look at the meaning of the term kosen-rufu, it will be clear that this is not some utopian or pie-in-the-sky view. *Ko* of kosen-rufu means "widely," as among all people in society. *Sen* of kosen means "to speak and talk," suggesting that peace will be accomplished primarily through dialogue. *Ru* means "to flow." Buddhism is a dynamic, flowing thing, not static, dogmatic, or rigid. As we have seen, the Buddhism of Shakyamuni was refined and enhanced by Nichiren Daishonin, and Nichiren's Buddhism has been refreshed and interpreted for today by Daisaku Ikeda. Buddhism evolves and adapts to suit the environment in which it flourishes. *Fu* of kosen-rufu means to "carpet" society, that is, leave no place unreached, no person untouched. Therefore, kosen-rufu means both the spread of Buddhism and the stage when Buddhism is widely spread.

Kosen-rufu, or world peace, is not a set goal but a process. In practical terms, kosen-rufu describes a situation in which one-third of the world practices Buddhism, and one-third is supportive of Buddhism while not actively practicing. The remaining one-third, whether neutral, hostile, or otherwise engaged, is not important under this formulation. When two-thirds of the society favors Buddhism, kosen-rufu already exists. But this is not a fixed state. Even in a society where kosen-rufu has been accomplished, the truths of Buddhism must still be transmitted to new generations.

The organization that supports this Buddhism throughout the world, the Soka Gakkai International, aims to promote harmony and end war through activities based on peace, culture and education. True culture and education stem from the recognition that life itself is the greatest of all possessions. In the gosho known as "The Gift of Rice," Nichiren Daishonin wrote, "Life itself is the highest and most precious of all treasures in the universe." Therefore, there can be no crime greater than the taking of life. The first two presidents of the

Soka Gakkai took to heart Nichiren's words, which sprang from the ordeals and persecutions he was forced to endure, and they made them the guiding principle of their lives.

The SGI has maintained its status as a longtime non-governmental organization (NGO) at the United Nations. After each gongyo (morning and evening practice), Nichiren Buddhists conclude with a prayer for world peace. Once a month, in communities across the nation, Nichiren Buddhists hold a group gongyo for world peace, typically involving dozens of members (sometimes many more) chanting together. Each year, Daisaku Ikeda, the founding president of the SGI, submits a detailed peace proposal. These treatises are remarkable for the depth of their understanding and the specificity of their proposals.

The Peace Ahead

In his 2006 peace proposal, Ikeda tackles such diverse and critical topics as global warming and desertification, nuclear proliferation and disarmament education, and the need to reform and strengthen the United Nations. His Buddhist-based view of world peace issues is grounded in three core principles:

•the need for a gradualist approach
•an emphasis on dialogue
•a focus on personal character or integrity as a pivotal concern

This last point is critical to understanding the Buddhist approach to peace. If a people cannot see the dignity, creativity, and potential of their own lives, they won't value it in others. People who do not treasure their own lives negatively affect nature, causing disharmony; the same is true of their interaction with others. Ikeda writes:

> We must never lose sight of the fact that a third millennium imbued with the respect for the sanctity of life, free from nuclear arms and war and rich with the rainbow hues of diversity, will come into being only through the efforts of empowered and

responsible citizens who don't wait for someone else to take the initiative.[1]

✳

Not too long ago, civilization was said to be on the brink of annihilation. Two massively armed superpowers were locked in an apparent death struggle of mutual assured destruction. Today the world has taken a giant step back from that dreadful risk. The imminent danger has been greatly reduced, if not altogether eliminated. The sword of mutual assured destruction no longer hangs over everyone like a bad dream. But new challenges await. Rogue states and outlaw rulers keep turning up with alarming frequency, from Idi Amin and Pol Pot to Slobodan Milosevic, Saddam Hussein and Kim Jong Il. So the world is at a delicate stage in which small states now threaten the larger peace in ways not dreamed of during the Cold War. As Ikeda puts it in his 2006 peace proposal, the next five years, to 2010, are critical for disarmament efforts. He identifies three threats: 1) emergence of a nuclear black market; 2) determined efforts by more countries to acquire technology to produce fissile materials; and 3) the clear desire of terrorists to acquire weapons of mass destruction. In addition to specific proposals, Ikeda emphasizes a more general shift from an attitude of confrontation to one of "creative coexistence." Ultimately, the destiny of human life rests with human beings. "Our greatest priority should be changing the people's mindset and behavior," Ikeda writes, "so they are grounded in a culture of peace."

Does that mean we are compelled to sit around and pray for peace and, essentially, do nothing? Not at all. The work of peace education and environmental activism requires the sort of long-term commitment and single-minded focus that are the strengths of practicing Buddhists. Ikeda encourages us to take very seriously the motto, "Think global, act local." He calls for a "whirlwind of dialogue" that reaches out across cultural and ideological divides, as individuals, one by one, begin to make small contributions to peace—which eventually multiply, exponentially, throughout society. While this process may seem futile or invisible on a macrocosmic level, it is not. To describe the way individual actions can dramatically affect the larger stage of human events, Ikeda uses the analogy of of trimtabs, the small, adjustable flaps found on the wings of airplanes and the keels of boats:

> As designer and philosopher R. Buckminster Fuller pointed out, a trimtab on a ship's rudder can be operated by the unaided power of a single individual; it can facilitate the movement of the rudder, thus enabling a change in direction of a massive ship. Humanism can play a similar role, redirecting the course of global society. As ripples of dialogue multiply and spread, they have the potential to generate the kind of sea change that will redirect the forces of fanaticism and dogmatism. The cumulative effect of such seemingly small efforts is, I believe, sufficient to redirect the current of the times—just as a small trimtab can adjust the course of a massive ship or plane. What is crucial is the hard and patient work of challenging, through the spiritual struggle of intense encounter and dialogue, the assumptions and attachments that bind and drive people.[2]

✳

Buddhists can confidently carry out the strategy emphasized throughout this book: chant and take action. David Kasahara, onetime regional leader of Nichiren Buddhists in the Northeast, said in a May 2006 lecture: "Prayer is not a feeble consolation. It is powerful, unyielding, and must be manifested in action. And action must be backed up by prayer." He added that traditionally the bodhisattvas, those in the ninth world just below Buddhahood, have the word *gyo* in their names (for example, bodhisattvas Jogyo, Anryugyo, and Muhengyo, who appear on the Gohonzon). In Japanese, *gyo* means "action." The world of Bodhisattva has been defined as a state of compassion and altruistic behavior in which people aspire to enlightenment yet are also determined to take action to help other human beings reach the same goal. What distinguished the historical Buddha's life, in the years after his enlightenment, was his dedication to the enlightenment of others. The last words of Shakyamuni Buddha in the "Life Span" chapter of the Lotus Sutra, recited daily in the practice of gongyo, are these:

> *At all times I think to myself:*
> *How can I cause living beings*
> *To gain entry into the unsurpassed way*
> *And quickly acquire the body of a Buddha?*

Bringing others to enlightenment, then, is the fundamental cause for world peace. What you do in addition to that will be based on your own wisdom and compassion.

The action you take is up to you. It can certainly include political action and peace activism, if these things square with your views. It might mean working to ameliorate and end the underlying causes of political strife—poverty, malnutrition, illiteracy, environmental depredation, and so on. It can even mean putting on a uniform and joining the armed forces. There are numerous Buddhists serving in the U.S. military. They bring humanism and respect for the dignity of life to this profession. Servicemen and -women have been engaged in numerous humanitarian missions around the world, most notably during the Southeast Asian tsunami of 2004. There is also a rare but noble tradition of pacifists serving in times of war. (The film *Sergeant York*, starring Gary Cooper, dramatized one such case, that of a Quaker torn between his ingrained pacifism and the compelling need to defeat the Germans.) It is not terribly far-fetched to envision a time when U.N. peace-keeping troops—the so-called "blue helmets"—will have many, many Buddhists in their ranks, especially among the U.S. contingent.

In the post-9/11 world, another area where Buddhists can take action would be educating and persuading religious and ideological extremists, including radical Muslims, toward a more pacifistic view.

(Remember, the condition of kosen-rufu depends on two-thirds of the people being at least supportive of Buddhist ideals.) Without Muslims moving in the Buddhist direction, peace will be more difficult to achieve. This is not as unlikely as it seems. To cite just one example: Working for three years as a foreign affairs official in Afghanistan, Eileen Olexiuk, a Nichiren Buddhist, was determined that her chanting of Nam-myoho-renge-kyo would "penetrate everything" in that war-torn nation, which had been the home base for Al Qaeda.

"I often chanted as I shivered in a sleeping bag," she writes in the *World Tribune*, a Buddhist weekly newspaper. "I chanted for appreciation for having the Gohonzon and for the wisdom to understand Afghanistan and its people, to establish trust and to give the most appropriate advice."[3] Initially assigned to two-week stints in Afghanistan while residing in Islamabad, Pakistan, she had to live in a guest house with no heat and sporadic water and electricity. "In Afghanistan, I worked under the constant threat of rocket attack and the roar of fighter jets and attack helicopters, while witnessing people suffering from unimaginable deprivations," Olexiuk writes.

While she vowed to achieve something positive amid incredibly negative conditions, the interesting thing is that so much of her struggle had to do with her inner life—the sort of struggle we all undergo, whether we are on the front lines of international conflict or living in comfort and security in North America. When she was transferred to a regular embassy post in Kabul in mid-2003, she had to chant to overcome her arrogance when a person half her age was appointed as her superior. Eventually, she and the young ambassador became a formidable diplomatic team, working together on security and human rights issues.

Her patience was frequently tested in a tribal-based nation that in many ways is still feudalistic. Women and girls were often exchanged for debts owed by male relatives—or substituted to serve jail time for male family members—and the country has one of the world's highest rates of illiteracy. She relied on her Buddhist practice to overcome her anger and arrogance and instead transform her weakness into the wisdom and courage of a person who doesn't back down easily in difficult situations. "I believe I was part of a value-creating exercise, and I felt I manifested the principles of Nichiren Buddhism in daily life," she adds. "As one of the longest-serving foreigners in Afghanistan with many positive relationships, I became known as the person to whom Afghans could go with their grievances and requests for advice."

Taking action is fundamental to Buddhist practice, but the nature of the action to be taken is not prescribed, as in other faiths. Anger, the root cause of war, begins in the heart. Through thousands, millions, and billions of positive individual causes, large and small, Nichiren Buddhists seek to create the effects of peace and harmony in the world.

A Critique of Pure Pacifism

The world changed on Sept. 11, 2001. On this, everyone seems to agree. What to do about it is another matter. The dilemma has been particularly sharp for Buddhists, who have long cherished the implicit pacifism of the Buddha's teachings. Throughout history, Buddhism has spread across borders and continents without firing a shot or shedding a drop of blood. However, in the wake of 9/11, there were articles, including in *The New York Times*, suggesting that Buddhism had been marginalized or rendered irrelevant by those events. It seemed naive to propose anything less than active measures to prevent the further mass killings of innocents.

In the months after 9/11, I wrote an article for *The Wall Street Journal* ("I'm a Buddhist, but Not a Pacifist in War on Terror") in which I stated that it is a misconception to think Buddhism demands a passive response to evil in all situations. I made a distinction between "monastic" Buddhists, who apply a kind of doctrinaire or absolute pacifism to the world—including, for example, removing the earthworms from a construction site before the foundation can be dug—and "lay Buddhists," a category that includes most Westerners, who sometimes swat a mosquito and do not hesitate to defend the innocent, even if a degree of force is required. The crucial question posed by that article is whether one stands by and takes no action when further innocent lives could be lost. If you can save ten lives by taking one, should you not do so? When faced with an implacable enemy who commits unprovoked acts of war against innocent civilians, with tremendous loss of life, what is a reasonable person to do? Nothing? I wrote:

> Most of the peace activists I know subscribe to a belief roughly similar to Mohandas Gandhi's "passive resistance," that is, substituting some form of nonviolent mass protest, combined with respect and understanding for the enemy, as an alternative to war. But Gandhi (who was a Hindu) insisted that his method of resistance—which he termed *satyagraha*, from two Sanskrit words meaning "holding firmly to the truth"—should only be used if it held out some prospect of being effective. There were cases in which satyagraha would be futile, Gandhi said, but resistance to evil was obligatory in all cases.[4]

As we know, passive resistance is not likely to be effective against determined terrorist networks whose very goal is to take innocent human life. In fact, terrorists depend to a certain extent on passivity, most notably in their assumptions about the behavior of airline passengers during hijackings.

Absolute pacifism is not widespread in the real world, because the level of violence in society is such that reason simply does not support it. Even vigorously antiwar people usually favor having a police force in their communities (although some are quite critical of police procedures). To take a hypothetical situation, as described in the *Wall Street Journal* piece, suppose a gunman or group of gunmen were holding pupils and teachers hostage, in a Columbine-type situation, at your local school. Suppose also that they were killing innocent children one by one. (None of this is inconceivable, unfortunately. It has happened.) Let's assume also that you have children attending this school, and they are unaccounted for. Finally, imagine a police sharpshooter has a gunman in his telescopic sight—or, even, that *you* have the gunman in your sights. Your child could be next. Should the trigger be pulled?

Many people would say yes, although their reasons may vary. Intuitively we seem to know that *taking* the life of a mass murderer is perhaps less evil than *allowing* the further deaths of innocents. With no perfect choices available, an argument about lesser evils comes into play. Nichiren Daishonin addressed this very point seven hundred years ago. "The nature of killing varies," he wrote. "If one kills the person who has murdered one's father, mother, sovereign, or teacher, although the offense remains the same, what would have been a grave offense probably becomes a lighter one instead." In other words, irrespective of our Christian notions of morality, certain *karmic* distinctions can be made. Violence is a negative cause leading to negative effects, but some kinds of defensive violence may have less negative effects. It is always evil to take a life, but it is less evil to take a life in order to save other lives.

Of course, determined pacifists reject such reasoning and say "no" to the question posed above about a Columbine-type standoff. They would argue that it is precisely the presence of an armed police force (or even armed parents) that created the violence-prone conditions for such a situation to arise in the first place: didn't the families of the Columbine killers keep guns in their homes? Weren't they part of a "culture of violence" for which we are all responsible in some measure? A society that takes life in retribution for violence or disorder just gives rise to more violence. It is an endless cycle. This is a fairly common pacifist view of the use of defensive force, but it does not allow for the element of *time*.

The present moment is as it is. Life takes place in the here and now. We cannot dial back time in order to make social conditions perfect. The policeman on the beat cannot deal with all past injustices in a single moment in time. Nor can nations operate within a fantasy of an ideal world. Police carry weapons because they sometimes need to defend against brutal killers. Some armies exist to repel other, putatively more aggressive, expansionist armies. This is the reality of the world today. Clearly for pacifism to be viable, there must exist an already somewhat peaceful milieu. That is, until the world has reached a certain threshold of peacefulness, absolute pacifism as a rational strategy may not be entirely feasible—at least not in all situations.

A rough analogy can be made to the American West, at one time a lawless place where might made right. Then law-abiding citizens began banding together in the common interest of order and security, and certain legendary lawmen appeared on the scene—Wyatt Earp, Wild Bill Hickok, and so on. They established a semblance of law and order. It was a flawed system, but only after order had been established could regular citizens begin individually to disarm. Otherwise it would have been imprudent to do so. Similarly, on the world stage, a semblance of order has begun to emerge, with its own cast of outlaws (nuclear proliferators) and rough justice (ethnic and regional conflicts). The law and order so far established has been far from perfect.

Since the publication of the *Journal* article, I have interviewed several Tibetan Buddhist monks from the Himalayan Mountains, and none supported the idea of absolute pacifism. They all allowed for certain circumstances—saving an innocent child from a molester, or preventing one young man from killing another in anger, for example—when force would be justified. Not to defend innocent life is itself a crime, they said. Even monastic Buddhists find it extremely difficult to uphold absolute pacifism in carefully defined specific cases.

If absolute pacificim is insupportable in individual cases, then we need to be skeptical of its logic in the international realm. In his book *The End of Faith*, the philosopher Sam Harris is as critical of dogmatic pacifism as he is of dogmatic faith:

> While it may seem moral enough when the stakes are low, pacifism is ultimately nothing more than a willingness to die, and to let others die, at the pleasure of the world's thugs. It should be enough to note that a single sociopath, armed with nothing more than a knife, could exterminate a city full of pacifists. There is no doubt that such sociopaths exist, and they are generally better armed.[5]

But to throw the idea of pacifism out the window merely because it is sometimes impossible is not completely logical either. Pacifism is inherently a gradualist program that can only succeed where a degree of pacification has taken root. One can maintain a steadfast belief in pacifism, with the hope that the day is coming when there are enough people who share this view that the position becomes more viable. If pacifism is casually or routinely abandoned, then that day may never come.

By addressing the limits of pacifism, especially doctrinaire pacifism, my *Journal* article proved controversial in Buddhist circles. I was referred to as a "Buddhist hawk," among other things. But the tension between pacifism and the human responsibility to resist evil is quite real and difficult to reconcile. All Buddhists grapple with it to some degree. After all, the first of the five precepts in Shakyamuni's teaching is that of "non-injury."

Acutely aware of this, Ikeda in his 2006 Peace Proposal examines the difficult choices made by Albert Eintein, who was an avowed pacifist but also was instrumental in creating the atomic bomb. Einstein, an admirer of Gandhi, had once declared, "I would rather be cut to pieces than shoot someone on command." However, eventually Einstein came to the conclusion that failing to resist the Nazis would be tantamount to supporting their murderous rampage and that it was necessary for the Alllies to develop nuclear weapons lest Germany develop them first. When, against his wishes, nuclear weapons were dropped on Hiroshima and Nagasaki, Einstein regretted his involvement, calling it the "one great mistake in my life." His sense of responsibility and guilt, Ikeda writes, drove his efforts as a peace activist in the postwar years, when he worked to abolish nuclear weapons. Einstein himself, one of history's greatest minds, was forced to equivocate on the issue of pacifism versus resistance to evil.

In 2005, the Dalai Lama, spiritual leader of the Tibetan Buddhists, surprised many pacifists when he said in a speech at Stanford University that "some wars might be just."[6] In response to a question from the audience, the fourteenth Dalai Lama (whose real name is Tenzin Gyatso), allowed that the Allied victory in World War II "saved Western civilization," and that the conflicts fought in Korea and Vietnam were "honorable" from a moral standpoint. These comments might give many pacifists and traditional Buddhists pause. He went on to say that waging war purely for the cause of freedom can also be justified (although he ruled it out in the case of Tibet's dream of winning autonomy from China).

Asked about the United States–led invasion of Iraq, Gyatso said that it would take a few years before it became clear whether the U.S. military action was the right course. If handled improperly, he said, the situation in Iraq could go from "today, one [Osama] bin Laden, next few years 10 bin Ladens, then 100 bin Ladens." He noted that both the conduct of a war and the concept of international collective security were extremely important. His comments reinforce the notion that Buddhism is not monolithic or doctrinaire on the subject of force in the interests of justice.

This is a subject on which people of good will may disagree. But Buddhists, perhaps more than others, seem compelled to take an unflinching look at these issues. In a 2005 article in a Buddhist magazine, Al Albergate, a vice general director of the SGI-USA, the lay organization of Nichiren Buddhists in America, addressed the question of the use of force in Buddhist tradition. He pointed out that the goal of Mahayana Buddhism had always been to bring about a world where human beings refrain from violence and live in harmony and peace. He went on to relate the story of Simha, a general in ancient India who questioned the Buddha about, first, whether it was wrong to punish criminals, and, second, if it was wrong to go to war to protect one's home and family.

The historical Buddha, Shakyamuni, responded that those who deserve punishment must be punished, but a magistrate should mete out punishment without hatred. The Buddha then added that all war is lamentable, but he did not say "that those who go to war in a righteous cause after having exhausted all means to preserve the peace are blameworthy. He must be blamed who is the cause of war."[7] Furthermore, the Buddha told Simha that although Buddhism involves the surrender of the self, it does not require surrender to evil powers. (It should be noted that the Shakya clan, of which

Shakyamuni was a member, was wiped out when they chose not to defend themselves against aggressors.)

The Buddha said we must "kill the will to kill." It is never "good" to kill. But, as Albergate points out, these propositions do not lead to inflexible definitions of right and wrong, as in other faiths. Buddhist principles are not like commandments from a supreme being, but rather teachings intended to guide human beings to liberation from suffering. The Buddha himself encouraged his followers to test the validity of his principles in their lives. "It is appropriate, therefore, to question whether the Buddhist prohibition against harming other living beings is an absolute moral principle," Albergate writes, adding that Ikeda, in his 2004 peace proposal, allowed that "it may sometimes be possible to break an impasse through the use of military force or other forms of 'hard power.'"

This was an isolated passage. In his broader argument, Ikeda stated that military action alone is not the answer to war and terrorism. Summing up his own article on just-war theory and the response of Nichiren Buddhists, Albergate continues, "I believe President Ikeda is saying that one should be a pacifist and continue working toward a nonviolent world, while recognizing the occasional use of force as a 'necessary evil' in a world where not everybody holds pacifist views."[8]

Some of the conditions for pacifism are taking shape, including interludes of international consensus (however fleeting) at the United Nations Security Council, which make possible successful attempts at collective security and disarmament. For example, the United Nations nuclear-inspection regime, the International Atomic Energy Agency (IAEA), might seem at times to be stalemated or even impotent when secretive nations with nuclear ambitions defy its decrees. But the IAEA has enjoyed notable successes in getting nuclear-equipped nations to disarm, including Ukraine, South Africa, and, more recently, Libya. In addition, the laws of war and the rules of engagement during war have come under increasing international and media scrutiny. These are all reasons for hope, not despair.

A critique of pure pacifism is just that—a critique. It in no way represents the official position of Nichiren Buddhists in general, the

Soka Gakkai International, or anyone other than the author. Nobody, least of all the Buddhist, loves war. Yet we have Buddhists serving in the American military. Nobody can be happy with the idea that America (or Great Britain or Australia) is involved in overseas military engagements, year after year. Yet reasonable people, too, must examine the real dangers posed by religious and ideological extremists who now have the means to kill vast numbers of people—and declare themselves determined to do so. This is the unsettling reality of the new global situation.

The concept of military intervention itself has taken on certain humanitarian aspects, as nations seek to refine their weaponry, avoid collateral damage to innocent civilians, and assist in the plight of refugees from war- and disaster-torn areas. The long-cherished dream of collective security is also edging closer to reality. In some ways, the goal of a globally administered police, based on a consensus of nations, is being reached, through many missteps and stumbles. The next step is to be rid of war completely. Meanwhile, Buddhists continue to stand for the principle that real change in the world begins with the transformation of the individual.

Notes on Chapter 7

[1] Ikeda, *Faith into Action*, 287.

[2] "Toward a New Era of Dialogue," SGI President Ikeda's 2005 Peace Proposal.

[3] Eileen Olexiuk, "Bringing Buddhism to the Front Lines," *World Tribune* (May 12, 2006), 4.

[4] *The Wall Street Journal* (March 28, 2002), 20.

[5] Harris, *The End of Faith*, 199.

[6] *Agence France-Presse* (November 5, 2005).

[7] Al Albergate, "Just War? Can a Buddhist Ever Justify the Use of Force?", *Living Buddhism*, Vol. IX, no. 2 (April 2005), 22.

[8] Ibid., 26.

8

TIPS ON PRACTICE
The Daily Struggle

THE OBJECT OF BUDDHIST PRACTICE IS to become truly yourself, to uncover and polish the essential you.

Those just starting out experience the same joy and benefits as longtime practitioners. However, after practicing twenty, thirty years or more, you develop quite a history of struggle and victory. Morning after morning, evening after evening, you get in front of the Gohonzon and chip away at your negative karma. Sometimes it's difficult, nothing seems to work, and the practice seems like a needless austerity. This is your own karma stopping you like a brick wall. But there are ways to break through. If karma can be compared to rock, then there are certain hammers and chisels, fine stone mason tools, so to speak, to make the work of reshaping your destiny not just easier but more creative.

Drawing on the experiences of Buddhist friends, Buddhist publications, and the guidance of SGI leaders, these are some tips on practice:

✳ What to Think About ✳

It is only natural for the mind to wander when one is chanting. Daydreams and fantasies continually enter into one's thoughts. Negative feelings may intrude, too. Illness, family problems, financial obligations, and career worries—all will come to mind while chanting. Such concerns arise from the heart and will be solved through one's earnest prayer. Using these thoughts constuctively, one can make a plan for the next day or reflect on one's actions the previous day.

Gradually, as one sincerely practices Buddhism, the mind becomes clearer and one's life is purified. Eventually, one begins to regard the Gohonzon with greater and greater clarity, leading to a more transparent view of one's own mind and life. Nichiren said, "master your mind, don't let your mind master you." When you chant to the Gohonzon, you are mastering your mind. When you perform a vigorous gongyo, you are taming the stream of consciousness, the torrent of unbroken thoughts and emotions that pour forth unceasingly from within life.

Some of our thoughts tend to be erroneous, emotionally charged, or self-destructive. The beauty of chanting is that it does the work of meditation, of returning you to your true or higher self, quite automatically. Initially, when one is learning how to chant just the phrase Nam-myoho-renge-kyo, it is very difficult to think about other things while chanting. The phrase itself precludes other thoughts you might have. The chatter of your mind diminishes. Before long, however, you will be able to chant Nam-myoho-renge-kyo and think your usual thoughts. It is a bit like patting your head and rubbing your stomach at the same time. When chanting Nam-myoho-renge-kyo becomes second nature, you will be able to do this. Then you begin learning gongyo and reciting the sutra—portions of the *Hoben* and *Juryo* chapters of the Lotus Sutra—and once again you will find it impossible to chant and think your usual thoughts at the same time. The restless river of consciousness necessarily ceases while you master the sutra. Your egotistic thoughts recede. Your Buddha nature awakens.

It is a good idea to keep your goals, both daily and long-term ones, in mind when chanting to the Gohonzon. But don't obsess about them or allow them to dominate, that is, to get in the way of your personal connection, or fusion, to the Gohonzon. Your goals should be there, perhaps just over your shoulder, with the Gohonzon, the mirror of your enlightenment, clearly in view.

When doing gongyo, you do not have to strive constantly to control the stream of thought or master the mind. Gongyo *is* mastery. By doing gongyo, you are already mastering your mind.

✳ Posture ✳

One's attitude in front of the Gohonzon is important. Praying to the Gohonzon means worshiping the life of the Buddha within yourself. Therefore, sit erect with your back as straight as possible. The gosho reads, "When you bow to a mirror, the image in the mirror bows to you." In other words, by fusing your life with the Gohonzon, the state of Buddhahood wells up within you. You do not want to slump or slouch. The Lotus Sutra states: "Sit upright and recall the ultimate reality," and "In their heartfelt desire to see the Buddha, their lives they do not begrudge." That is, even if you are tired and grouchy, your attitude toward the Gohonzon should be one of respect and appreciation. There will be times when this is difficult. But gongyo is a discipline. Any practice or discipline demands a degree of dedication.

When chanting, place your palms together, chest high, with your fingertips touching—symbolizing the mutual possession of the Ten Worlds. Your two hands also symbolize the fusion of objective reality (*kyo*) and subjective wisdom (*chi*). Although chanting Nam-myoho-renge-kyo has a powerful rhythm, try not to rock back and forth while chanting. You do not have to add any rhythmical "body English" to your practice. This can be distracting to other practitioners and also to you. Be as still as possible. That does not mean you have to be as rigid as a statue. Chanting and performing gongyo involve discipline and flexibility. If your child needs an answer to a question, or the telephone rings, naturally you can stop to answer. You can pause to handle various things as they come up. But when you do go back to chanting to the Gohonzon, try to be as still as possible. Experienced practitioners often stop in the middle of a very focused chanting session to scribble a note or a reminder to themselves. That is okay, too.

Keep in mind that chanting is like training, including to some extent, training yourself in single-mindedness. Obviously, there is a sense in which chanting is meditative practice. There is also a yogic element to it. One exhales during the words and inhales in between, but no conscious attempts to control one's breath are necessary. You can chant while seated on the floor, or you can use a chair. Lounging on a sofa or in a soft easy chair is not recommended, however. Twenty-five years ago, most Nichiren Buddhists chanted while seated on the floor in the Japanese lotus position—knees on the floor, thighs parallel, and hindquarters resting on the backs of the ankles (sort of an upright version of the "child's pose" in yoga). Cushions were strategically placed to relieve pressure, but it still got uncomfortable after a while. It's not a good idea if you have bad knees.

Nowadays at most Buddhist meetings chairs are set up for people to sit on while chanting. Many people also use chairs when chanting at home. It depends on the individual—and the state of one's joints. If you do use a chair, be sure to set up the Gohonzon so it is high enough (the second character, reading down the middle, should be at eye level or above). Also, it is better not to cross your legs while chanting. Some people use specially made small wooden benches to support them while chanting from the floor; others find that bean bag chairs or pillows can be helpful—whatever assists you in being comfortable and erect while chanting.

✳ Speed ✳

When we chant daimoku and perform gongyo, we are fusing our lives with the universe and striving to reveal our fullest potential. Naturally we want to perform this action with vigor and a strong pace. How fast you chant and recite the sutra is up to you. But it should be vigorous and steady, like a galloping horse, to use an image favored by Daisaku Ikeda, who writes:

> When you chant to the Gohonzon, do so rhythmically and with a fresh feeling. A good gongyo has an appealing sound to anyone. Avoid doing gongyo in a loud voice. It should not be slow like a cow's walk or so fast you don't even know what you're saying.

Doing gongyo in a weak voice or dozing off in the middle is also not acceptable. Do gongyo vigorously and clearly so that it sounds like the gallop of a horse. This kind of prayer enables you to fuse with the Gohonzon, thus opening the way to infinite benefit.[1]

When you are chanting with others, the pace of gongyo is determined by a person designated to sit right in front of the Gohonzon and lead the prayer. When in group situations, one should never chant more loudly than the leader. If the leader has a soft voice, chant even softer. Everyone strives to match the leader's pitch and rhythm as closely as possible. Over time, most practitioners memorize the entire sutra book and are thus able to chant gongyo from memory. This can be very helpful at airports and train stations, when you have no time to do anything but a very quick and quiet gongyo. But in most situations, it not necessary or desirable to rush. In fact, slowing things down can have its own benefits. If you are chanting with a newcomer, it may be necessary to do a "slow gongyo" to enable that person to keep up. When we do slow gongyo frequently—that is, when we teach others how to pronounce gongyo correctly—we receive the inestimable benefit of perfecting our own gongyo.

Detailed instructions on correctly reciting and pronouncing gongyo are contained in the booklet *The Liturgy of Nichiren Daishonin's Buddhism* (available for $2 at SGI community centers nationally). Most Nichiren Buddhists have multiple copies of this indispensable little book. You can also download a digital recording from the SGI website (www.sgi-usa.org). Above all, attend Buddhist meetings, where you can really experience and learn the correct pace and pronunciation of gongyo. There is no substitute for chanting with others.

✳ Consistency ✳

Because it is easy to practice, Nichiren Daishonin's Buddhism is available to everyone. However, because it is hard to practice, it contains the power to lead people to enlightenment. The prime point of Buddhist practice is chanting daimoku and reciting gongyo twice a day. Anyone can learn to chant and pronounce gongyo. But it is difficult to do it every day, twice a day. The goal should be never to miss gongyo. That would mean doing gongyo 730 times a year. But if you do miss gongyo, it is not the end of the world. You may notice a little drag on your life condition that day. As Ikeda writes: "If you miss gongyo, no matter what you attempt, your actions are like hacking at the air. No matter how sharp your sword, you never can sever the chains of destiny which imprison your life." But you need not feel guilty. We lead busy lives. Sometimes it is impossible to take time out and make an effective prayer. Just redetermine to carve out the time and do an even more powerful gongyo at the next available opportunity. Ikeda adds:

> On some occasions, you may be unable to do gongyo or you may be able only to just chant daimoku. Nevertheless, so long as you maintain faith you will not experience negative effects on account of your occasional failure to carry out a complete practice of gongyo. While you should not take advantage of this statement or misconstrue it as condoning a lax or lazy attitude, you do not have to be overly strict or inflexible in your pratice.[2]

Ikeda has often emphasized that the daily ritual of gongyo is really the only opportunity the human being has to connect to the macrocosm. We can worship nature all we like, hike to the highest mountaintops, but we never really connect to the universe as we do during gongyo. "The powerful reverberations of your gongyo attune you to the pulsing wavelength of the macrocosmic life," he writes. "It is the cry of your ichinen summoning forth 'Buddha'— the ultimate reality of the life of the universe. When you face the Gohonzon and chant daimoku, you yourself become the entity of Buddha." That is why it is important to make this connection consistently every day.

✳ The Altar ✳

The altar where practitioners keep their butsudans containing the Gohonzon should be kept clean and tidy. Everything on the altar is there for a purpose, often symbolic, and contributes to the ideal environment for bringing forth one's Buddha nature.

Buddhists traditionally make three offerings on their altars: candles, incense, and evergreens (symbolic of the "three truths" of Buddhism—nonsubstantiality, temporary existence, and the Middle Way). One or two candles can be lit for illumination during morning and evening gongyo (electric candles are fine, too). One to three sticks of incense may be burned. The sticks should be placed flat in the incense tray and burned from left to right. (Smokeless incense can be used.) Evergreens can be cut or purchased at a florist and placed in one or two vases, flanking the butsudan. A water cup with a lid should be placed at the center of the altar in front of the butsudan. Fill it in the morning before gongyo; empty in the evening. This tradition of offering fresh water in Buddhism dates to ancient India, a hot country where water was precious. An offering of food is also traditional—in recognition of Nichiren's disciples, whose offerings of food sustained him. These typically consist of one to several pieces of fruit carefully arranged on a plate, but sometimes rice and other foods are offered. Fruit should be removed and consumed when it is ripe. When making an offering, the practitioner should sound the bell, then chant daimoku three times. The kind of bell you use to mark the beginning and end of your prayers is up to you, but be sure not to make the gonging so loud it disturbs others.

When you sound the bell and begin chanting before the Gohonzon in the morning, sometimes you may feel listless, tired, and uninspired. First, dust and refresh the items on your altar. Refill the water cup. If you haven't done so lately, change the evergreens or the water in the greens. You do this to restart your life. Sometimes performing gongyo in the morning is like trying to start a lawnmower that has been sitting in the garage all winter. Through trial and error with lawnmowers and other gas-powered tools, you eventually learn that, first, you have to drain off all the old gas, which becomes degraded over time; then you have to top up the oil and perhaps clean the air filter. Finally, you must open the choke lever all the way. Likewise, no matter how many times you pull on the rope to start yourself in the morning, the engine of your enlightenment may just sputter and cough. You end up just going through the motions. Taking care of your altar and going through the rituals of refilling the water cup and dusting (buy a duster and keep it handy) can make a difference in jump-starting your practice each morning. These actions refresh your existence. No "cause" you make toward improving and maintaining your altar is wasted. As Nichiren stated in his gosho "On Attaining Buddhahood," even offering flowers and incense can bring benefit. (Nichiren Buddhists generally offer flowers, symbolic of perishability, on their altars only on October 13th, the anniversary of Nichiren's death.)

The various accessories on the altar are symbolic of the five senses: sight (candles), sound (bell), smell (incense), touch (prayer beads), taste (food offering). Nowadays, some practitioners substitute artificial or potted plants for the fresh evergreens. Others dispense with the incense and candles because they are allergic or have children around and worry about fire hazards. The particulars of how the practitioner arranges and maintains the altar are somewhat individual. But the benefits in having a beautiful altar are great.

✳ Cause Cards ✳

Again and again Buddhists emphasize the importance of chanting for specific, measurable goals. That does not mean one cannot chant for more abstract aims like world peace or the happiness of others; in fact, as discussed, linking one's individual goals to the larger goals of Buddhism is vital. But it is also desirable to keep track of one's specific progress and individual milestones in the practice. One way is to make "cause cards," little written reminders or lists of one's objectives, to be placed on one's altar. These optional cards can be written on regular index cards, post-its, or other kinds of paper. They can be quite specific–"Score 90 percent or above on my nursing final exam"–or they can be more broadly phrased–"Better relations with my parents"–depending on what you are setting out to accomplish. What you put on your cause cards is your business. (Many pracititioners consider their lists private and remove them when friends come over to chant.) As these various goals or targets are accomplished, the practitioner crosses them out, just as on a grocery shopping list.

If you do not quite know what to put on your list at the outset, here is a default suggestion: #1, *I will not begrudge my life.* So much unhappiness is based on holding grudges–toward bosses, rivals, neighbors, family members–but the most essential grudge we hold tends to concern ourselves. (*I am no good. My life is a mess. My career is a shambles. Nobody will ever love me.*) Buddhism effects a change deep within your life in which you see yourself differently, begin to realize the uniqueness of your life, and stop regarding *yourself* with a constant grudging attitude. But you need to be a partner in this process. Therefore, begin to appreciate what you have and who you are. Life is precious. Just to be born a human being is a very fortunate thing. Your own life is of inestimable value. *Do not begrudge your life.* Add that one to your list, and see what happens.

Everyone has long lists of things they want to accomplish at work, at home, financially, romantically, socially, and spiritually. Write these goals or causes down on your cause cards, place them on the altar, and check and recheck the list as your life progresses. When people practice in this systematic, goal-directed manner, they are often amazed by the results.

✳ Tosos ✳

How much you chant depends on your schedule and other factors. Just chanting for five minutes a day can be difficult. But there is no doubt that an occasional marathon session can have a positive effect on your life. When Buddhists chant Nam-myoho-renge-kyo for an extended period it is called a *toso.* Typically several Buddhist friends gather together for a toso and chant prodigiously for a common goal, like world peace or the success of an upcoming cultural presentation, or perhaps for the health of a fellow Buddhist. It is also common for individual participants in the toso to dedicate their prayers, or daimoku, to certain personal goals as well–thus linking their individual desires with the common goals of the group. Tosos can lead to breakthroughs in one's life. Definitely try chanting for an hour or two or more on an occasional basis. When chanting Nam-myoho-renge-kyo, both quality *and* quantity count.

✳ **Obstacles** ✳

Obstacles will arise. Any time you attempt to move ahead in life you will meet some form of resistance. But you can take a great leap forward when you meet a difficult situation.

Buddhist practice can be likened to an airplane taking off. An airplane actually takes off more easily into a headwind—the wind provides extra lift to the wings. Similarly, obstacles can be viewed not as impediments but as natural forces in the environment that make you raise your life condition higher and higher. Life without obstacles might seem attractive, but it would entail no growth. Buddhists use life's obstacles to change their karma and move forward. Without obstacles, it would be more difficult to see one's karmic tendencies—to perceive one's weaknesses—and overcome them.

Of course, some problems seem never to go away. Although you chant resolutely to resolve certain situations in life, there will always be those knotty ones that persist. First, check all three aspects of your practice—faith, practice, and study. These three components are often compared to the landing gear on an airplane. Unless all three wheels are down, an airplane will be unable to take off. If even one wheel is not engaged, the plane will list to one side, its wing dragging along the ground. Without practicing all three aspects of Buddhism, you will be unable to achieve lift-off and attain cruising altitude. When your practice is strong and life is going smoothly, you have the inner resources to meet your personal challenges, and you are thus able to be a "vehicle" to carry others toward enlightenment.

Even if you are chanting prodigious amounts of daimoku, if you are neglecting the other two aspects of practice, eventually your benefits will be incomplete. In terms of faith, are you doing a complete gongyo, morning and evening, seven days a week? Without a very consistent daily practice, one cannot expect to receive full benefit from Buddhism. Next, do you attend and participate in Buddhist meetings? In other words, do you practice for and with others? Maybe you are one of those introverted types who feel somewhat uncomfortable in group situations. Perhaps you have a tremendous dread of speaking in front of a group. In that case, it could be that this karma—this uneasiness or anxiety in a group situation—is precisely the underlying karma that you need to address head-on. Therefore, attend more meetings, and volunteer to speak as often as possible about your own experiences in Buddhism. Attack your weakness at the root.

Likewise, do you find it difficult to read and study about Buddhism? Many people do. It reminds them of school, childhood learning problems, or—whatever. They just don't like to study. But study is an important part of this practice. Without practice and study, Nichiren said, there can be no Buddhism. If you have an inner resistance to study, then it is all the more imperative that you study hard, in order to reverse this karma.

So first, check on the basics of your practice. Make sure you are practicing with all three components fully engaged. Then you will have the breakthroughs you seek.

✳ Chanting for Others ✳

There is no such thing as a self-centered Buddhist—it is a contradiction in terms.

As President Ikeda points out, practicing for others has noble ancient roots. Shakyamuni himself recommended various meditations aimed at alleviating the suffering of others. In Buddhism, we chant for other people with the same sincerity that we chant for ourselves. This is doubly important in cases of people who appear to be causing us problems. If you have a difficult boss, a recalcitrant child, a contentious lover, a litigious neighbor—chant first for *their* happiness. Most of us spend a tremendous amount of time and effort trying to *change* other people for our own sake. This is like banging your head against the wall in order to get the neighbors to lower the stereo.

Many people are unaware that they are responsible for their inability to get along with others. Nearly everyone has a person in the immediate environment with whom he or she has strained relations. Often it is the very person to whom we are closest. Chanting sincere daimoku for the other person's sake will result in underlying changes in the relationship. That is the only kind of change you can reliably cause to happen. Chanting for the happiness of others, even those whom we dislike, does not come naturally. However, the sincere effort to alter one's narrow view is often the first step in resolving the problem. You are the one who is changing, from the inside out. The other person, perhaps at a subconscious level, will notice and respond to these changes.

Approaching difficult interpersonal problems in this tactical manner may seem distant and artificial—there you are, in front of your Gohonzon, furiously chanting for a rival's happiness or enlightenment, when you really want them to fall off a cliff! But in a very important sense it makes the situation less emotionally charged. As human beings, we have a tendency to sentimentalize things, to be hostage to our *feelings* about various situations. This misguided emotionalism diminishes with Buddhist practice as we begin to identify with the other person, to see things from the other person's point of view. The more we are concerned about others, the less we are caught up in our selfish views.

✳ Detailed Caring ✳

When we practice sincerely for the sake of others as well as for ourselves, we quickly notice how important small gestures and detailed knowledge of other people can be. It is not enough simply to hope or wish for the best for others. There is a world of difference between being "nice," in the conventional sense, and manifesting the real compassion of detailed caring about others. We must also show through our actions that we have some specific understanding and sensitivity to their needs, hopes, and dreams. Detailed caring may include something as small as not sounding the bell when you perform gongyo late in the evening, because you know it disturbs your spouse. It could be that a demanding coworker is constantly cross with you and insists on your staying late to work. If you care enough to find out, you may learn this is because he or she has a sick child at home and is in a constant state of anxiety about getting home to deal with the situation. To support your colleague sincerely, perhaps you need to complete the work early so you can tell him or her: "It's okay. I have everything under control. You can go home early." The difference between conventional expressions of sympathy or caring and this kind of Buddhist empathy or understanding can be subtle and counterintuitive. For example, coddling someone who is feeling sorry and self-indulgent about his or her financial situation might be less compassionate than offering strict words of encouragement about finding a paying job. Knowing the difference is a form of detailed caring. Only by chanting determined daimoku to the Gohonzon can we develop the wisdom to know what to say—or when just to listen.

✳ Meetings ✳

The image of monks meditating in caves or on mountaintops has long been associated with Buddhism. However, it is extremely difficult for a person to practice Buddhism in isolation. The lone practitioner, unconnected to his fellows in faith, eventually develops his or her own ideas about Buddhism. When practicing something as beautifully subtle and mysterious as the Lotus Sutra, everyone needs a reality check from time to time. Fundamental to Nichiren Buddhist practice is the monthly discussion meeting. Thousands of such meetings take place in individual Buddhists' homes across the United States each month. Larger meetings are held on an occasional basis in major venues like Lincoln Center's Avery Fisher Hall in New York or the Ikeda Auditorium in Santa Monica, California. But the key to one's early practice is the discussion meeting. A typical discussion meeting includes explanations of the basics of practice, brief presentations on study topics and Buddhist activities in the area, and first-hand experiences in practice. More than anything else, such experiences in practice—examples of "actual proof" of the power of

Buddhism—serve to encourage, enlighten, and inspire us to continue. As Nichiren wrote: "In judging the relative merits of Buddhist doctrines, I, Nichiren, believe that the best standards are those of reason and documentary proof. And even more valuable than reason and documentary proof is the proof of actual fact."[3] (To find a discussion meeting in your area, go to www.sgi-usa.org.)

✳ Home Visits ✳

Most of the time, we chant alone, in the privacy of our homes. But it is also a very good idea to get out there and chant with other people. In addition to the various meetings that a Nichiren Buddhist might attend, there is also the informal practice of chanting with another Buddhist at his or her home. Such "home visits" can be real eye-openers. And the "opening of the eyes" is a prime goal of Buddhism. In the context of Buddhist strategy to "chant and take action," it is one of the best forms of action. When you chant with other people, it becomes a quick check on the quality and pronunciation of your own daimoku and gongyo, not to mention your thoughts and ideas about Buddhism. Making a home visit to another Buddhist practitioner—or allowing another Buddhist to visit you—can be a refreshing or watershed moment in your practice.

To put this in perspective, let's return to the concept of the Ten Worlds. It has been noted that the defining quality of the lower six worlds—the ones most of us dwell in most of the time—is that in them, one is pretty much at the mercy of one's external circumstances. Things happening outside of us determine whether we are in the state of, say, Rapture, or whether we descend into, say, Anger or Hunger at any given moment. It is not easy to escape from the lower worlds. However, when we undertake to go on a home visit, consciously deciding to take an action in support of another's Buddhist practice, we are, perhaps for the first time in a long time, *acting on* our environment. One could characterize this act as one of almost pure intention, because on the face of things, it is an action you are taking that is entirely without reference to the self—that is, your own desires, dreams, ambitions, and so on. The fact that you would rather be watching television than making a home visit to a person you perhaps barely know actually enhances the significance of the cause you are making. Making a home visit (or, again, having one in your own home) almost always involves overcoming a bit of inertia. The process is almost Newtonian. A body at rest tends to stay at rest. A body in motion tends to remain in motion. When you are out there visiting and chanting with others, your life is in motion—and great things begin to happen.

✳ Anxiety ✳

When you are practicing Buddhism correctly, you will sometimes feel sudden pangs of—what to call them?—anxiety, discomfort, distaste, even anger in the midst of your efforts. These seem to bubble up from nowhere. (In Buddhist slang, we used to call the onset of such negative feelings a "karma attack.") You might hear someone say something at a meeting that does not gibe with your own views. You may confront a situation that is not at all what you chanted for—in fact, is the exact opposite of the result you desired. Expeiencing anxiety of this sort from time to time is perfectly normal.

Picture for a moment your life as a glass of water with a layer of sediment on the bottom. Let's call that sediment your karma. When you start attending Buddhist meetings and chanting Nam-myoho-renge-kyo with vigor, it is like stirring up the glass. The particles at the bottom are disturbed and cloud the liquid. In other words, you stir up your negative karma. The good thing is, you are finally able to *see* it and take constructive steps to correct it. Eventually, when you stir a glass continually, the sediment will dissipate and evaporate, leaving just clear water. Therefore, it is important to continue to chant your way through your various anxieties and steadily advance toward a brilliant, clear condition of life.

✳ Slander ✳

Misfortune comes from one's mouth, Nichiren said. Nowadays our lives tend to be full of slander. It is practically a national pastime. We speak ill of our superiors at work, our teachers at school, the quarterback of our favorite team, our family, and, of course, our leaders. Slander of politicians has become so commonplace and reflexive, it is almost surprising that any person of talent and dignity would ever run for office.

Nichiren wrote, "It is an undeniable fact that fire can at once reduce even a thousand-year-old field of pampas grass to ashes, and the merit one has formed over a hundred years can be destroyed with a single word."[4] As we have seen, the life of the samurai Shijo Kingo was profoundly affected, nearly ruined, by the slander of his colleagues. Nichiren counseled Shijo not to be swayed by such despicable actions—and not to slander in return. The only thing that can destroy benefit for a person who is practicing correctly is slander. If major benefits seem hard to win, look deeply in your life for slander. Ikeda writes:

> There are cases when we wonder why merit doesn't reveal itself in spite of our earnest and high degree of faith. At such times, rather than suspecting that you may entertain doubt about the Gohonzon, it is better to ask yourself whether you are guilty of any slander. Because a person who is contemptuous, hating, jealous, or holds grudges will realize no benefit.[5]

As philosophers since Socrates have pointed out, slander is intrinsically harmful to the person who utters it. Even if your words are out of earshot of the people you scorn, what you say has invisible effects on you and on your relationships with those persons. Even if they cannot hear you, the targets of your unkind or critical words will sense something different about you next time you meet. The ichinen in your face tells no lies. No slander goes completely unnoticed.

Above all, never slander yourself. We are all potentially Buddhas, and slander is unworthy of such a respectworthy being. By carefully checking ourselves for the subtle and not-so-subtle slanders that are part of everyday life, we can eliminate a major source of misfortune.

✳ From This Moment On ✳

In Buddhism, the past is less important than the here and now. We are guided by the principle of *hon'nin myo*, which in Japanese means "from this moment on" (like the Cole Porter song). This concept suggests that whatever has happened in the past, the important thing is to start from this moment to change for the better. Hon'nin myo also means "mystic principle of true cause," in the sense that, since all existence is based on cause and effect, then the most important thing (the only thing) you can do is start right now to make the best possible causes for your life. The "true cause" for individual happiness is chanting Nam-myoho-renge-kyo to the Gohonzon. Buddhism is not a backward-looking practice, obsessed with the mistakes of the past. It a dynamic, forward-looking practice that urges one to forge ahead with renewed vigor. With this from-this-moment-on spirit, we can make a fresh start every day.

✳ Appreciation ✳

The key attitude in front of the Gohonzon is one of appreciation. Nearly every one of Nichiren's hundreds of gosho or letters begins with an expression of heartfelt gratitude or appreciation, usually for various offerings he has received—rice cakes, sake, coins, and robes— but also for the trust and faith that people place in him at personal risk to themselves. Therefore "repaying debts of gratitude" is an important theme in Nichiren Buddhism. In our own relatively comfortable lives, we can continually offer gratitude to the Gohonzon for the opportunity to become enlightened.

How can a person develop a sense of appreciation when it does not seem to come naturally? It is similar to instilling good manners in a child. When a child is taught proper table manners at a very early age, the child may regard the whole exercise as silly and against nature. (Why not just eat with one's hands?) Over time, however, good manners become automatic, and long after the early, tentative efforts are forgotten, the results continue to speak for themselves. We admire people with perfect manners. Good manners are in themselves estimable. Similarly, if we begin chanting with appreciation and work

Original	本	Hon
Cause	因	Nin
Mystic	妙	Myo

on developing this habit, day in and day out, eventually our lives will be filled with appreciation. That, in itself, is estimable.

When you chant with an attitude of complaint, the benefit will perhaps be weak or incomplete. When you chant with an attitude of appreciation to the Gohonzon, all prayers become powerful. In a sense, happiness *equals* appreciation. That is one of the great messages of Buddhism.

When we were in school, many of us studied or saw a performance of the play *Our Town* by Thornton Wilder, one of the most popular of all American dramas. On the surface, *Our Town* seems a rather spare, even banal portrait of small-town New England life, but the play achieves universal resonance in its final act. The heroine, Emily Webb, who has died in childbirth, reappears in a graveyard scene in which the dead observe the living. When Emily decides to go back and relive a single day in her life, a twelfth birthday spent at home with her family, the visit becomes too heart-rending and overwhelming, because she realizes in reliving those unremarkable moments with her loved ones that no living being truly *appreciates* life, even the mundane details of home life—with mom and dad and little brother, the ups and downs, the little triumphs and tribulations. We do not cherish our existence nearly enough.

As we have said earlier, Nichiren declared that Buddhism is no different than the affairs of daily life. He equated the practice of

Buddhism with the details of living life. In essence, one's ichinen, or moment-to-moment attitude in life, is really the key fact in Buddhism, the basis of future happiness. Nichiren Buddhism offers a systematic approach to cherishing our highest selves and developing appreciation for each moment of life.

To practice correctly is to practice with appreciation. The more you appreciate your life and your Buddhist practice, the happier you will become.

NOTES ON CHAPTER 8

[1] Daisaku Ikeda, "Gongyo, the Prime Point," *NSA Quarterly*, Vol. IV, No. 2 (Spring 1976), 132.

[2] Ikeda, *Faith into Action* (World Tribune Press, 1999), 115.

[3] *The Major Writings of Nichiren Daishonin* (Tokyo: Soka Gakkai, 1999), 599.

[4] *The Major Writings*, 636.

[5] *Faith into Action*, 165.

GLOSSARY

arhat *(är-hət)*—in Hinayana Buddhism, one who has completely overcome suffering and its causes, and attained the highest of the four stages leading to enlightenment.

bodhisattva *(bō-dē-SAHT-və)*—a person who practices Buddhism for the enlightenment of others. In Sanskrit, *bodhi* means "enlightenment" and *sattva* means "a living being." (In Japanese, *bosatsu*.) Also Bodhisattva is the ninth, or next to the highest, of the Ten Worlds.

bodhi tree—the *pipal* or fig tree in Buddhagaya, India, beneath which Shakyamuni Buddha was said to have achieved his enlightenment. The pipal is a tall evergreen with heart-shaped leaves and can reach nearly one hundred feet in height. The *bodhi* (enlightenment) tree is regarded as sacred by many Buddhists.

Buddha *(BÜ-dah)*—an "awakened one," a person who is enlightened to the ultimate truth of life and the nature of all phenomena. The word itself predates the historical Buddha, Shakyamuni, but it came to be applied exclusively to him. Numerous Buddhas are named in the various Mahayana Buddhist scriptures.

Buddhahood–the state of enlightenment and the goal of Buddhist practice. Also the tenth or highest of the Ten Worlds.

Buddha nature–the inherent cause or potential within each human being to attain Buddhahood. Unlike some schools, Nichiren Buddhism holds that everyone possesses this potential.

bushido *(BÜSH-i-dō)*–the code of honor followed by the samurai, or warrior aristocrats, in Japan. It valued chivalric duty over human life.

butsudan *(BÜT-suh-dän)*–literally "house of the Buddha," the wooden box on a practitioner's altar used to house the Gohonzon.

Dai-Gohonzon *(dī-gō-HŎN-zŏn)*–the object of worship inscribed by Nichiren Daishonin on October 12, 1279, on a large block of wood, and the template or forerunner for the silk-screened scrolls (Gohonzon) enshrined in the home of Nichiren practitioners.

daimoku *(dī-MŌ-kū)*–the chanting of the title of the Lotus Sutra, Nam-myoho-renge-kyo, known as the primary or essential practice of Nichiren Buddhism.

dharma *(DÄR-mä)*–the law, teaching, doctrine, or ultimate truth of Buddhism.

engaku *(ĕn-GÄ-kū)*–literally "cause-awakened ones," or those who perceive the chain of causation. It also describes the eighth world, or Realization, in which we come to an undestanding of the nature of reality through our own efforts. Such enlightenment, achieved independently of the teachings of a Buddha, is considered partial.

esho funi *(EH-shō-FŪ-nē)*–a Japanese term indicating the oneness of human beings and their environment. The first word is a contraction of *shoho* ("man") and *eho* ("environment"). *Funi* indicates that the two are inseparable aspects of the same reality. For example, when a person is angry, everything surrounding that person tends to seem unpleasant or hostile. One's mind therefore reflects one's circumstances and vice versa.

Gohonzon *(gō-HŎN-zŏn)*–the supreme object of worship in Nichiren Daishonin's Buddhism, a scroll based on the original Dai-Gohonzon, kept in the home of millions of practitioners worldwide. It depicts both the Ten Worlds concept and the theory of *ichinen sanzen*, and materializes Nichiren's enlightenment. It also functions as a mirror for revealing the practitioner's own Buddha nature.

gongyo *(GŎNG-yō)*–literally "assiduous practice" in Japanese. It refers both to the practice of chanting *daimoku* (Nam-myoho-renge-kyo) and reciting two sections of the Lotus Sutra. Gongyo is performed in both the morning and the evening.

gosho *(GŌ-shō)*–the writings of Nichiren Daishonin, comprising both religious treatises and letters to his disciples. *Gosho* literally means "honorable writings." In Japan, the word is used to honor the books and writings of the founders of Buddhist schools.

Gautama *(gō-TÄ-mä)*–the family name of the historical Buddha, it means "Best Cow."

Hinayana *(hĭn-ä-YÄN-ä)*–the earlier teachings of Shakyamuni Buddha, also called Theravada Buddhism, still widely practiced in southern Asia.

hosshaku kempon *(hō-SHÄK-kū kĕm-pŏn)*–to reveal one's true identity (*kempon*) while discarding one's transient identity (*hosshaku*). This signifies the realization of one's essential or Buddha nature as one's true self.

honzon *(HŎN-zŏn)*—an object of fundamental respect or worship. Can be applied to anything people center their lives around, from romantic attachments to an all-consuming interest to a career.

ichinen *(ĒCH-ĭ-nĕn)*—life at this moment; also one's moment-to-moment determination or will to win in life.

ichinen sanzen *(ĒCH-ĭ-nĕn SĂN-zen)*—literally "three thousand worlds in a momentary state of existence," the fundamental theory of life revealed in the Lotus Sutra, systematized by the Chinese philosopher T'ien-t'ai, and manifested on the Gohonzon.

jigyo keta *(JĬG-yo KĀ-tä)*—practice for oneself (*jigyo*) and practice for others *(keta)*. In Nichiren Buddhism, both are vital components of a complete practice—sometimes compared to the Earth's rotation and its orbit around the sun.

kalpa *(KĂL-pä)*—in Hindu cosmology, an unimaginably long period of time. Sometimes calculated as approximately 16 million years.

karma *(KĂR-mä)*—a Sanskrit word meaning "action" and also denoting the inner human potentials created through one's actions. Karma represents the workings of cause and effect, or karmic causality, and entails the totality of one's actions, throughout many existences, in terms of thoughts, words, and deeds. In Buddhism, karma is not, as popularly believed, deterministic, and does not imply the absence of free will. By making good causes, one can alleviate the negative effects from the past and change them into good karma.

Kosen-rufu *(KŌ-sĕn-RŪ-fŭ)*—literally "to widely spread" the humanistic ideals of Buddhism. The term is used by Nichiren Buddhists to denote both the process and the achievement of world peace. While the goal of individual practice is enlightenment or Buddhahood, the larger goal of the lay organization of Nichiren Buddhism, the Soka Gakkai International, is to secure lasting peace for all humankind, or *kosen-rufu*.

Lotus Sutra—a major work of Mahayana Buddhism widely revered throughout Asia, consisting of eight volumes and twenty-eight chapters, also known as the "Sutra of the Lotus of the Wonderful Law." It was the second-to last teaching of Shakyamuni Buddha (the Nirvana Sutra was the last). The definitive translation, from Sanskrit to Chinese, was by the scholar Kumarajiva in 406 A.D. and became the basis for T'ien-t'ai's teaching in China and Nichiren Buddhism in Japan, where the teacher Dengyo (767-822) established the Tendai School based on the Lotus Sutra, which became one of the major schools. The first fourteen chapters are known as the "theoretical teaching," and the last fourteen the "essential teaching." Portions of the "Expedient Means" (second) chapter and the "Life Span" (sixteenth) chapter are recited daily by Nichiren Buddhists.

Mahayana *(mä-hä-YÄ-nä)*—one of the two main streams of Buddhist teachings (the other is Hinayana), *Mahayana* means "great vehicle," as in a vehicle to carry people to enlightenment. Mahayana refers to the later teachings of Shakyamuni and emphasizes practice for the sake of others, or bodhisattva practice, in contrast to Hinayana schools, which focus more on personal awakening.

mandala *(män-DÄ-lä)*—a devotional object with images of Buddhas, bodhisattvas, or Buddhist doctrines. In Nichiren Buddhism, the Gohonzon is a mandala.

Mappo *(MÄ-pō)*—the third epoch that began 2,000 years after the death of the historical Buddha—also the period in which we are living today. Often described as an age of strife and conflict, when Buddhism has lost its power and influence, and many heretical teachings are rampant, Mappo coincides with the advent of Nichiren in Japan. (The other two millennial periods are Shoho and Zoho; see chart, p. 71.)

mudras *(MŪ-drəs)*—various signs and gestures made with the hands in some schools of Buddhism, particularly what Nichiren termed "esoteric" schools.

Nam-myoho-renge-kyo *(näm-myō-hō-rĕn-gĕh-kyō)*—the rhythm of the universe, the supreme law that underlies all phenomena, derived from the title of the Lotus Sutra, the penultimate teaching of Shakyamuni Buddha. When chanted by Nichiren Buddhists, the words enable all people to revitalize their lives, harmonize with their surroundings, and uncover the mystic truth within. Although its full meaning cannot be comprehended intellectually or described in words, it can be literally translated: *Nam* means "devotion to"; *myoho* indicates the "mystic law"; *renge* refers to the lotus flower or the simultaneous nature of cause and effect; and *kyo* means "the Buddha's teaching" or "sound" (since the original *sutras*, or teachings, were expounded and transmitted orally).

Nembutsu *(nem-BŪT-sū)*—the term applied to those schools of Japanese Buddhism (Jodo, Pure Land) that teach salvation and rebirth in the so-called Pure Land of perfect bliss. As a practice, Nembutsu believers invoke the name of Amida Buddha (or Buddha of Infinite Light), a figure from the sutras, as the means to ensure transmigration to the pure land.

Nichiren *(NĒ-chē-rĕn)*—the founder of a school of Buddhism based on the Lotus Sutra who revealed Nam-myoho-renge-kyo as the essence of the historical Buddha's teaching. Determined to establish the primacy of the Lotus Sutra, Nichiren (1222-1282) came into conflict with the authoritarian and aristocratic forces that dominated his era. His name means "Sun Lotus" in Japanese. He is often referred to as the *Daishonin*, or "great sage." (See Chapter 2 for a detailed biography.)

Pali Canon *(PÄ-lē)*—the original language of the Buddhist scriptures, Pali texts are the basis for Theravada (Hinayana) Buddhism.

Sado Island *(SÄ-dō)*—a desolate island in the Sea of Japan used as a natural prison for heretics and other exiles, where the reformist monk Nichiren was banished for offending the local ruling clan. It was believed impossible for anyone to return from Sado alive.

Shakyamuni *(SHĀK-ē-yǝ-mū-nē)*—born 2,500 to 3,000 years ago (scholars differ) in Lumbini Gardens, in the foothills of the Himalayas, in what is now southern Nepal. He was the son of Shuddhodana, the king of the Shakya clan, hence he came to be known as Shakyamuni, "sage of the Shakyas." His given name was Siddhartha (Goal Achieved). According to Buddhist scriptures, although he was raised in a royal household, he early became aware of human hardships and determined to abandon the comfort and luxury of secular life and seek a solution to the "four sufferings"—birth, sickness, old age, and death. After attaining enlightenment under a pipal or fig tree at around the age of thirty, he spent the remainder of his life preaching and traveling throughout India. He died at age eighty in Kushinagara, in a grove of sal trees. In Nichiren Buddhism, he is referred to as the historical Buddha, or the first documented Buddha in history.

Shijo Kingo *(SHĒ-jō KĬN-gō)*—a samurai and loyal follower of Nichiren. His full name and title were Shijo Nakatsukasa Saburo Saemon-no-jo Yorimoto. He was a retainer serving Lord Ema of the ruling Hojo clan in Kamakura, near present-day Tokyo. Skilled in both medicine and martial arts, he was the recipient of many of Nichiren's most important treatises and letters, called gosho. He attended Nichiren on his deathbed. (For a fuller account of Shijo Kingo's life, see Chapter 2.)

shiki shin funi *(SHĒ-kē-shĭn-FŪ-nē)*—the inseparability or oneness of body and mind. *Shiki* means the physical aspects of life, which are visible, and *shin* signifies quality or spirit, which is invisible. *Funi* means "two but not two." The principle is a core one in Buddhism and gives rise to a holistic view of human pyschology and health.

Soka Gakkai *(SŌ-kǝ GĀK-ī)*—the lay organization of Nichiren believers, founded in 1930 in Japan by Tsunesaburo Makiguchi (1871-1944). The words mean "value creating society." In 1975, in response to a growing worldwide membership, the Soka Gakkai

International (SGI) was founded, with Daisaku Ikeda as its first president. The organization has more than twelve million adherents in 190 nations and territories. Its goals are a peaceful world and the happiness of humanity.

Ten Worlds—a fundamental principle of Buddhism that depicts the inner life of human beings in terms of Ten Worlds or life conditions: Hell, Hunger, Animality, Anger, Humanity, Rapture, Learning, Realization, Bodhisattva, and Buddhahood. The first six are known as the Six Paths or Six Lower Worlds. In Nichiren Buddhism, these are not fixed or static conditions, but remarkably fluid life moments. Indeed, Nichiren pracititioners hold that all ten life conditions "mutually possess" one another, suggesting that the life condition or world of Buddhahood lies dormant even in the midst of total despair (Hell). The goal of Buddhist practice is to surmount the lower worlds and consistently manifest the tenth, Buddhahood (or Enlightenment), as one's predominant tendency.

T'ien-t'ai *(tē-en-TĪ)*—the founder of a school of Buddhism in China named for Mount T'ien-t'ai, where he retired and established his monastery in 575 A.D. His real name was Chih-i. He produced a scholarly classification of the various Buddhist sutras, placing the Lotus Sutra at the apex of meaning and importance, and developed the theory of *ichinen sanzen*, or three thousand worlds in a single moment of life (see entry above). He attracted a wide following and lectured on the Lotus Sutra at the imperial court. The T'ien-t'ai influence on Japanese Buddhism was substantial, since a majority of the Japanese monks who came to China to learn about Buddhism studied at the temples of Mount T'ien-t'ai. His most important work was the *Maka Shikan*.

Vajrayana *(väj-rä-YÄ-nə)*—the "diamond vehicle" or Tantric school of Buddhism. The Sanskrit word *tantra* means "loom" or "weave of cloth." Tantric Buddhism was formalized in India but came to prominence in Tibet. It involves what Nichiren termed "esoteric" practices, including *mantras* (magical formulas), *mudras* (hand gestures), *mandalas* (ritual diagrams), and various other rituals.

Zen—a school of Mahayana Buddhism based on meditation founded by Bodhidharma in sixth-century China, embraced in feudal Japan by the warrior classes, who were attracted to its ideals of strict discipline and spiritual self reliance. The word *zen* means "meditation." In Zen Buddhism one strives for enlightenment through direct perception of one's mind, independent of doctrinal study or reference to the sutras.

ABOUT THE AUTHOR

WOODY HOCHSWENDER, a former reporter for *The New York Times* and senior editor of *Esquire*, has been a practicing Buddhist for more than thirty years. His previous book, *The Buddha in Your Mirror*, co-authored with Greg Martin and Ted Morino, has been translated into Spanish and Italian. He regularly contributes humor, commentary, and style articles to the *Wall Street Journal*, the *Chicago Tribune*, the *Times,* and other publications. He lives with his wife and daughter on a small farm in northwestern Connecticut.